An Introduction to DATABASE SYSTEM

An Introduction to DATABASE SYSTEM

Dr. Anil Tandon

ANMOL PUBLICATIONS PVT. LTD.
NEW DELHI-110 002 (INDIA)

ANMOL PUBLICATIONS PVT. LTD.

Regd. Office: 4360/4, Ansari Road, Daryaganj,
New Delhi-110002 (India)
Tel.: 23278000, 23261597, 23286875, 23255577
Fax: 91-11-23280289
Email: anmolpub@gmail.com
Visit us at: www.anmolpublications.com

Branch Office: No. 1015, Ist Main Road, BSK IIIrd Stage
IIIrd Phase, IIIrd Block, Bangalore-560 085 (India)
Tel.: 080-41723429 • Fax: 080-26723604
Email: anmolpublicationsbangalore@gmail.com

An Introduction to Database System

First Edition, 2010

ISBN 978-81-261-4468-6

PRINTED IN INDIA

Printed at Mehra Offset Press, Delhi.

Contents

Preface

This book is designed specifically for a single semester, first course on Database Systems. It explains each term associated with the subject with very simple example, lucid language and a lot of illustrations. The book covers all the essential aspects of database systems, and also covers the areas of RDBMS. There are very few books, which cover all the theory and practice of database systems.

This book covers both these aspects. It contains over 400diagrams, making the book unique in terms of its visual approach. With this, even the most difficult concepts become a lot easier to understand. The book covers all the modern topics, such as OODBMs, database systems and the Internet, Data warehousing, Mobile databases, Multimedia databases, Deductive databases, and more.

A highlight of the text is the inclusion of a chapter on the concepts of symmetrical and asymmetrical configurations related to high-availability subsystem and basic copy model of Replication Technology along with two-phase commit protocol used in distributed databases. This takes the students beyond the average discussion of this technology.

Author

Chapter 1

Introduction to Programme

DATABASE

A collection of Programmes that enables you to store, modify, and extract information from a database. There are many different types of DBMSs, ranging from small systems that run on personal computers to huge systems that run on mainframes.

The following are examples of database applications:

- Computerized library systems
- Automated teller machines
- Flight reservation systems
- Computerized parts inventory systems

From a technical standpoint, DBMSs can differ widely. The terms *relational, network, flat,* and *hierarchical* all refer to the way a DBMS organizes information internally. The internal organization can affect how quickly and flexibly you can extract information.

Requests for information from a database are made in the form of a *query,* which is a stylized question. For example, the query Select All Where Name = "Smith" And Age > 35

Requests all records in which the Name field is Smith and the Age field is greater than 35. The set of rules for constructing queries is known as a *query language*. Different DBMSs support different query languages, although there is a semi-standardized query language called *SQL (structured query language)*. Sophisticated languages for managing database systems are called fourth, or *4GLs* for short. The information from a database can be presented in a variety of formats. Most DBMSs include a *report writer programme* that enables you to output data in the form of a report. Many DBMSs also include a graphics component that enables you to output information in the form of graphs and charts.

There are two approaches to data storage:

1. File-based
2. Database

FILE-BASED APPROACHES

File-based approaches to data storage are based on relatively simple data structures, such as the Indexed Sequential Access Method (ISAM), and are usually implemented for a single application.

Files are generally created on an as needed basis to service the data needs of an application.The files are associated with an application. The same data may be repeated on many files and stored under different names.

For example, an accounting application may refer to customer name while a purchasing application may refer to buyer name. The physical storage characteristics of the same data may be different for different applications.

For example, one application may allow 20 characters for name while another application allows 25 characters for the same name. Different business units are responsible for different data.

DISADVANTAGES OF A FILE-BASED APPROACH

Updates to files may result in inconsistent data across the organization. For example, if an accounting application updates a customer name without notifying other application areas that also maintain customer name, customer name will be stored differently for different applications.

A file-based data storage approach makes it difficult for other applications to access data not owned by their application. Data owned by other applications may be stored in a format not consistent with the retrieval capabilities of another application. File-based approaches to data storage are tied to applications rather than the entities to which the files refer. File-based approaches do not recognize relationships between entities until such information is needed by an application.

DATABASE APPROACHES

Database approaches to data storage support the sharing of data across multiple applications with multiple users. Databases are structured in a way that is meaningful to an organization. For example, if an organization maintains information on suppliers and the geographic areas they service, there would be a link in the database between the suppliers and geographic areas.

Databases reduce data redundancy. A Database Management System (DBMS) is the software that handles all database accesses. A DBMS presents a logical view of the data to the users. How this data is stored and retrieved is hidden from the users. A DBMS ensures that the data is consistent across the database and controls who can access what data.

CATEGORIES OF DATABASE MANAGEMENT SYSTEMS

HIERARCHICAL DATABASES

Description of Hierarchical Database

In the hierarchical structure, data is represented by a simple tree structure. The record type at the top of the tree is usually known as the "root." The simple hierarchical structure consists of a root and a single dependent record type.

In general, the root may have any number of dependent records, each of which may have any number of lower-level dependents, and so on, to any number of levels. The hierarchy view contains records of different types connected by links. Hierarchical relationships of records are explicitly defined in the data structure.

A parent record can have many child records but a child record can have only one parent. There are no many-to-many relationships between records. No dependent record within a hierarchical data structure can exist without its parent record. For this reason, records must be seen in context. Examples of hierarchical DBMSs include IBM's Information Management System (IMS) and System 2000.

Strengths of Hierarchical Databases

The advantages of a hierarchical database are:

- Efficient representation of hierarchical structures,
- Efficient single key search and access time (if the hierarchical structure corresponds to application views of the data),
- Fast update performance where locality of reference exists (locality of reference states that performance is significantly enhanced when the processing is close to the data being processed).

WEAKNESSES OF HIERARCHICAL DATABASES

The disadvantages of a hierarchical database are:

- Lack of flexibility (non-hierarchical relationships are awkward to represent; redundancy may be required),
- Poor performance for non-hierarchical accesses,
- Lack of maintainability (changing relationships may require physical reorganization of data).

NETWORK DATABASES

DESCRIPTION OF NETWORK DATABASE

In a network database structure, data is represented by records and links. There is no limit to the number of immediate parent segments or the number of immediate child segments a given record occurrence may have. The network database structure allows the modelling of many-to-many relationships. DMS and IDMS are examples of network databases.

STRENGTHS OF NETWORK DATABASES

The advantages of a network database are:

- Efficient representation of some structures (varies widely with physical implementation),

- More flexibility than a hierarchical approach (all relationships can be represented without redundancy).

WEAKNESSES OF NETWORK DATABASES

The disadvantages of a network database are:

- Machine performance (physical implementations that perform well for one type of network may perform poorly for another type),
- Maintainability (changing relationships may require physical reorganization of data),
- Lack of robustness. A failure in the system can leave dangling references to data which must somehow be recovered,
- Update overheads in multikey databases.

RELATIONAL DATABASES

The relational model for databases provides the basic DBMS characteristics. In addition, an RDBMS also conforms to Codd's model.

Relational Database Characteristics

Dr. Codd established 12 rules to which a DBMS must conform to be considered relational. DBMSs vary in the way in which they comply with these rules, however, commercial relational databases generally conform to these rules.

STRENGTHS OF RDBMS

Flexible and well-established. Sound theoretical foundation and use over many years has resulted in stable, standardized products available. Standard data access language through SQL. Costs and risks associated with large development efforts and with large databases are well understood.

The fundamental structure, i.e., a table, is easily understood and the design and normalization process is well defined. Representations of complex structures allow creation of a model that more closely resembles its real world counterpart. Storage of complex objects results in better performance. The model exhibits better coupling and cohesion characteristics. This results in a more maintainable and flexible database.

WEAKNESSES

Performance problems associated with re-assembling simple data structures into their more complicated real-world representations. Lack of support for complex base types, e.g., drawings. SQL is limited when accessing complex data. Knowledge of the database structure is required to create ad hoc queries. Locking mechanisms defined by RDBMSs do not allow design transactions to be supported, e.g., the "check in" and "check out" type of feature that would allow an engineer to modify a drawing over the course of several working days. Lack of maturity in the products.

This leads to more risk in employing the product. There is also a lack of product standardization. Database standards are emerging. There is no equivalent of SQL for object-oriented databases. Work is being done on establishing standards. There is much less experience with project development. Hence, there is a lack of information on costs and schedules. In addition, there is added training required for the team because of the lack of familiarity with the object paradigm. There is no consistent, solid theoretical basis to support ODBMS products. This raises questions about the completeness of the implementations. In addition, there is a plethora of analysis and design approaches.

OBJECT DATABASES

With the increased awareness of the object-oriented paradigm, many DBMSs claim to be object-oriented databases. The object-oriented model provides the basic DBMS characteristics. In addition Object-oriented Database Management Systems provide the following features.

MANDATORY

- *Support for Complex Objects*: An ODBMS must provide support for data types that allow storage of complex objects. An RDBMS supports only basic types, (e.g., integer, character), that are assembled into table rows to define objects.

- *Identity*: An object must be uniquely identified.
- *Encapsulation*: Hiding information and only allowing access through the public interface is a basic concept in object-orientation. Strict implementations enforce access to data through Programmes, however, some ODBMS products allow query access to the data.
- *Classes and Types*: An ODBMS must allow definition of classes and data types by the user. In addition these must not be restricted by the implementation. User defined types must be treated the same as the product supplier's base types in the database functionality.
- *Inheritance*: Inheritance is a basic concept in object-orientation that is a major factor in re-use. Inheritance of data and methods is a primary feature of an object-oriented programming language (OOPL).
- *Dynamic Binding and Polymorphism*: This characteristic allows different implementations of semantically similar methods with the same name in different classes.
- *Computational Completeness*: The integrated language must be computationally complete. For example, SQL is relationally complete since a SELECT statement can be constructed to retrieve any subset of data within an RDBMS. SQL is not computationally complete (it is sometimes called a data sublanguage) since there are computations that cannot be done using SQL constructs. The ODBMS language cannot have this restriction.
- *Extensibility*: The user must be able to add non-restricted types to the database.

SELECTING A DATABASE

Database technology may not always be needed, depending on the sophistication of the system's data structures, complexity of data, and the need for features provided by databases. In selecting a database, it is important to consider, in addition to the actual data management capabilities, the extent of the development environment provided or supported.

Since the physical view of data can be separated from the application view, the development environment provided or supported will have a significant effect on the ability to generate new applications or maintain existing applications using this data. Application engineers and developers do not need to know about the storage structure or access strategy of data to develop or modify applications.

Support for a standard query language, such as SQL, is also an important criteria. By developing applications using a standard query language, flexibility is achieved since the underlying database product can be changed or modified without necessarily affecting the applications that access the data. Note, however, that some DBMSs have added functionality not supported by the standard query language.

DATABASE SYSTEM VS FILES SYSTEM

INTRODUCTION

Database File System; It is a new type of file system that does away with places where you store your files. Actually do not think of it as a file system, instead think of it as a document system. And while being precise, it is not database system either, it is a faceted system. It is a file system geared toward serving the user and is meant to make your live easier. It supports 'locating' files the way you think about them.

Did you work on that file last month? Find all files you worked on last month. Was it a word document? Find all word documents you worked on last month. Was it for a certain project. Find all word documents from that project you worked on last month. That is the thinking the DBFS supports.

This is implemented in KDE and integrates right into its very core. The open-file and save-file dialogs are replaced with those from the DBFS. A file manager application (KDBFS) is added. The DBFS sits right on top of the hierarchy you use today. It indexes your files and keeps track of them. Saving a word document in the DBFS creates that same document on your hierarchy based system in the 'Documents' directory. But you need not know there is a traditional file system in your KDE, it looks as though there is not.

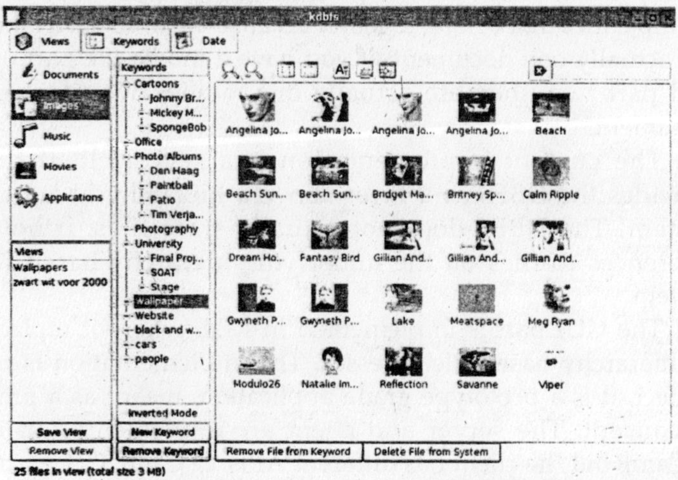

Fig. This is How it Looks; Click to Enlarge.

The searches are very fast, which gives direct feedback when browsing your files. And instead of directories the DBFS uses keywords. Keywords work somewhat like directories, but they can do much more. The keywords, as the DBFS uses them, are like a superset of directories.

Locating a file amongst gigabytes of files is hard. Hierarchy based file system create locations and unless you know where to look, you will not find your file. The DBFS tries to place the responsibility of finding files at the computer, so you don't have to remember where you stored it.

Look at what Apple is trying to do with their Spotlight!, or Microsoft with their WinFS!. Or look at google!, iTunes!, and others (like this announcement!). Searching is the new browsing. The DBFS takes a different approach by breaking away from directories. Still all these different types of search technologies definitely have a place inside the DBFS (in the future). But there are more things, beside searching, to making file management easier. Being document oriented for example. In the DBFS this is two fold. First, the DBFS does not store system files: No shared libraries, no font files or others like that.

These are not documents, not files you look up at a day to day basis, and have no place in a file system. Second, multiple files that belong together because the need each other, are actually one document. If you have a movie file part one and part two, they are actually one movie; two files, one document.

The current implementation is a server/client that provides the DBFS as a layer above a hierarchy based file system. The DBFS does not actually store files, it holds references to files on the underlying hierarchy based file system.

The GUI part is implemented in KDE where it replaces all hierarchy based file accesses. The implementation is not perfect, it is a prototype grade application, meant as a proof of concept. The server and client are implemented using O'Caml, but the client has different APIs: O'Caml, C, C++ and Objective-C.

Testing the DBFS is somewhat involved. Most people will need to compile a completely new KDE environment including QT. This is explained step-by-step in the README. It is important to use O'Caml 3.07 and KDE 3.2.3 (both have a newer version).

There are two more reasons that make the DBFS a good idea. One is that — when implemented — properties like owners, security, sharing and encryption have the same interface as keywords. Drag a special keyword 'private' to a file, and it is now private. No need to learn a new set of tools, no weird security that works through hierarchy.

A second good thing is that there are no locations, only file properties. Most applications can generate the file properties of a file. If you see the current version of the save-file dialog, it is very simple. This enables applications to always save every file you create in them, which enables a new type of computer usage. Today computers are dualistic; they have a screen area, this is where you input information, but it is violate. And they have a disk area which is permanent storage, but you need to explicitly save to that storage. There used to be a good reason for this behaviour, but today there is nothing wrong with storing every keystroke you input.

The DBFS allows the desktop to do away with that dualistic nature of the computer by just saving every file you start. If your file was just a temporary sketch then throw it in the trash, just like a scribble you write on paper, which you throw away afterwards. Instead of a save-file dialog there should be a file-properties dialog, where you change the file-name and file-type and assign keywords.

APPROACH

There are number of characteristics that differ from traditional file management system. In file system approach, each user defines and implements the needed files for a specific application to run. For example in sales department of an enterprise, One user will be maintaining the details of how many sales personnel are there in the sales department and their grades, these details will be stored and maintained in a separate file.

Another user will be maintaining the salesperson salary details working in the concern, the detailed salary report will be stored and maintained in a separate file. Although both of the users are interested in the data's of the salespersons they will be having their details in a separate files and they need different Programmes to manipulate their files.

This will lead to wastage of space and redundancy or replication of data's, which may lead to confusion, sharing of data among various users is not possible, data inconsistency may occur.

These files will not be having any inter-relationship among the data's stored in these files. Therefore in traditional file processing every user will be defining their own constraints and implement the files needed for the applications. In database approach, a single repository of data is maintained that is defined once and then accessed by many users. The fundamental characteristic of database approach is that the database system not only contains data's but it contains complete definition or description of the database structure and constraints. These definitions are stored in a system catalog, which contains the information about the structure and definitions of the database. The information stored in the catalog is called the metadata, it describes the primary database.

Hence this approach will work on any type of database for example, insurance database, Airlines, banking database, Finance details, and Enterprise information database. But in traditional file processing system the application is developed for a specific purpose and they will access specific database only.

The other main characteristic of the database is that it will allow multiple users to access the database at the same time and sharing of data is possible. The database must include concurrency control software to ensure that several users trying to update the same data at the same time, it should maintain in a controlled manner. In file system approach many programmers will be creating files over a long period and various files have different format, in various application languages.

Therefore there is possibility of information getting duplicated, this redundancy is storing same data multiple times leads to higher costs and wastage of space. This may result in data inconsistency in the application, this is because update is done to some of the files only and not all the files. Moreover in database approach multiple views can be created. View is a tailored representation of information contained in one or more tables. View is also called as "Virtual table" because view does not contain physically stored records and will not occupy any space.

A multi-user database whose users have variety of applications must provide facilities for defining multiple views. In traditional file system, if any changes are made to the structure of the files if will affect all the Programmes, so changes to the structure of a file may require changing of all Programmes that access the file. But in case of database approach the structure of the database is stored separately in the system catalog from the access of the application Programmes. This property is known as programme-data independence. Database can be used to provide persistent storage for programme objects and data structures that resulted in object oriented database approach.

Traditional systems suffered from impedance mismatch problem and difficulty in accessing the data, which is avoided in object oriented database system. Database can be used to represent complex relationships among data's as well as to retrieve and update related data easily and efficiently.

It is possible to define and enforce integrity constraints for the data's stored in the database. The database also provides facilities for recovering hardware and software failures. The backup and recovery subsystem is responsible for recovery.

It reduces the application development time considerably when compared to the file system approach and availability of up-to-date information of all the users. It also provides security to the data's stored in the database system.

CONCEPT AND ARCHITECTURE

ARCHITECTURE OF A DATABASE SYSTEM

A database consists of one or more tables, each containing data stored as individual records. Different database architectures determine how the tables and records are organized or related to one another.

The first database architectures - Hierarchical and Networked - have largely been superseded by the Relational, Object-Oriented and Object-Relational architectures. The Relational Data Model, developed by Todd Codd in 1969, allows multiple tables to be related to one another within a database.

For example, one customer's information could be recorded in separate tables such as "Personal Information",

"Marketing Efforts", and "Service Requests". The information stored in these tables will then relate back to the customer's main record. A relational database management system (RDBMS) also offers flexibility in terms of how the customer's data can be viewed.

To access the information stored in relational databases, users can either build queries using the Structured Query Language (SQL), or they can utilize a user interface that translates their requests into SQL and displays the results. While the American National Standards Institute (ANSI) approved an early version of SQL as a standard, many RDBMS's also use customized, proprietary forms of the language.

The Object-Oriented database model emerged in the mid-1980s due to the dissatisfaction of some database users with the structural limitations of RDBMS's. The Object-Oriented model defines each piece of data and its associated processes as an individual object. According to the basic tenets of this model, all information about an object is stored in one place instead of being stored across multiple tables, as is done in the relational model.

An Object-Oriented Database Management System (OODBMS) also integrates more easily with applications that have been written with an Object-Oriented programming language such as C++ or Java. Despite the advantages of the Object-Oriented approach, no standard model for the construction of an OODBMS yet exists.

For this reason, at least in part, RDBMS's still dominate the database market. One effort to combine the best parts of the RDBMS and OODBMS is the Object-Relational Database Management System (ORDBMS). This model allows developers to incorporate the best parts of an RDBMS and an ODBMS.

An ORDBMS works with objects like an ODBMS, but also allows SQL-based querying like an RDBMS. Market Leaders As of June 2001, the Oracle Corporation controlled 33.8% of the database market, IBM held 30.1% and Microsoft had 14.9%. While Oracle once dominated the market, the allegiance has been shifting as major enterprise application vendors such as SAP, PeopleSoft and Siebel Systems have pushed their primary application development efforts to IBM's DB2 database. IBM's recently completed acquisition of Informix has consolidated the number of players in the database market. It remains to be seen what impact the various open source DBMS's will have on the market, and the extent to which they will erode the market share of the current leaders.

The Future of Databases Databases play an important role in both data management and data storage in today's Information Age. The high value placed on information-gathering by companies as well as individuals requires efficient methods of storing and accessing information. Database architectures and products will need to be even more highly scalable to accommodate and support this increasing production of data in the future.

According to Michael Lesk, the huge amount of data would take several billion gigabytes or several thousand petabytes to store. Today, the importance and impact of databases is unquestioned, as government organisations, academic institutions and business entities create and maintain extensive databases containing all kinds of information ranging from natural-language text documents, statistical tables, financial data, and multimedia objects to data of a scientific and technical nature.

Many databases are composed of metadata, which means the records hold data about data such as information about the size and character of another database rather than primary source content such as a person's name and address. Database technologies, including architecture and access methods, are rapidly developing to keep pace with this demand for information management mechanisms.

Database designers and managers face many challenges that reflect the complexity of the burgeoning information environment. Database technologies must handle massive amounts of data, extract useful information from these repositories, and have the ability to reflect relationships between data maintained in different databases.

In addition, the architecture and system must provide integrity, recovery, concurrency and security. To answer these challenges, the three fundamental database models, hierarchical, network and relational, have served as a foundation for developing more powerful and flexible data models, such as the extended-relational and object-relational models.

Well defined architecture and data schema assure efficient, logical data storage which increases database capacity and extends the capabilities of query languages and other access methods. In addition, data mining creates useful information by identifying related data within the vast stores. Researchers now wrestle with the complexities of relational issues and interoperability. Researchers are now able to use meta data more efficiently to improved data dissemination. Researchers are also able to use federated strategies for distributed databases.

The architecture of DBS can be represented by the quintuple (data sources, application server, DB server with a DBMS, application server, DB and repository); Database Management Systems (DBMSs) are a ubiquitous and critical component of modern computing, and the result of decades of research and development in both academia and industry. *Architecture of a Database System* presents an architectural discussion of DBMS design principles, including process models, parallel architecture, storage system design, transaction system implementation, query processor and optimizer architectures, and typical shared components and utilities.

Successful commercial and open-source systems are used as points of reference, particularly when multiple alternative designs have been adopted by different groups. Historically, DBMSs were among the earliest multi-user server systems to be developed, and thus pioneered many systems design techniques for scalability and reliability now in use in many other contexts.

While many of the algorithms and abstractions used by a DBMS are textbook material, *Architecture of a Database System* addresses the systems design issues that make a DBMS work. *Architecture of a Database System* is an invaluable reference for database researchers and practitioners and for those in other areas of computing interested in the systems design techniques for scalability and reliability that originated in DBMS research and development.

As mentioned above, business processes act as data sources in commercial systems, while at statistical offices data is supplied by surveys, periodic reports or a census. Similarly, in science the data is generated by observations or measurements collected by field or simulation experiments.

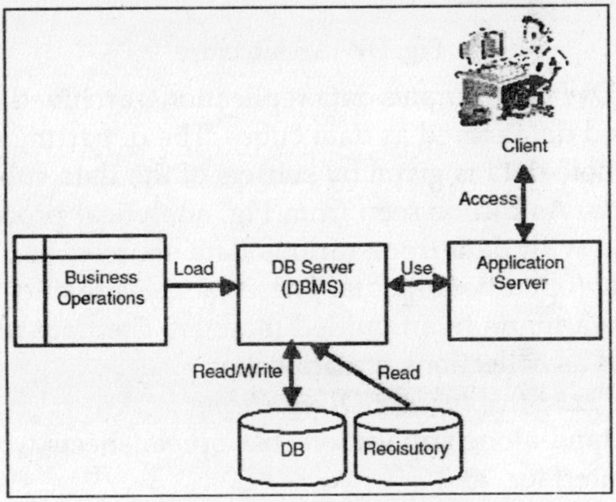

Fig. Architecture of a DBS

As an example from business we consider a company, which manages wages and salaries of its employees. The data is generated by bookkeeping, the DBMS administers the real and metadata, processes queries, and controls transactions. The application server is responsible for running the software for wage and salary computation, while the client is used as a presentation layer. The main components of the architecture of any OLAP application are heterogeneous data sources S like internal or external databases or files, an OLAP server with DWMS, DW, Repository and Data Marts, and OLAP clients. The DWMS is responsible for load management, query management and warehouse management.

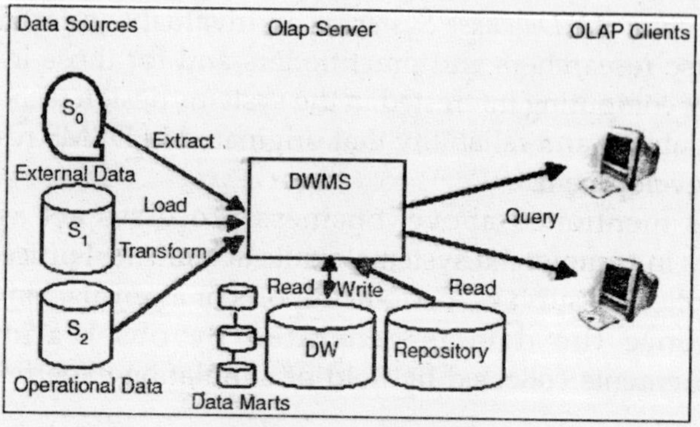

Fig. DW Architecture

The DW incorporates data replications, archived data and aggregated data stored as data cubes. The departmental view on the whole data is given by subsets of the data cube, called data marts. As can be seen from Fig. analytical processing is concerned with data from various data sources, i.e., external or internal (operational) data. These sources are integrated by ETL in data marts in an unified manner. The data marts can be viewed as collections of data cubes.

There exist two types of OLAP clients:

- Stand-alone applications like spreadsheets with a DW interface, and
- Web clients that use an Internet browser and often applets.

DATABASE SYSTEMS CONCEPTS

One way to keep the information on a computer is to store it in the permanent files. The system has a number of application Programmes, each of them is defined to manipulate the data files. These application Programmes have been written on request of the users in the organization.

New application will be added to the system as the need arises. The system just described is called the file-based system. Consider a traditional banking system which using the file-based system in managing the organization's data in the picture below. As we can see, there are different departments in the Bank, each of them have their own applications which manage and manipulate different data files. For Banking system, the Programmes can be the one to debit or credit an account, , find the balance of an account, add a new mortgage loan or generate monthly statements etc.

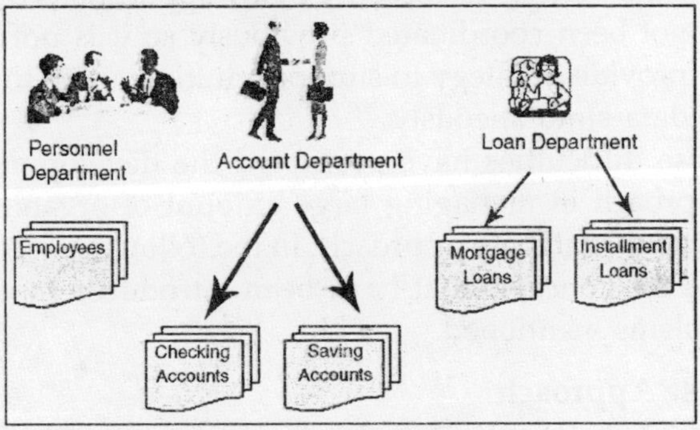

Fig. File-based Approach for Banking System

Keeping organizational information in this approach has a number of disadvantages, including:

- *Data Redundancy*: Since files and applications are created by different programmer of various departments over long period of time, it might lead to several problems:
- Inconsistency in data format
- The same information may be kept in several different place (files).
- Data inconsistency which means various copies of the same data are conflicting ; waste storage space and duplication of effort
- Data Isolation
- It is difficult for new application to retrieve the appropriate data which might be stored in various files.
- Integrity problems
- Data values must satisfy certain consistency contraints which are specified in the application Programmes.
- It is difficult to add change the Programmes to enforce new constraint

- Security problems
- There are constraint regarding accessing privileges
- Application is added to the system in the ad-hoc manner so it is difficult to enforce those constraints
- Concurrent – access anomalies
- Data may be accessed by many applications that have not been coordinated previously so it is not easy to provide a stategy to support multiple users to update data simutaneously

These difficulties have prompted the development of a new approach in managing large amount of organizational information – database approach. In the following section, we shall see the concepts that have been introduced to get over the problems mentioned.

Database Approach

Database and database technology play an important role in most of social areas where computer are used, including business, education, medicine etc. To understand the fundamental of database system, we start from introducing the basic concepts in this area.

Fundamental Concepts

Database is a shared collection of related data which will be used to support the activities of particular organization. Database can be viewed as a repository of data that is defined once and then is accessed by various users.

A database has the following properties:

- It is a representation of some aspect of the real world; or perhaps, a collection of data elements (facts) representing real world information.
- Database is logical coherent and internally consistent.
- Database is designed, built, and populated with data for a specific purpose.

Database Management System (DBMS) is a collection of Programmes that enable users to create, maintain database and control all the access to the database. The primary goal of the DBMS is to provide an environment that is both convenient and efficient for user to retrive and store information. Application programme accesses the data stored in the database by sending requests to the DBMS.

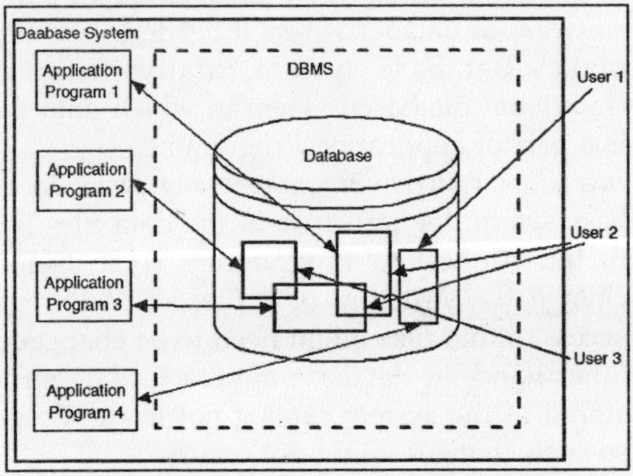

Fig. The Components of a Database System.

With the database approach, we can have the traditional banking system as shown in the following picture.

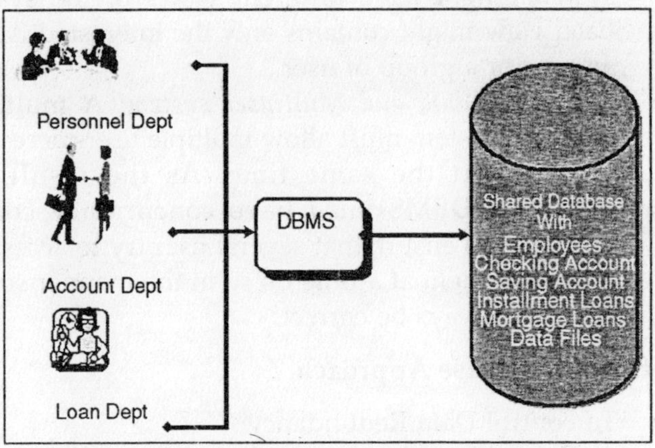

Fig. Database Approach for Banking System.

Characteristics of Database Approach

There are a number of characteristics that distinguish the database approach with the file-based approach. In this section, we describe in detail some of those important characteristics:

- *Self-Describing Nature of a Database System*: Database System contains not only the database itself but also the descriptions of data structure and constraints (meta-data). These information is used by the DBMS software or database users if needed. This seperation makes database system totally different from traditional file-based sytem in which data definition is a part of application Programmes
- *Insulation between Programme and Data*: In the filed base sytem, the structure of the data files is defined in the application Programmes so if user want to change the structure of a file, all the Programmes access to that files might need to be changed. On the other hand, in database approach, data structure is stored in the system catalog not in the Programmes so such changes might not occurs.
- *Support multiple views of data*: A view is a subset of the database which is defined and dedicated for particular users of the system. Multiple users in the system might have different views of the system. Each view might contains only the interested data of an user or a group of user.
- *Sharing of data and Multiuser system*: A multiuser database system must allow multiple users access the database at the same time. As the result, the multiuser DBMS must have concurrency control strategies to ensure that several user try to access the same data item at a time do so in the manner so that the data always be correct.

Benefits of Database Approach

- To control Data Redundancy
  - In the Database approach, ideally each data item is stored in only one place in the database
  - However, in some case redundancy is still exists to improving system performance, but such redundancy is controlled and kept to minimum
- Data Sharing

- The integration of the whole data in an organization leads to the ability to produce more information from a given amount of data
- Enforcing Integrity Constraints
  - DBMSs should provide capabilities to define and enforce certain constraints such as data type, data uniqueness.
- Restricting Unauthorised Access
  - Not all users of the system have the same accessing privileges.
  - DBMSs should provide a security subsystem to create and control the user accounts.
- Data Independence
  - The system data descriptions are separated from the application Programmes.
  - Changes to the data structure is handled by the DBMS and not embedded in the programme.
- Transaction Processing
  - The DBMS must include concurrency control subsystem to ensure that several users trying to update the same data do so in a controlled manner so that the result of the updates is correct.
- Providing multiple views of data
  - A view may be a subset of the database. Various users may have different views of the database itself.
  - Users may not need to be aware of how and where the data they refer to is stored
- Providing backup and recovery facilities
  - If the computer system fails in the middle of a complex update programme, the recovery subsystem is responsible for making sure that the database is restored to the stage it was in before the programme started executing.

DATA MODELS

Data Model is a collection of concepts that can be used to describe the structure of database. Structure of database means data types, relationships and constraints. In addition, most data model include a set of basic operations for specifying retrievals and modifications on the database. Data Model provides a means to achieve Data Abstraction. Data Abstraction is refers to the hiding of certain details of how the data are stored and maintained.

With several levels of abstraction, the user's view of the database is simplified and this leads to the improved understanding of data.

There are three levels of abstractions:

1. *View level*: The highest level of abstraction describes only part of the entire database. Many users will not be concerned with the large database. Instead, they need to access only a part of it so that view level abstraction is defined. There are many views for the same database.
2. *Logical level*: This level describes what data are stored in the whole database.
3. *Physical level*: The lowest level of abstraction describes how the data are actually stored.

CATEGORIES OF DATA MODEL

- *High-level Conceptual Data models*: Provide concepts that are close to the way people perceive data to present the data. Typical example of this type is entity – relationship model which use main concepts like entities, attributes, relationships. An entity represents real-world object such as an employee, a project. An entity has some attributes which represents properties of entity such as employee's name, address, birthdates. A relationship represents association among entities for example a works on relationships between employee and project.
- *Record-based Logical Data models*: Provide concepts that can be understood by the user but not too far from the way data is stored in the computer. Three well-known data models of this type are relational data model, network data model and hierarchical data model.

- The Relational model represents data as relations. Here is an example of relational schema for the SUPERMARKET database

Emps (Ename, Salary)	Managers (Ename)
Depts (Dname, Dept#)	Suppliers (Sname, Saddr)
Items (Iname, Item#)	Orders (O#, Date)
Works_In (Ename, Dname)	Manages (Ename, Dname)
Carries (Iname, Dname)	Placed_By (O#, Cname)
Customers(cname,Caddr, Balance)	Includes (O#, Iname, Quantity)
Supplies (Sname, Iname, Prices)	

- The Network model represents data as record types and also represents a limited type of one to many relationship, called set type. Figure shows a schema in network model notation

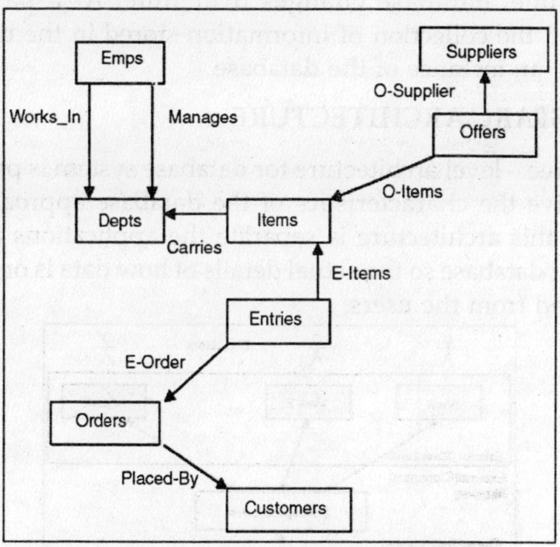

Fig. Sample Schema in Network Model

- The Hierarchical model represent data as hierarchical tree structures. Each hierarchy represents a number of related records. Here is the schema in hierarchical model notation.

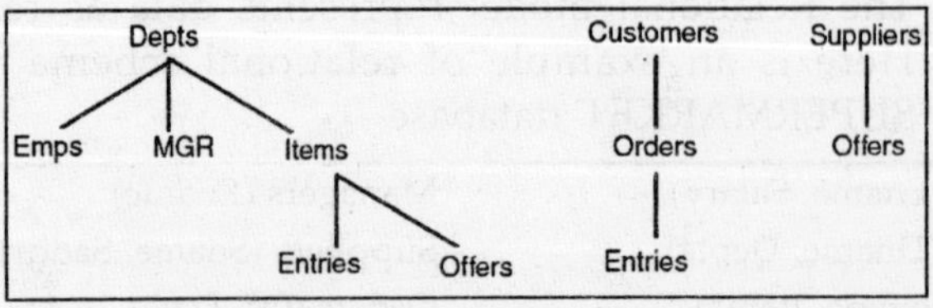

Fig. Sample Schema in Hierarchical Model Notation

- *Physical Data models*: Provide concepts that describe how data is actually stored in the computer.

Database Instances and Schemas

The description of the database which is designed in the early stage and is not expected to change frequently is called the database schema. Database system have severals schemas. Since information can be inserted to or deleted from database at anytime, database changes over time. At a particular moment, the collection of information stored in the database is called an instance of the database.

ANSI/SPARC ARCHITECTURE

Three – level architecture for database system is proposed to archive the characteristics of the database approach. The goal of this architecture is separate the applications and the physical database so the actual details of how data is organized are hided from the users.

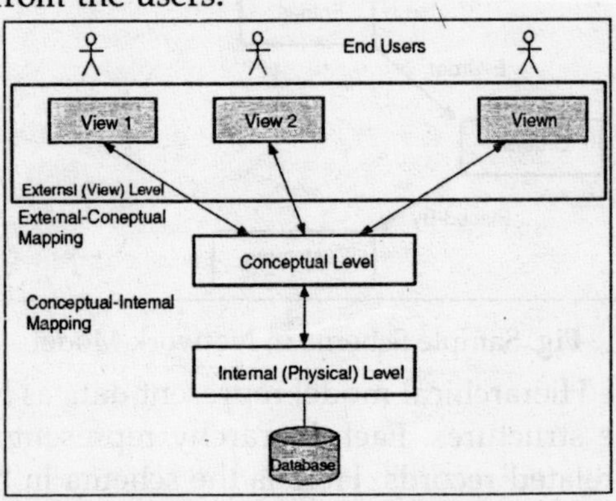

Fig. Three- level Architecture

As we can see from above picture, there are three levels of schemas in the database architecture

External Level

- In this highest level, there exists a number of views which of is defined a part of the actual database.
- Each view is provided for a user or a group of users so that it helps in simplified the interaction between the user and system.
- *Conceptual level*: Conceptual Schema in this level describes the logical structure of the whole database.
- The entire database is described using simple logical concepts such as objects, their properties or relationships. Thus the complexity of the implementation detail of the data with be hided from the users.
- *Internal level*: Internal Schema in this level describes how the data are actually stored, how to access the data.

Data Independence

Data Independence is the ability to modify the schema in one level without affecting the schema in the higher level.

There are two levels of data independence:

- Logical data independence is the ability to make change in the conceptual schema without causing a modify in the user views or application programme.
- Physical data independence is the ability to make change in the internal schema without causing a modify in the conceptual schema or application programme.

Physical data independence seem to be easier to achieve since the way the data is organized in the memory affect only the performance of the system. Meanwhile, the application programme depends much on the logical structure of the data that they are access.

Database Language

Data Definition Language (DDL): This is used to define the conceptual and internal schemas for a database system.

- It is not procedural language, rather a language for

describing the types of entities and relationships among them in terms of a particular data model.

- *Data Manipulation Language (DML)*: This is used to manipulate the database, which typically include retrieval, insertion, deletion, and modification of the data.

DATABASE USERS

End Users

People whose jobs require access to database for querying, updating and generating report.

An end users might by one of the following:

- Naïve users who use the existing appication Programmes to perform their daily tasks
- Sophisticated users are who use their own way to access to the database. This mean they do not use the application programme provided in the system. In stead, they might define their own application or describe their need directly in a query languages.
- Specialized users maintain the personal database by using ready –make programme packages that provide easy-to-use menu.

Application Programmer

People implement specific application programme to access to the stored data. This kind of user need to familiar with the DBMSs to accomplish their task.

Database Administrators

A person or a group of people in the organization who is responsible for authorizing the access to the database, monitoring its use and managing all the resource to support the use of the whole database system

CLASSIFICATION OF DATABASE SYSTEMS

The database management systems can be classified based on several criteria:

- *Based on data model*: The most popular data model in

today commercial DBMSs is relational data model. Almost wellknown DBMSs like Oracle, MS SQL Server, DB2, MySQL are support this model. Other traditional models can be named hierarchical data model , network data model. In the recent year, we are getting familiar with object-oriented data model but this model has not had widespread use. Some examples of Object-oriented DBMSs are O2, ObjectStore or Jasmine.

- Based on number users we can have single user database system which support one user at a time or multiuser syste,s which support multiple users concurrently
- Based on the ways database is distributed we have centralized or distributed database system
- Centralized database system : Data in this kind of system is stored at a single site.
- Distributed database sytem: Actual database and DBMS software are distributed in various sites connected by a computer network.
- Homogeneous distributed Database Systems
- Use the same DBMS software at multiple sites
- Data exchange between various sites can be handle easily
- Heterogeneous distributed Database Systems
- Different sites might use differents DBMS softwares
- There is a software to support data exchange between sites

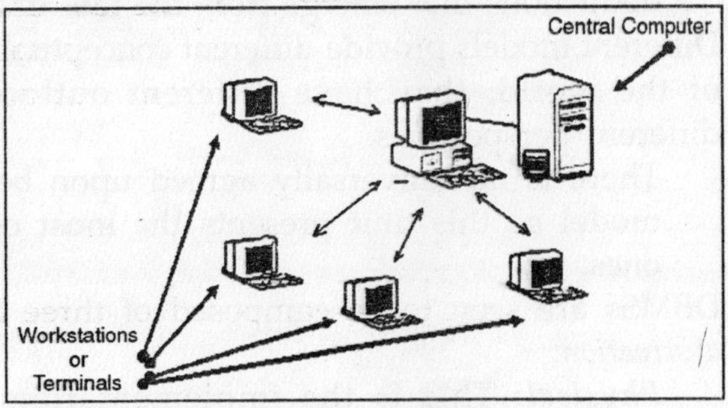

Fig. Centralized Database System

DATA MODELS

INTRODUCTION

- A *data model* is mathematical formalism consisting of two parts.
  - A notation for describing data, and
  - A set of operations used to manipulate that data.
- A data model is a way of organizing a collection of facts pertaining to a system under investigation.
- Data models provide a way of thinking about the world, a way of organizing the phenomena that interest us.
- They can be thought of as an abstract language, a collection of words along with a grammar by which we describe our subject.
  - By choosing a language, we pay the price of being constrained to form expressions whose words are limited to those in the language and whose sentence structure is governed by the languages grammar.
  - We are not free to use random collections of symbols for words nor can we put the words together in any *ad hoc* fashion.
- A major benefit we receive by following a data model stems from the theoretical foundation of the model.
  - From the theory emerges the power of analysis, the ability to extract inferences and to create deductions that emerge from the raw data.
- Different models provide different conceptualizations of the world; they have different outlooks and different perspectives.
  - There is no universally agreed upon best data model so this unit presents the most common ones.
- DBMSs are seen to be composed of three *levels of abstraction:*
  - *Physical*: This is the implementation of the database in a digital computer. It is concerned

with things like storage structures and access method data structures.

- *Conceptual*: This is the expression of the database designers model of the real world in the language of the data model.
- *View*: Different user groups can be given access to different portions of the database. A user groups portion of the database is called their *view*.

TYPES OF DATA MODELS

COMMON DATA MODELS

- This section presents an overview of the most common data models

Entity-Relationship Model

- The Entity-Relationship (ER) model is generally attributed to (Chen 1976).
- The ER model envisions the world as comprised of *entities* that are associated with each other by *relationships*. All of the entities of a particular type are collected together into *entity sets*.
- Entity sets and relationships can be depicted graphically in an ER-diagram.

Entities

- Entities are distinguishable real-world objects such as employees, maps, airplanes, or bus schedules.
  - Distinguishable means that all entities can be uniquely identified.
  - Entities have common attributes that define what it means to be such an entity.
  - Any particular real-world object does not necessarily have a single or best representation as an entity.
    a. For any given real-world object, different modelers can choose different sets of

attributes of the object that are of interest to their particular situation.

b. This results in the same object being modeled differently.

- Entities are collected into *entity sets.*
  - Entity sets are depicted as rectangles in *ER diagrams.*
  - Their attributes are depicted as ellipses attached to the rectangles by lines.

Relationships

- A relationship is a list of entity sets.
  - *Notation*: Two entity sets *A* and *B* that stand in relationship r is written *A* r *B*. See the next bullet for examples.
- Types of relationships
  - *Aggregating relationships*:

a. *One-one*: if *A* r *B* and r is one-one then each entity of *B* is in relationship with at most one entity of *A* and vice-versa.

b. For example, if *CAPTAIN* commands *VESSEL* and commands is one-one then, in our model, each vessel has at most one captain and each captain commands at most one vessel at a time.

c. *Many-one*: If *A* r *B* and r is many-one then each entity of *A* is in relationship with at most one entity of *B* but not vice-versa.

d. For example, if *CREW* assigned-to *VESSEL* and assigned-to is many-one then, in our model, a vessel has many crew members but a crew member is assigned to only one vessel.

e. *Many-many*: If *A* r *B* and r is many-many then each entity of *A* can be in relationship with any number of *B* entities and vice-versa.

f. For example, if *VESSEL* patrols *REGION* and patrols is many-many then, in our model, a vessel patrols many regions and a region is patrolled by many ships.

- Is a (read is a) relationships: if *A* isa *B* then *A* is a specialization of *B*, or, conversely, *B* is a generalization of *A*.

g. For example, if *CAPTAIN* isa *CREW* then, in our model, captains have all the attributes of crew members but not vice versa.

h. The isa relationship allows hierarchies to be established among entity sets.

- A Relationship is depicted by a lozenge with lines connecting it to the relevant entity sets.
- The Entity-Relationship model lacks an underlying formalism and is, therefore, used more for general conceptualization than for creating physical models
  - (indeed, some authors do not acknowledge the ER model as a data model at all).
  - It is not uncommon for a conceptual design to be expressed in the ER model and then translated into another model for implementation.

THE NETWORK MODEL

- The network data model is based upon the concept of a *structure* such as is found in programming languages like C or Pascal.
  - ER entities can be modeled as structures with the entitys attributes corresponding to the structures fields.
  - Entities are distinguished by their location, *i.e.*, the physical address of the structure that is holding them. Thus, two structures of identical value represent two separate entities.
- Entity sets can be implemented as files whose records match the structures.
- Relationships are created with explicit linkages (*viz.* pointers) from structure to structure.
- Codasyl is an example of a DBMS based on the network model.
- The network model has neither formal semantics nor a high-level query language. Database manipulation

was done via custom Programmes often written in COBOL.

- Network model databases are hand-coded and, therefore, can be very efficient in their space utilization and query execution times; all the relationships are hardwired or pre computed and built into the structure of the database itself.
- The price for such performance is inflexibility and great difficulty of use (among many other things).

THE RELATIONAL MODEL

- The relational model was introduced by Codd (1970) and has been the inspiration of an entire generation of database management systems that are based on the concept of a *relation* which is a set of *tuples*.

Tuples

- A tuple is a set of facts that are related to each other in some way (perhaps only by the fact theyve been put together in a set).
- Each fact in a tuple is a datum whose value comes from a specified domain (*e.g.*, the domain of all integers, the domain of all character strings of length 255 or less, *etc.*)
- Formally, let $D_1, \ldots, D_n$ be n sets of values constituting n domains (n is usually greater than zero but that is not strictly necessary). A *tuple* t is a set of values $t = \{d_1, \ldots, d_n\}$, such that d_1 is an element of $D_1, \ldots$, and d_n is an element of D_n. The domains are called *attributes*.

Relations

- Formally, let $D_1, \ldots, D_n$ be n domains. A *relation* R is a set of tuples over the Cartesian product $D_1 \times \ldots \times D_n$.
- In English, a relation is a (possibly complete) subset of all the possible tuples formed by the Cartesian product of the domains.
- Since tuples are sets (of values) and a relation is also

a set (of tuples), relations are sets of sets.

- A file is a list of records
- A table is a list of rows
- A relation is a set of tuples

- Relations are naturally represented as tables.
  - Tables are not relations because relations cannot have duplicate tuples and there is no such stricture on tables. However, it is perhaps convenient to think about relations as tables so long as the distinction remains clear.
  - Most (if not all) commercial relational DBMSs violate this principle: they allow duplicate tuples.
- The use of relations as a data modeling tool becomes apparent when we have a relation, say, *OUR_DEM* with fields {*quadname, zone_code, mappingcenter*}.
  - It happens that the USGS has a digital elevation model named Placitas NM in UTM zone 13 that was created by the Forest Service Mapping Centre.
  - Then, the presence of a tuple in the *OUR_DEM* relation whose
    a. *Quadname* attribute has the value Placitas NM
    b. *Zone_code* attribute has the value 13, and
    c. *Mappingcenter* attribute has the value FS,
  - Indicates that we have the Placitas DEM in our possession.

Tuples, Relations and Keys

- *Relations are sets of tuples*: Consequently, no two tuples that are elements of the same relation can have identical values for all their attributes. That is to say, there are no duplicate tuples in a relation.
- All tuples in a relation can be distinguished by the values of their attributes.
  - Any set of attributes whose values *necessarily* uniquely identify a tuple are said to be a *key*.
- Database designers choose some attribute set to be a key for their databases relations.
  - This key is known as the *primary key*.

- If the primary key of one table appears as an attribute of a different relation, the key is known as a *foreign key* in the other relation.
- A key uniquely identifies its tuple. Therefore, a tuples key is often used as a surrogate for the entire tuple.

Relationships

- Not surprisingly, the relational model represents relationships with relations.
- Figure shows a relational database that was designed from the ER-diagram developed above.
  - Key attributes are denoted in bold face.
- If you wish to work with these examples, you can download either.
  - *The Microsoft Access97 .mdb file by SAVING the files at:*
  - *ASCII text for the tables by clicking their names below.*
    a. The attribute names are on the first row, character strings are delimited with double quotes (") and the fields are comma delimited.
- Aggregating relationships are represented by embedding the primary key of one relation into another relation as a foreign key:
  - *one-one*: if *A* r *B* and r is one-one then the primary key of *A* can be embedded in *B* or vice versa or both.
    a. For example, suppose *CAPTAIN* commands *VESSEL* and that commands is one-one.
    b. Suppose further that *cptn_name* is the primary key of *CAPTAIN* and *vessel_name* is the primary key of *VESSEL*.
    c. Then, *CAPTAIN* could have an attribute commands whose value is that of *vessel_name* for the vessel that captain commands.
    c. It is equally reasonable to have an attribute *commanded by* in *VESSEL* whose value is that of name for the captain commanding the vessel.
  - *Many-one*: if *A* r *B* and r is many-one then the

primary key of *B* can be embedded in *A* but not vice versa.

a. For example, suppose *CREW* assigned-to *VESSEL* and assigned-to is many-one.

b. Suppose further that *crew_name* is the primary key of *CREW* and *vessel_name* is the primary key of *VESSEL*.

c. Then, *CREW* could have an attribute *assigned_to* whose value is that of *vessel_name* for the vessel this crew member serves on.

d. However, *VESSEL* cannot have an attribute *roster* because *roster* would have to be a set (many crew members per vessel) and the relational model stipulates that all domains are atomic; no collections.

– *Many-many*: if *A* r *B* and r is many-many then neither primary key can be embedded the other table. Again, the difficult lies in the atomicity rule for domains. So, for a many-many relationship, we must create a separate relation whose attributes include but are not limited to the primary keys from *A* and *B*.

a. For example, if *VESSEL* patrols *REGION* and patrols is many-many.

b. Suppose further that *vessel_name* is the primary key of *VESSEL* and *region_name* is the primary key of *REGION*. Then we have a third relation *PATROLS* with attributes *vessel_name* and *region_name*.

c. Such relations are sometimes called *join supports*

d. Such relations are no different in any way from any other relation

- *Isa relationships are handled as the other relationships*:

– *One-one*: Suppose *CAPTAIN* isa *CREW*.

a. Then there is a one-one relationship between *CAPTAIN* and *CREW* so the primary key of *CREW* can be used as the key in *CAPTAIN*.

b. The one-one nature of this relationship

indicates that the two tuples really give details of the same entity; they are sort of like a single tuple that has been split in two.

– *Many-one*: Suppose we are modeling WWII combat vessels, known collectively as "ship(s) of the line" (SOTL). It happens that a ship design can be used as the plan for many individual vessels (obviously).

a. The design is known as a class and the vessels made to that design are said to belong to that class.

b. For example, the USS Missouri belongs to the Iowa class of battleships.

c. We model this relationship with a relation *SOTL* which has a single tuple for each class of warship. Thus, *VESSEL* isa*SOTL*.

d. The *SOTL* relation has attributes that are common to all ships of the line. For WWII vessels, this might include attributes such as the number of primary guns, size of the primary guns, *etc.*

e. The tuple in *SOTL* for the Iowa battleships gives information that is common to all Iowa class battleships (*e.g.*, nine 16-inch guns, *etc.*).

f. The tuple in *VESSEL* for the *USS* Missouri holds the information specific to that vessel including the fact it belongs in the Iowa class.

g. Therefore, the primary key of *SOTL* is embedded in *VESSEL*, not vice versa.

h. Compare many-one isa relationships with one-one isa relationships.

i. Ullman restricts relationships to be one-one.

Query Languages

- Codd invented two early languages for dealing with relations: one was algebraic and the other was based on first-order predicate logic. These languages have the same expressive power.

- *Relational Algebra*
  a. [an] algebraic notation where queries are expressed by applying specialized operators to relations
  b. See for a presentation of the relational algebra.
- *Relational Calculus*
  a. [a] Logical notation where queries are expressed by writing logical formulas that the tuples in the answer must satisfy.
  c. See for a presentation of the relational calculus.

- The most common commercial query language is the *Structured Query Language,* or *SQL.*
  - Despite its reputation as a relational query language, SQL does not fully support the relational model (it includes things that are not in the model and omits things that are. Relational Database Management System (RDBMS)
- A *relational database management system* is a DBMS based on the relational model as defined.
- There is no commercially available DBMS that fully implements the relational model as defined. Some are coming closer. Not everyone agrees that this strict lack of conformance is a Bad Thing.

Advantages of the Relational Model

- Codd presents many advantages of the relational model. Some of them are highlighted below:
- The relational model is truly a mathematically complete data model. This solid theoretical underpinning is responsible for.
  - *Ad hoc* query languages whose queries can be automatically compiled, executed, and optimized without resorting to programming.
  - *Correctness*: The semantics of the relational algebra are sound and complete
  - Predictable: the consistent semantics enables users to easily anticipate the result of a given query
- *Adaptability*: Making a change in the structure of the

tables in the network model requires programmatic making changes to all the databases queries. As a result, the network model is inflexible in the extreme.
  - The relational model cleanly separates the logical from the physical model and this decoupling mitigates or eliminates these problems.
  - Also, the relational models integrity constraints are very helpful in ensuring that structural changes did not adversely effect the meaning of the database.
- *Multiple views*: it is straightforward to present different user groups different views of the same database.
- *Concurrency*: A full theory of transaction concurrency control exists which depends upon the theoretical formalisms of the relational model.
  - This theory guarantees the correct execution of concurrent queries (indeed, it defines what is correct)

OBJECT MODEL

Definition

- The word object is similar to the Entity-Relationship concept of an entity although object is more general.
  - I recommend taking object in the spirit of objects in the physical world.
  - Objects are things but they are not limited to physical, tangible things. For example, data structures (*e.g.*, a hash table) can be objects.
  - All objects are distinct and, like the network model, are made distinct by an identifying attribute, the *object ID*.
- Like the other models, the object model assumes that objects can *conceptually* be collected together into meaningful groups. These groups are called *classes*.
- An object grouping is meaningful because objects of the same class must have common attributes, behaviors, and relationships with other objects.

- Unlike entity sets and relations, classes do not actually hold the objects of that class.
  - Classes are purely conceptual.
  - There is nothing in the object model that is equivalent to either a entity set or a relation (there could be but its not required by the model).
- Like the network model, the relationships among objects are specified via a physical link (pointer) between objects.
- According to Rumbaugh *et al*. (1991), The object model describes the structure of objects in a system their identity, their relationships to other objects, their attributes, and their operations.
- The DARPA Open OODB project proposes the following as the essential features of the OO data model.
  - *Object Identity*: The ability of the system to distinguish between two different objects that have the same state. The state of an object can be shared by several objects via object identity.
  - *Encapsulation:* a kind of abstraction that enforces a clean separation between the external interface (behaviour) of an object and its internal implementation. Encapsulation requires that all access (or interaction) with objects be done by invoking the services provided by their external interface.
  - *Complex State*: The ability to define data types whose implementation has a nested structure. The state of an object could be built from records of primitive types, other objects, or [collections] of objects.
  - *Type Extensibility*: The ability to define new data types from previously defined types by enhancing or changing the structure or behaviour of the types. Type inheritance is a mechanism used to define new types by enhancing already existing behaviour.

- *Genericity*: The types of the object data model with which the object query language collaborates must be generic. That is, as a new type is added to the system, it must be queriable.

- There is no universally agreed upon object data model but *The Object-Oriented Database System Manifesto* (Atkinson, *et al.* 1989) gives a framework being considered from which to derive a standard.
- According to Rao, The object-oriented database (OODB) paradigm is the combination of object-oriented programming language (OOPL) systems and persistent systems. The power of the OODB comes from the seamless treatment of both persistent data, as found in databases, and transient data, as found in executing Programmes.
  - Note that the emphasis with OODB, like the network model, is towards programmers, not end users.
  - This point is further emphasized by the primary interface to OODBs being OOPLs.
- I suggest for a good introduction to object-oriented design and analysis.

Inheritance (isa) Relationships and Typing

- Many object-oriented models take classes to be a typing mechanism (for example, Eiffel and C++.
- The *type* of an object is its *class*; an object is an *instance* of its class.
  - For example, the number 2.3 is an instance of the class of rational numbers.
- Interpreting classes to be types implies the inherent ability of users to create their own data domains.
- Inheritance can be viewed from two perspectives:
  - *incremental*: the process of adding attributes and functions to an existing class (the *base class*).

    a. New attributes/functions can added to the New class that were not in the base class.

    b This is a technique for code reuse.

c. No typing information is implied by this relationship.

d. For example, suppose that there is a class *PERSISTENT* that has the functionality of automatically storing its objects in a database. Any class that inherits *PERSISTENT* magically gains the ability to do likewise.

– *Subtyping*: a technique for arranging class definitions in a hierarchy satisfying the condition that members of the subclass are also members of the superclass.

a. Subtyping constitutes the isa relationship.

b. Old attributes/functions can change type so long as the new type is more specific (it inherited either directly or indirectly) than the original base class.

c. Old attributes/functions cannot be removed.

d. Old functions can be provided with new implementations so long as the interface to the function remains unchanged (or is changed via specialization as indicated above)

- Various object models span the gambit of inheritance relationships:
  - Full repeated multiple inheritance.
  - Single inheritance.
  - No inheritance.

Encapsulation

- Objects *encapsulate* their attributes and the behaviors. *This implies*:
  - There is no interaction with an object that does Not go through a publicly published interface
  - Objects manipulate their own state; the definition of class includes the object's behaviour manifested as functions and procedures.
  - An objects state *cannot* be manipulated by anything external to them (at least, not without permission).

- For example, in a non object-oriented language such as C, let's say a programmer writes a procedure to change the values of a structure holding the position of a graphics primitive.
  - In an object-oriented language, the programmer creates a graphics primitive class that has its positional information along with an internal procedure that changes its own position.
  - The programmer sends a message to the object requesting it to change its own position.
- The advantage of encapsulation is that the implementation of any behaviour can be changed without effecting any other class in the system. This helps de-couple the classes and reduces the complexity of the system.

Comparison to the Relational Model

- The object model differs from the relational model in (at least) the following ways:
  - The object model allows complex objects to be attribute domains; this is prohibited in the relational model.
  - The only complex type available in the relational model is the relation.
    a. The object model restricts all system entities to be objects which is a more general concept than a relation (relations can be objects but not all objects are relations).
  - The relational model allows no duplicate tuples and, consequently, entities are identified by their attribute values.
    a. The object model assumes the existence of an object ID which uniquely identifies its object and is, possibly, invisible to the user.
  - Objects are instances of classes and classes constitute the typing system of the model.
    a. There is no concept of class-level typing in the relational model; everything is a relation.

b. The relational model supports user-defined domains but this is applied at the attribute level whereas, with the object model, the class is also a type.

c. The equivalent in the relational world would be for relations to constitute types, as well.

- There is no generally accepted formal object model.

a. The relational model is well-defined, sound, and complete.

- Relations hold all tuples. There is no equivalent for objects; there is no set or anything else that contains all the objects of a class.
- There are many higher-order, non-programming query languages for the relational model. There are few equivalents for the object model.
- The object model is aimed more at programmers than at end users; the reverse is true of the relational model.

DATABASE LANGUAGE AND INTERFACE

DATA INDEPENDENCE

Data independence is a form of database management that keeps data separated from all Programmes that make use of the data. As a cornerstone for the idea of a DBMS or database management system, data independence ensures that the data cannot be redefined or reorganized by any of the Programmes that make use of the data.

In this manner, the data remains accessible, but is also stable and cannot be corrupted by the applications using it. Database management within the environment of a centralized DBMS relies on the process of data independence. While data transparency still exists as far as the ability of different applications to access and use the data for completing tasks, no programme or application can read and then begin to make changes to the data itself. The consistency of the data makes the overall process of maintaining and managing a single database or multiple databases within a single environment much easier.

The concept of data independence is different from another approach referred to as data dependence. With this approach, the data used to run an application is actually represented in the source code for the programme. The ability of the data to be modified by the programme, and vice versa, means that the data is not considered constant and may be changed either by initiating the change through modifications to the source code or through using the programme in other ways to adapt the core data.

One of the functions of data independence is to restrict access to the storage structure of the data by the user applications. By effectively hiding the specifics of the structure from the applications, the potential for any one application to alter the nature of the data becomes impossible. Thus, the essential data retains its integrity and remains consistent no matter how many databases or database applications access the core data.

Data independence is normally thought of in terms of two levels or types. Logical data independence makes it possible to change the structure of the data independently of modifying the applications or Programmes that make use of the data. There is no need to rewrite current applications as part of the process of adding to or removing data from then system. The second type or level of data independence is known as physical data independence. This approach has to do with altering the organization or storage procedures related to the data, rather than modifying the data itself.

Accomplishing this shift in file organization or the indexing strategy used for the data does not require any modification to the external structure of the applications, meaning that users of the applications are not likely to notice any difference at all in the function of their Programmes.

DATABASE LANGUAGE

A generic term referring to a class of languages used for defining and accessing databases. A particular database language will be associated with a particular database management system. There are two distinct classes of database language: those that do not provide complete programming facilities and are designed to be used in association with some general-purpose programming language (the *host language*), and those that do provide complete programming facilities (*database programming languages*). Some products adopting the former approach seek to minimize host-language programming by the provision of fourth-generation language (4GL) facilities.

A database language must provide for both logical-schema specification and modification (*data description*) and for retrieval and update (*data manipulation*). In some cases, particularly products derived from the CODASYL network database standard, these aspects are treated distinctly as the *data description language* (DDL) and the *data manipulation language* (DML). Modification to the storage is also generally separately provided.

DATA INTERFACE

Using a foreign language is challenging for most of us. Clearly there are many benefits of knowing languages for when we travel, but finding the time to learn them seems elusive. The situation with relational databases is seemingly similar. We know that so much information is now stored in databases in an organization, that it is tempting to think that we could do our jobs better if only we had the computer skills to work more directly with them.

Unfortunately, getting better database querying skills can involve a significant investment of time. Most databases now are based on relational database technology. The idea behind a relational database is very simple: It is just composed of tables of information, and so absorbing information from a small database is often easy. Each row is an example on which we have information, and the information is given in the entry for each column.

In this way, a table in a relational database is no different to a table we might draw on a piece of A4 paper. Whilst using simple relational databases is straightforward, problems arise when we have larger tables – ie. tables that do not fit on a manageable number of pages.

Consider a telephone directory. We might consider this as a table. Each subscriber is a row in the table, and the columns are for name, address, area, and telephone number. In a sense such a big table is manageable because the rows are sorted according to the alphabetical order of the names. Having such an order allows us to quickly find the number of someone in the books.

But consider trying to find a particular number in a telephone book, or trying to find all the people who live in particular road. And these are relatively simple queries you could ask. The formal language for querying relational database is usually SQL.

There are simpler querying facilities for querying and manipulating data in many databases packages such as "query by example" and the ability to select a column and then order all the items in the table according to the ordering in that column.

That would solve our problem of finding a person by their telephone number in the previous paragraph. But it is only part of the answer. SQL provides the most expressive way of querying and manipulating data in a database. Obviously English (or indeed any natural language) is more expressive than SQL. But the problem with English is that it is too expressive. There are many ways of saying the same thing using different words, abbreviations, phraseology, and grammatical constructions.

Furthermore, in using English there are many ways of saying things in indirect ways. For example, using metaphor, analogy, euphemisms, and humour. Yet it seems very appealing to be able to query a relational database using natural language.

If we accept that we need to use relatively restricted subset of English, then it is possible to develop useful natural language interfaces with some degree of flexibility and robustness. A natural language interface for a database needs to incorporate both syntactic knowledge and semantic knowledge. The syntactic knowledge is relatively well-established for this kind of task and includes grammar of the language, conjugations, declensions, rules of agreement and rules of word order.

It is normally knowledge that is common to all database interfaces, and so is relatively stable knowledge. It can be built into the software tools by the software developers, and normally doesn't need amending.

In contrast, most semantic knowledge is dependent on the application. Simple examples are the ability to deal with synonyms in a context sensitive way. For example, in a database on names and addresses, we don't want to treat the uses of *bank* in *Barclays Bank and Kew Gardens Seed Bank* as symonymous in questions like "Give me the names of banks and building societies that have branches in the Borough of Richmond".

Whilst handling semantic knowledge is a complex and open-ended problem. There have been plenty of promising experimental natural langauge database interfaces developed that combine syntactic and semantic knowledge. Unfortunately these developments have not led to overwhelming commercial success so far.

As long ago as 1985, Ovum (an independent IT consultancy) published a report predicting that "By 1987 a natural language interface should be a standard option for users of database management systems and 'Information Centre' type software, and there will be a reasonable choice of alternatives". With hindsight this prediction appears incorrect because the advantages of graphical and form-based query techniques were under-estimated.

However, as the limits of these other approaches are reached, it is likely there will be increased interest in natural language querying. Currently, there are products on the market for building natural language interfaces for pc-based relational databases. Though it is still very much a niche market with suppliers being very small companies such as Elf with its Access ELF product for Microsoft.

The Access ELF software incorporates syntactic knowledge together with a general-purpose lexicon. When configuring the software for a particular database, the lexical knowledge is updated. Some is by the system analysing the entries in the tables and analysing queries to the database, and some is by the users directly updating the lexical knowledge. Using this knowledge, the software is able to understand and process quite complex queries. For example, for a typical customer orders database it can handle the following types of query.

- Which customers have placed more orders than average?"
- Which customers have placed fewer than 10 orders?"
- Which customers have ordered tofu but not Longlife tofu?"
- Make a list of the clients that use Federal Shipping exclusively"
- Which customers ordered tofu in the week of 5 April?"

In general getting software to handle such queries can be very useful. But it is not difficult to find queries that can confound an interface. As a result natural language interfaces for databases are still regarded as a niche technology. But it is likely that this will change rapidly over the next few years with developments in artificial intelligence and computational linguistics providing more intelligent and more robust solutions. In particular, there has been much research into developing semantic knowledge using techniques such as semantic networks and automated learning technology. Currently, much of this new technology is being directed at natural language search engines such as Ask Jeeves (www.askjeeves.co.uk) , and given the current economics of the web, it is not surprising that some technology start ups, such as Easy Ask, have shifted their focus from selling natural language interfaces to selling natural language search engines. But as the web drives information technology forward, it likely natural language interfaces to databases will become better and more widely used.

What is a Relational Database?

Relational databases are the most commonly used kind of database. In a relational database, information is stored in tables. Each table has one or more columns, and one or more rows. We can consider each row as an example and each entry in a column in the row gives details about the example.

For example, we can have a customer database where each row represents an individual customer, and each entry in the row gives details about that customer such as name, address, and telephone number. The basic idea is simple and yet so much business information easily falls into this format. This largely explains the ubiquity of relational databases in commercial information systems.

What is SQL?

SQL stands for Structured Query Language. To illustrate SQL, let us consider a table of customers that has columns Name, House number, Road, Town, County, Postcode, Telephone Number, Fax number, and Email. We call this table Customers. Now consider the following SQL. This will retrieve all rows from the Customers table.

```
Select
From Customers
```

Now consider the following SQL query. This will retrieve all rows where the entry for the County column is East Sussex.

```
Select
From Customers
Where County = East Sussex
```

So far so good. But the language does quickly get much more complicated. This is not a criticism of SQL. Indeed the language is very clear if you are prepared to invest the time to learn it. However it is by necessity very precise so as to avoid the ambiguities that arise in natural language. Furthermore, it does not directly handle synonyms and common-sense abbreviations. For example, consider the following query which many would regard as equivalent to the query above.

```
Select
From Customers
```

Where County = E Sussex

Here, common-sense would dictate that East Sussex and E Sussex are equivalent. But in SQL this equivalence needs to be made explicit. Making all the desirable semantic knowledge explicit can be challenging.

Kind of Natural Language

Within the focused domain of an SQL database, natural language interfaces can be constructed that can understand and respond correctly to a wide range of queries. To illustrate, let us consider the Customer table:

We start with the simplest query:

Select *

From Customers

Even trying to handle a simple query such as this could be posed in many different ways such as:

What customers do we have?

List all customers?

Please give me all customers?

Who are our customers?

I want a list of all our customers?

Can I have list of all customers?

This list could easily grow to a list of a few hundred different ways of asking the same question! But by using appropriate knowledge of the recursive nature of grammar, it is possible to have a system that can "understand" the vast majority of possible versions of this query. In the same way, this can be scaled up to handle more complex queries such as:

DATA DEFINITIONS LANGUAGE

Stands for "Data Definition Language." A DDL is a language used to define data structures within a database. It is typically considered to be a subset of SQL, the Structured Query Language, but can also refer to languages that define other types of data.

A Data Definition Language has a pre-defined syntax for describing data. For example, to build a new table using SQL syntax, the Create command is used, followed by parameters for the table name and column definitions. The DDL can also define the name of each column and the associated data type. Once a table is created, it can be modified using the Alter command. If the table is no longer needed, the Drop command will delete the table.

Since DDL is a subset of SQL, it does not include all the possible SQL commands. For example, commands such as Select and Insert are considered part of the Data Manipulation Language (DML), while access commands such as Connect and Execute are part of the Data Control Language (DML). Of course, if you are working with a database, knowing the names of each language is not important as long as you know the correct syntax.

The Data Definition Language (DDL) is used to create and destroy databases and database objects. These commands will primarily be used by database administrators during the setup and removal phases of a database project. Let's take a look at the structure and usage of four basic DDL commands:

The Data Definition Language (DDL) is used to create and destroy databases and database objects. These commands will primarily be used by database administrators during the setup and removal phases of a database project. Let's take a look at the structure and usage of four basic DDL commands:

CREATE

Installing a database management system (DBMS) on a computer allows you to create and manage many independent databases. For example, you may want to maintain a database of customer contacts for your sales department and a personnel database for your HR department.

The CREATE command can be used to establish each of these databases on your platform. For example, the command: Create Data Base employees creates an empty database named "employees" on your DBMS. After creating the database, your next step is to create tables that will contain data. (If this doesn't make sense, you might want to read the article The command: Create Table personal_info (first_name char(20) not null, last_name char(20) not null, employee_id int not null) establishes a table titled "personal_info" in the current database. In our example, the table contains three attributes: first_name, last_name and employee_id. Don't worry about the other information included in the command — we'll cover that in a future article.

USE

The USE command allows you to specify the database you wish to work with within your DBMS. For example, if we're currently working in the sales database and want to issue some commands that will affect the employees database, we would preface them with the following SQL command: USE employees. It's important to always be conscious of the database you are working in before issuing SQL commands that manipulate data.

ALTER

Once you've created a table within a database, you may wish to modify the definition of it. The ALTER command allows you to make changes to the structure of a table without deleting and recreating it. The "money" argument specifies that an employee's salary will be stored using a dollars and cents format. Finally, the "null" keyword tells the database that it's OK for this field to contain no value for any given employee.

DROP

The final command of the Data Definition Language, DROP, allows us to remove entire database objects from our DBMS. For example, if we want to permanently remove the personal_info table that we created, we'd use the following command:

Drop Table personal_info

Similarly, the command below would be used to remove the entire employees database:

Drop Data Base employees

Use this command with care! Remember that the DROP command removes entire data structures from your database.

If you want to remove individual records, use the DELETE command of the Data Manipulation Language. That's the Data Definition Language in a nutshell. In the next section of this article, we'll take a look at how the Data Manipulation Language is used to manipulate the information contained within a database.

DML

A data modeling language to define the schema of each database hosted in the DBMS, according to the DBMS database model. The four most common types of models are the:

- Hierarchical model,
- Network model,
- Relational model, and
- Object model.

Inverted lists and other methods are also used. A given database management system may provide one or more of the four models. The optimal structure depends on the natural organization of the application's data, and on the application's requirements (which include transaction rate (speed), reliability, maintainability, scalability, and cost).

The dominant model in use today is the ad hoc one embedded in SQL, despite the objections of purists who believe this model is a corruption of the relational model, since it violates several of its fundamental principles for the sake of practicality and performance. Many DBMSs also support the Open Database Connectivity API that supports a standard way for programmers to access the DBMS.

Before the database management approach, organizations relied on file processing systems to organize, store, and process data files. End users became aggravated with file processing because data is stored in many different files and each organized in a different way. Each file was specialized to be used with a specific application. Needless to say, file processing was bulky, costly and nonflexible when it came to supplying needed data accurately and promptly. Data redundancy is an issue with the file processing system because the independent data files produce duplicate data so when updates were needed each separate file would need to be updated. Another issue is the lack of data integration. The data is dependent on other data to organize and store it. Lastly, there was not any consistency or standardization of the data in a file processing system which makes maintenance difficult. For all these reasons, the database management approach was produced. Database management systems (DBMS) are designed to use one of five database structures to provide simplistic access to information stored in databases. The five database structures are hierarchical, network, relational, multidimensional and object-oriented models.

The hierarchical structure was used in early mainframe DBMS. Records' relationships form a treelike model. This structure is simple but nonflexible because the relationship is confined to a one-to-many relationship. IBM's IMS system and the RDM Mobile are examples of a hierarchical database system with multiple hierarchies over the same data. RDM Mobile is a newly designed embedded database for a mobile computer system. The hierarchical structure is used primary today for storing geographic information and file systems.

The network structure consists of more complex relationships. Unlike the hierarchical structure, it can relate to many records and accesses them by following one of several paths. In other words, this structure allows for many-to-many relationships.

The relational structure is the most commonly used today. It is used by mainframe, midrange and microcomputer systems. It uses two-dimensional rows and columns to store data. The tables of records can be connected by common key values. While working for IBM, E.F. Codd designed this structure in 1970. The model is not easy for the end user to run queries with because it may require a complex combination of many tables.

The multidimensional structure is similar to the relational model. The dimensions of the cube looking model have data relating to elements in each cell. This structure gives a spreadsheet like view of data. This structure is easy to maintain because records are stored as fundamental attributes, the same way they're viewed and the structure is easy to understand. Its high performance has made it the most popular database structure when it comes to enabling online analytical processing (OLAP).

The object oriented structure has the ability to handle graphics, pictures, voice and text, types of data, without difficultly unlike the other database structures. This structure is popular for multimedia Web-based applications. It was designed to work with object-oriented programming languages such as Java.

OVERALL DATABASE STRUCTURE

A collection of interrelated data together with a set of Programmes to access the data, also called database system, or simply database. The primary goal of such a system is to provide an environment that is both convenient and efficient to use in retrieving and storing information.

A database management system (DBMS) is designed to manage a large body of information. Data management involves both defining structures for storing information and providing mechanisms for manipulating the information. In addition, the database system must provide for the safety of the stored information, despite system crashes or attempts at unauthorized access. If data are to be shared among several users, the system must avoid possible anomalous results due to multiple users concurrently accessing the same data.

Examples of the use of database systems include airline reservation systems, company payroll and employee information systems, banking systems, credit card processing systems, and sales and order tracking systems.

A major purpose of a database system is to provide users with an abstract view of the data. That is, the system hides certain details of how the data are stored and maintained. Thereby, data can be stored in complex data structures that permit efficient retrieval, yet users see a simplified and easy-to-use view of the data. The lowest level of abstraction, the physical level, describes how the data are actually stored and details the data structures. The next-higher level of abstraction, the logical level, describes what data are stored, and what relationships exist among those data. The highest level of abstraction, the view level, describes parts of the database that are relevant to each user; application Programmes used to access a database form part of the view level.

The overall structure of the database is called the database schema. The scheme specifies data, data relationships, data semantics, and consistency constraints on the data. Underlying the structure of a database is the logical data model: a collection of conceptual tools for describing the schema.

The entity-relationship data model is based on a collection of basic objects, called entities, and of relationships among these objects. An entity is a "thing" or "object" in the real world that is distinguishable from other objects. For example, each person is an entity, and bank accounts can be considered entities. Entities are described in a database by a set of attributes. For example, the attributes account-number and balance describe one particular account in a bank. A relationship is an association among several entities. For example, a depositor relationship associates a customer with each of her accounts. The set of all entities of the same type and the set of all relationships of the same type are termed an entity set and a relationship set, respectively.

Like the entity-relationship model, the object-oriented model is based on a collection of objects. An object contains values stored in instance variables within the object. An object also contains bodies of code that operate on the object. These bodies of code are called methods. The only way in which one object can access the data of another object is by invoking a method of that other object.

This action is called sending a message to the object. Thus, the call interface of the methods of an object defines that object's externally visible part. The internal part of the object-the instance variables and method code-are not visible externally. The result is two levels of data abstraction, which are important to abstract away (hide) internal details of objects. Object-oriented data models also provide object references which can be used to identify (refer to) objects.

In record-based models, the database is structured in fixed-format records of several types. Each record has a fixed set of fields. The three most widely accepted record-based data models are the relational, network, and hierarchical models. The latter two were widely used once, but are of declining importance. The relational model is very widely used. Databases based on the relational model are called relational databases.

The relational model uses a collection of tables (called relations) to represent both data and the relationships among those data. Each table has multiple columns, and each column has a unique name. Each row of the table is called a tuple, and each column represents the value of an attribute of the tuple. The size of a database can vary widely, from a few megabytes for personal databases, to gigabytes (a gigabyte is 1000 megabytes) or even terabytes (a terabyte is 1000 gigabytes) for large corporate databases.

The information in a database is stored on a nonvolatile medium that can accommodate large amounts of data; the most commonly used such media are magnetic disks. Magnetic disks can store significantly larger amounts of data than main memory, at much lower costs per unit of data.

To improve reliability in mission-critical systems, disks can be organized into structures generically called redundant arrays of independent disks (RAID). In a RAID system, data are organized with some amount of redundancy (such as replication) across several disks. Even if one of the disks in the RAID system were to be damaged and lose data, the lost data can be reconstructed from the other disks in the RAID system. *See* Computer storage technology

Logically, data in a relational database are organized as a set of relations, each relation consisting of a set of records. This is the view given to database users. The underlying implementation on disk (hidden from the user) consists of a set of files. Each file consists of a set of fixed-size pieces of disk storage, called blocks. Records of a relation are stored within blocks. Each relation is associated with one or more files. Generally a file contains records from only one relation, but organizations where a file contains records from more than one relation are also used for performance reasons.

One way to retrieve a desired record in a relational database is to perform a scan on the corresponding relation; a scan fetches all the records from the relation, one at a time.

Accessing desired records from a large relation using a scan on the relation can be very expensive. Indices are data structures that permit more efficient access of records. An index is built on one or more attributes of a relation; such attributes constitute the search key. Given a value for each of the search-key attributes, the index structure can be used to retrieve records with the specified search-key values quickly. Indices may also support other operations, such as fetching all records whose search-key values fall in a specified range of values.

A database schema is specified by a set of definitions expressed by a data-definition language. The result of execution of data-definition language statements is a set of information stored in a special file called a data dictionary. The data dictionary contains metadata, that is, data about data. This file is consulted before actual data are read or modified in the database system. The data-definition language is also used to specify storage structures and access methods.

Data manipulation is the retrieval, insertion, deletion, and modification of information stored in the database. A data-manipulation language enables users to access or manipulate data as organized by the appropriate data model.

There are basically two types of data-manipulation languages: Procedural data-manipulation languages require a user to specify what data are needed and how to get those data; nonprocedural data-manipulation languages require a user to specify what data are needed without specifying how to get those data. A query is a statement requesting the retrieval of information. The portion of a data-manipulation language that involves information retrieval is called a query language. Although technically incorrect, it is common practice to use the terms query language and data-manipulation language synonymously.

Database languages support both data-definition and data-manipulation functions. Although many database languages have been proposed and implemented, SQL has become a standard language supported by most relational database systems. Databases based on the object-oriented model also support declarative query languages that are similar to SQL.

SQL provides a complete data-definition language, including the ability to create relations with specified attribute types, and the ability to define integrity constraints on the data. Query By Example (QBE) is a graphical language for specifying queries. It is widely used in personal database systems, since it is much simpler than SQL for nonexpert users.

Forms interfaces present a screen view that looks like a form, with fields to be filled in by users. Some of the fields may be filled automatically by the forms system. Report writers permit report formats to be defined, along with queries to fetch data from the database; the results of the queries are shown formatted in the report. These tools in effect provide a new language for building database interfaces and are often referred to as fourth-generation languages (4GLs).

Often, several operations on the database form a single logical unit of work, called a transaction. An example of a transaction is the transfer of funds from one account to another. Transactions in databases mirror the corresponding transactions in the commercial world.

Traditionally database systems have been designed to support commercial data, consisting mainly of structured alphanumeric data. In recent years, database systems have added support for a number of nontraditional data types such as text documents, images, and maps and other spatial data. The goal is to make databases universal servers, which can store all types of data. Rather than add support for all such data types into the core database, vendors offer add-on packages that integrate with the database to provide such functionality.

A suite of Programmes which typically manage large structured sets of persistent data, offering ad hoc query facilities to many users. They are widely used in business applications. A database management system (DBMS) can be an extremely complex set of software Programmes that controls the organisation, storage and retrieval of data (fields, records and files) in a database.

It also controls the security and integrity of the database. The DBMS accepts requests for data from the application programme and instructs the operating system to transfer the appropriate data.

When a DBMS is used, information systems can be changed much more easily as the organisation's information requirements change. New categories of data can be added to the database without disruption to the existing system.

Data security prevents unauthorised users from viewing or updating the database. Using passwords, users are allowed access to the entire database or subsets of the database, called subschemas (pronounced "sub-skeema"). For example, an employee database can contain all the data about an individual employee, but one group of users may be authorised to view only payroll data, while others are allowed access to only work history and medical data.

The DBMS can maintain the integrity of the database by not allowing more than one user to update the same record at the same time. The DBMS can keep duplicate records out of the database; for example, no two customers with the same customer numbers (key fields) can be entered into the database. Query languages and report writers allow users to interactively interrogate the database and analyse its data.

If the DBMS provides a way to interactively enter and update the database, as well as interrogate it, this capability allows for managing personal databases. However, it may not leave an audit trail of actions or provide the kinds of controls necessary in a multi-user organisation. These controls are only available when a set of application Programmes are customised for each data entry and updating function.

A business information system is made up of subjects (customers, employees, vendors, etc.) and activities (orders, payments, purchases, etc.). Database design is the process of deciding how to organize this data into record types and how the record types will relate to each other. The DBMS should mirror the organization's data structure and process transactions efficiently.

Organizations may use one kind of DBMS for daily transaction processing and then move the detail onto another computer that uses another DBMS better suited for random inquiries and analysis. Overall systems design decisions are performed by data administrators and systems analysts. Detailed database design is performed by database administrators.

The three most common organizations are the hierarchical database, network database and relational database. A database management system may provide one, two or all three methods. Inverted lists and other methods are also used. The most suitable structure depends on the application and on the transaction rate and the number of inquiries that will be made.

Database machines are specially designed computers that hold the actual databases and run only the DBMS and related software. Connected to one or more mainframes via a high-speed channel, database machines are used in large volume transaction processing environments. Database machines have a large number of DBMS functions built into the hardware and also provide special techniques for accessing the disks containing the databases, such as using multiple processors concurrently for high-speed searches.

The world of information is made up of data, text, pictures and voice. Many DBMSs manage text as well as data, but very few manage both with equal proficiency. Throughout the 1990s, as storage capacities continue to increase, DBMSs will begin to integrate all forms of information.

Eventually, it will be common for a database to handle data, text, graphics, voice and video with the same ease as today's systems handle data. A database management system provides the ability for many different users to share data and process resources. But as there can be many different users, there are many different database needs. The question now is: How can a single, unified database meet the differing requirement of so many users?

A DBMS minimizes these problems by providing two views of the database data: a logical (external) view and physical (internal) view. The logical view/user's view, of a database programme represents data in a format that is meaningful to a user and to the software Programmes that process those data. That is, the logical view tells the user, in user terms, what is in the database. The physical view deals with the actual, physical arrangement and location of data in the direct access storage devices(DASDs). Database specialists use the physical view to make efficient use of storage and processing resources. With the logical view users can see data differently from how they are stored, and they do not want to know all the technical details of physical storage. After all, a business user is primarily interested in using the information, not in how it is stored.

One strength of a DBMS is that while there is typically only one physical view of the data, there can be an endless number of different logical views. This feature allows users to see database information in a more business-related way rather than from a technical, processing viewpoint. Thus the logical view refers to the way user views data, and the physical view to the way the data are physically stored and processed...

DBMS FEATURES AND CAPABILITIES

Alternatively, and especially in connection with the relational model of database management, the relation between attributes drawn from a specified set of domains can be seen as being primary. For instance, the database might indicate that a car that was originally "red" might fade to "pink" in time, provided it was of some particular "make" with an inferior paint job. Such higher arity relationships provide information on all of the underlying domains at the same time, with none of them being privileged above the others.

Throughout recent history specialized databases have existed for scientific, geospatial, imaging, document storage and like uses. Functionality drawn from such applications has lately begun appearing in mainstream DBMSs as well. However, the main focus there, at least when aimed at the commercial data processing market, is still on descriptive attributes on repetitive record structures. Thus, the DBMSs of today roll together frequently-needed services or features of attribute management. By externalizing such functionality to the DBMS, applications effectively share code with each other and are relieved of much internal complexity. Features commonly offered by database management systems include:

Query Ability

Querying is the process of requesting attribute information from various perspectives and combinations of factors. Example: "How many 2-door cars in Texas are green?" A database query language and report writer allow users to interactively interrogate the database, analyse its data and update it according to the users privileges on data.

Backup and Replication

Copies of attributes need to be made regularly in case primary disks or other equipment fails. A periodic copy of attributes may also be created for a distant organization that cannot readily access the original. DBMS usually provide utilities to facilitate the process of extracting and disseminating attribute sets. When data is replicated between database servers, so that the information remains consistent throughout the database system and users cannot tell or even know which server in the DBMS they are using, the system is said to exhibit replication transparency.

Rule Enforcement

Often one wants to apply rules to attributes so that the attributes are clean and reliable. For example, we may have a rule that says each car can have only one engine associated with it (identified by Engine Number). If somebody tries to associate a second engine with a given car, we want the DBMS to deny such a request and display an error message. However, with changes in the model specification such as, in this example, hybrid gas-electric cars, rules may need to change. Ideally such rules should be able to be added and removed as needed without significant data layout redesign.

Security

Often it is desirable to limit who can see or change which attributes or groups of attributes. This may be managed directly by individual, or by the assignment of individuals and privileges to groups, or (in the most elaborate models) through the assignment of individuals and groups to roles which are then granted entitlements.

Computation

There are common computations requested on attributes such as counting, summing, averaging, sorting, grouping, cross-referencing, etc. Rather than have each computer application implement these from scratch, they can rely on the DBMS to supply such calculations.

Change and Access Logging

Often one wants to know who accessed what attributes, what was changed, and when it was changed. Logging services allow this by keeping a record of access occurrences and changes.

Automated Optimization

If there are frequently occurring usage patterns or requests, some DBMS can adjust themselves to improve the speed of those interactions. In some cases the DBMS will merely provide tools to monitor performance, allowing a human expert to make the necessary adjustments after reviewing the statistics collected.

Chapter 2

Entity Relationship Model

ER MODEL CONCEPTS

Database Application Development is the process of obtain real-world requirements, analyse requirement, design the data and functions of the system and then implement the operations in the system. The figure below shows the main phases of the database application development process.

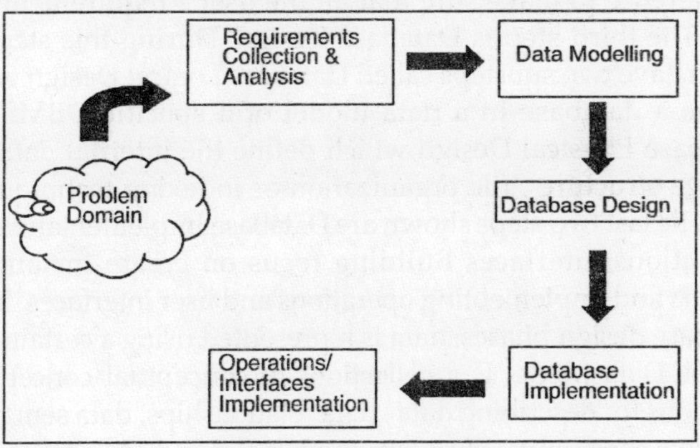

Fig. The main Phases of the Data Base Application Development Process

As we can see, the first step is Requirement Collection and Analysis. During this step, the database designers have to interview the customers (database users) to understand the be-built system, obtain and document the data and functional requirements. The results of this step is a document including the detail requirements of the users. Data Modeling is the next step in the process. This step is sometimes considered as a high-level and abstract design phase (conceptual design).

The aims of this phase are:

- Describes what data is contained in the database (E.g entities: students, lecturers, courses, subjects etc.)
- Describes the relationships between data items (E.g Students are supervised by Lecturers; Lecturers teach Courses)
- Describes the constraints on data (E.g Student Number has exact 8 digits; A subject has 4 or 6 unit of credits only)

The data items, the relationships and constraints all are expressed using the concepts provided by the high-level data model. Because these concepts donot include the implementation details so the results of the data modeling process is a (semi) formal representation of the database structure. This result is quite easy to understand so it is used as reference to make sure that all the user's requirements are met. The third step is Database Design. During this step, we might have two substeps called Database Logical Design which define a database in a data model of a specific DBMS and Database Physical Design which define the internal database storage structure , file organization or indexing techniques.

The last two steps shown are Database Implementation and Operations/Interfaces Building focus on create instance of schema and implementing operations and user interfaces. In the database design phases, data is represented using a certain data model. Data Model is a collections of conceptual concepts or notations for describing data , data relationships, data semantics and data constraints. Most data models also include a set of basic operations for manipulating data in the database.

As mentioned in the first lecture, data models are either:

- Conceptual models
  - Database is considered as a collection of entities (objects) of various kinds.
  - These model provide a flexible data structuring capabilities.
  - The typical examples of this model is entity-

relationship model, object-oriented model or semantic data model.

- Record based logical models
  - Database is considered as a collection of fixed – size record.
  - These models are closer to the physical level or file structure so they are easier to implement.
  - The three most well-known models of this kind are relational data model , network data model or hierarchical data model.
- Physical models
  - Provide concepts that describe the details of how data is stored in the computer's memory

ENTITY RELATIONSHIP MODEL (ER MODEL)

Entity Relationship Data Model has existed for 30 years original description: Chen, ACM Transactions on Database Systems. The ER model is well suited to data modelling for use with databases because it is fairly abstract and is easy to discuss and explain. ER models are readily translated to relations. ER models (or ER schemas) are represented by ER diagrams.

ER modeling is based on two concepts:

- Entities, that is, things. Eg. Prof. Ba, Course Database Sytem.
- Relationships, that is, associations or interactions between entities. Eg. Prof. Ba teachs course Database Systems.

EXAMPLE DATABASE

In this lecture, we will use a sample database called the COMPANY database to illustrate the concepts of Entity Relationship Model.

This database contains the information about employees, departments and projects:

- There are several departments in the company. Each department has an unique identification, a name, location of the office and a particular employee who manages the department.

- A department controls a number of projects, each of which has unique name, a unique number and the budget.
- Each employee has name, an identification number, address, salary, birthdate. An employee is assigned to one department but can join in several projects. We need to record the start date of the employee in each project. We also need to know the direct supervisor of each employee.
- We want to keep track of the dependents of the employees. Each dependent has name, birthdates and relationship with the employee.

ENTITY, ENTITY SET AND ENTITY TYPE

Entity is an object in the real world with an independent existence and can be differentiated with other object.

An entity might be:

- Object with physical existence. Eg a lecturer, a student, a car.
- Object with conceptual existence. Eg a course, a job, a position. An Entity Type defines a collection of similar entities An Entity Set is a collection of entities of an entity type at a point of time. In ER diagram, an entity type is represented by a name in a box.

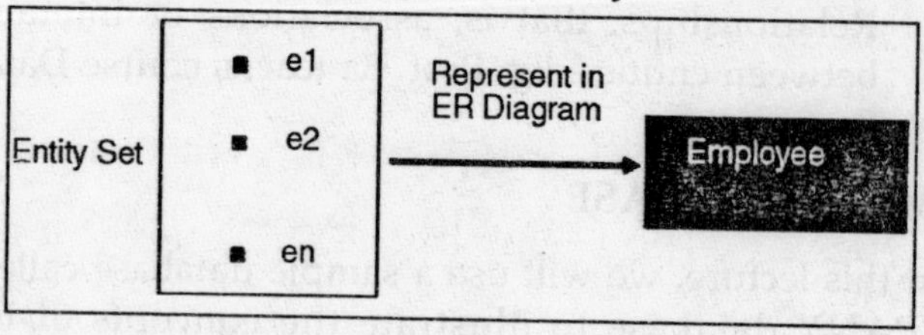

Fig. Entity Type in ER Diagram

ATTRIBUTES

Each entity is described by a set of attributes that model "properties of interest" E.g. Employee = (Name, Address, Age, Salary). Each attribute has a name, associate with an entity and is associated with a domain of legal values. However the information about attribute domain is not presented on the ER diagram. In the diagram, each attribute is represented by an oval with a name inside.

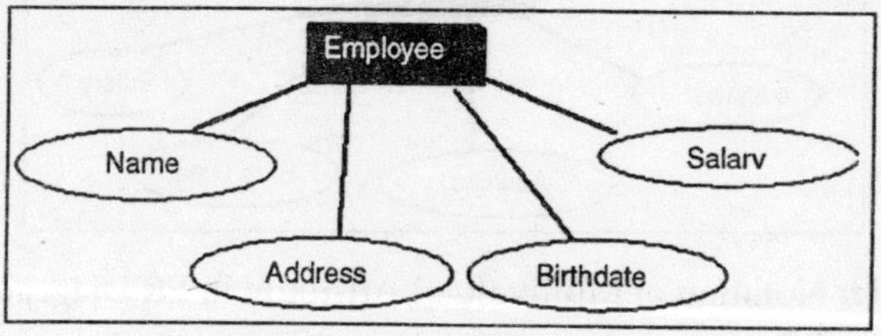

Fig. Attribute Diagram

Types of Attributes:

- Simple attributes are attributes that are drawn from the atomic value domains
  E.g. Name = {John}; Age = {23}
- Composite attributes: Attributes that consist of a hierarchy of attributes
  E.g. Address may consists of "Number", "Street" and "Suburb" ? Address = {59 + 'Meek Street' + 'Kingsford'}
- Single Valued attributes: Attributes that have only one value for each entity
  E.g. Name, Age for Employee
- Multivalued attributes: Attributes that have a set of values for each entity
  E.g. Degrees of a person: ' BSc' , 'MIT', 'PhD'
- Derived attributes: Attributes Contain values that are calculated from other attributes Eg. Age can be derived from attribute Date Of Birth. In this situation, Date Of Birth might be called Stored Attribute.

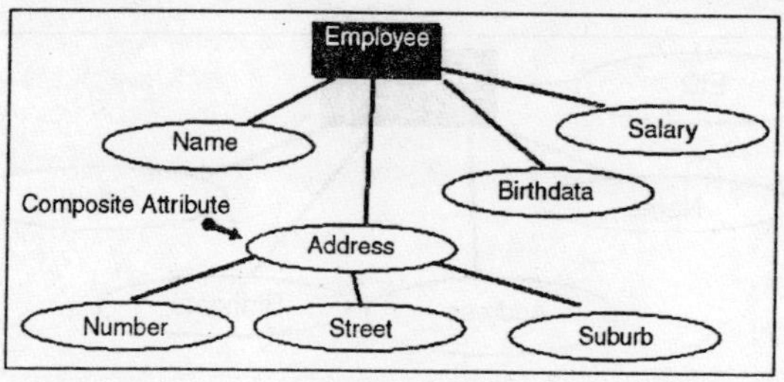

Fig. Notation of Composite Attribute in ER Diagram

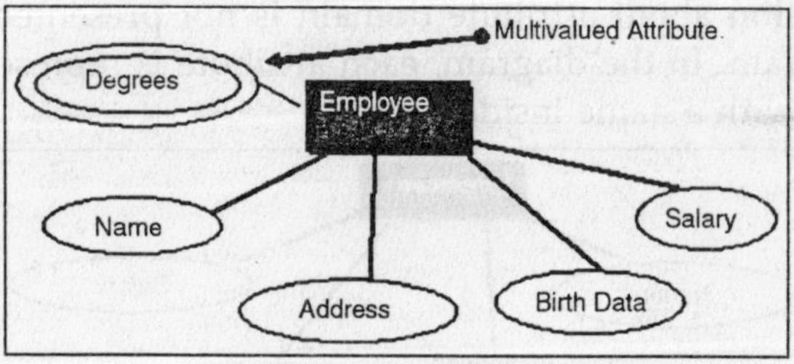

Fig: Notation of Multivalued Attribute in ER Diagram

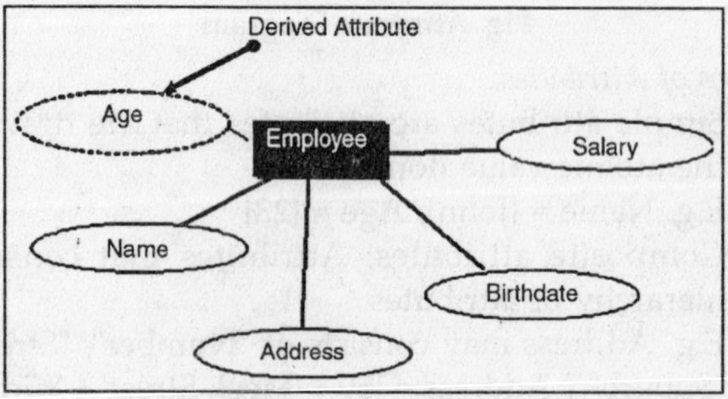

Fig: Notation of Derived Attribute in ER Diargam

Keys

An important constraint on the entities is the key. Key is an attribute or a group of attributes whose values can be used to uniquely identify individual entity in an entity set. For example, for the entity Employee = {EID, Name, Address, Age, Salary}

- Definite keys are any set that involving EID
- Possible keys might be {Name, Address}
- Unlikely keys: {Name}, {Age}

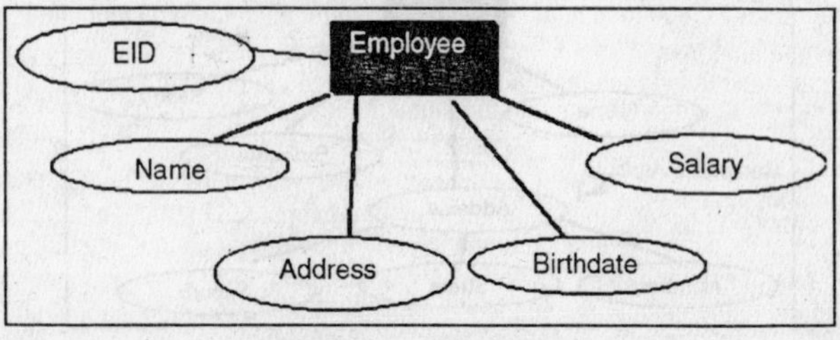

Fig. Key Notation

RELATIONSHIP SET AND TYPE

- Relationship is an association among several entities
  Eg. Employee (John) joins Project (Netlife)
- The set of similar associations at a point of time is called the Relationship Set
  Eg. the following "Joins in " is a relationship set
  Employee (John) joins in Project (Netlife)
  Employee (Mark) joins in Project (GreenNet)
  Employee (Sara) joins in Project (mFORM)
  Employee (Steve) joins in Project (Netlife)
- Relationship type is a collection of relationships among entities from a certain set of Entity Types

We can define the relationship type more formally.

Definition:

Consider n ? 2 possibly non-distinct entity types E1, E2, …, En.

A relationship is a tuple(e1, e2,…, en) is a subset of E1 x E2 x … x En.

A relationship type R is a subset of the Cartesian Product E1 x E2 x … x En.

R has degree n

In the ER diagram, relationship type is represented by a diamond with a name inside and connects by straight line to the rectangles representing entity type.

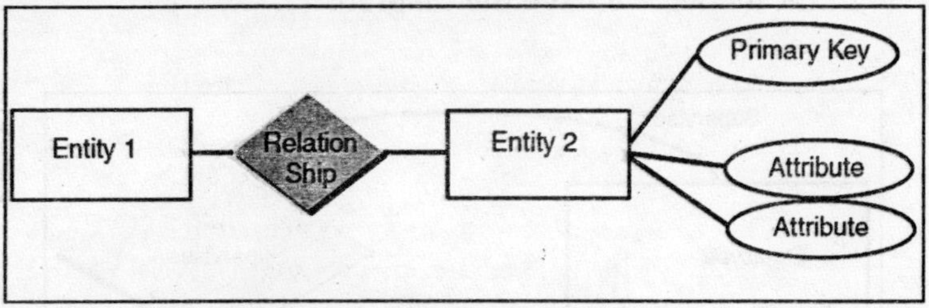

Fig. Relationship Type Notation

DEGREE OF RELATIONSHIP TYPE

The degree of a relationship type is the number of participating entyties types.

- Unary (Recursive) relationship type is the re ationship that involve only one entity type. However, the same entity type participates in a relationship type in different roles. For example, figure below shows the Supervise relationship type which relates an Employee and a Supervisor who is also an employee. So in this relationship, one employee has the role of supervisor, another has the role of supervisee.

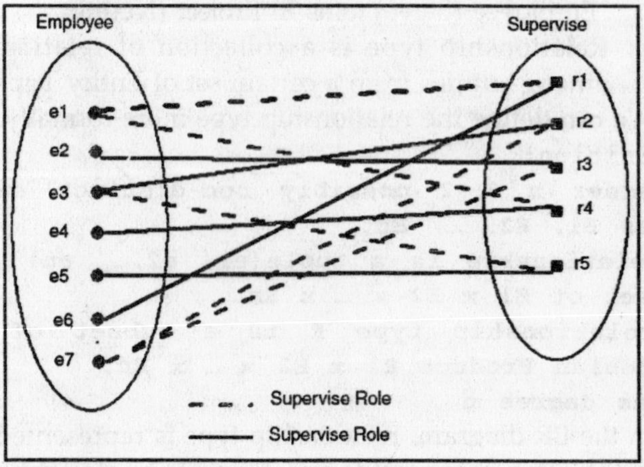

Fig. Supervise Relationship

In ER model, we have the diagram

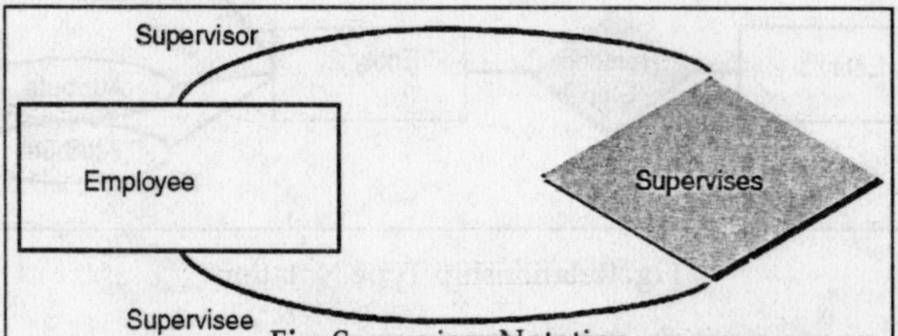

Fig. Supervisor Notation

- *Binary relationship type*: This relationship type has two entity types link together. This is the most common relationship.

For example the "Joins in" relationship between EMPLOYEE and PROJECT

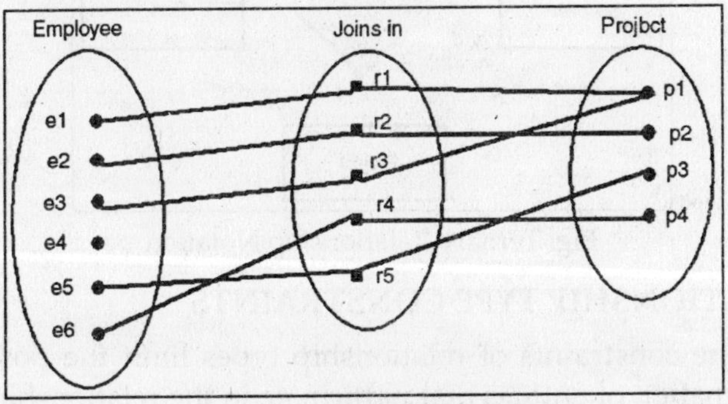

Fig. "Joins in" Relationship

The ER diagram for this relationship type is:

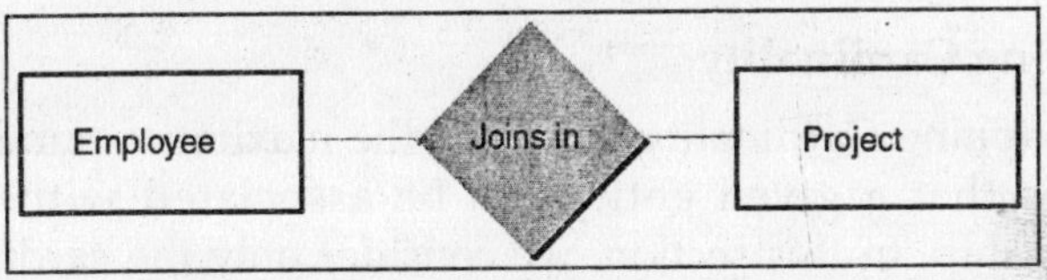

Fig. "Joins in" Relationship Notation

- Ternary relationship type: If there are three entity types link together, the relationship is called ternary relationship.

For example: The Supply relationship associates a SUPPLIER, a PART and a PROJECT.

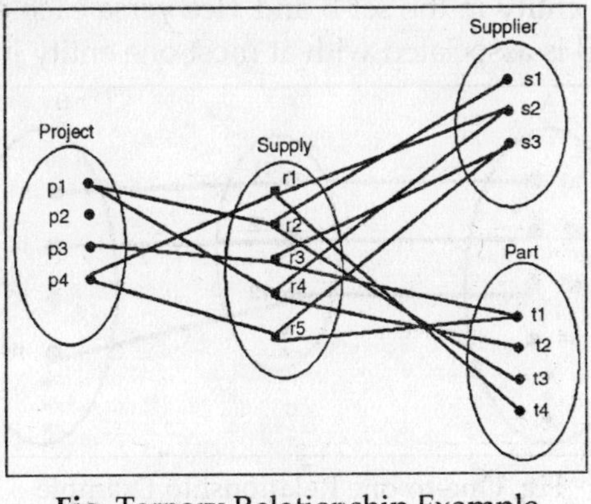

Fig. Ternary Relationship Example

The ER diagram for this relationship type is:

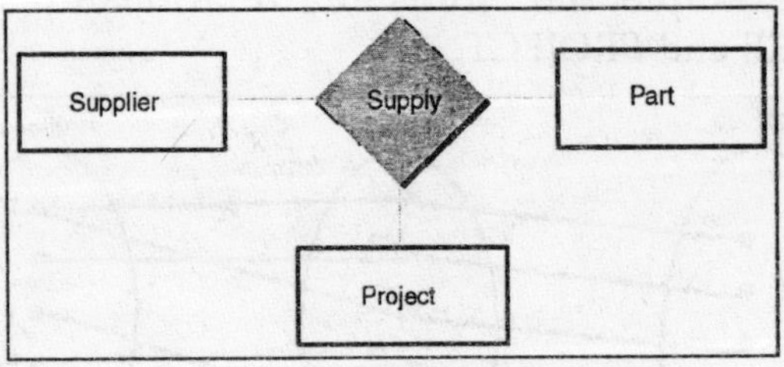

Fig. Ternary Relationship Notation

RELATIONSHIP TYPE CONSTRAINTS

The constraints of relationship types limit the possible combination of entities that participate in the relationship set. Two main types of constraints is mapping cardinality and participation.

Mapping Cardinality

Mapping Cardinality describes the maximum number of entities that a given entity can be associated with via a relationship. In this section, we consider only the cardinality constraint for the binary relationship. *The possible cardinality for binary relationship types are* : One - to- One (1-1) , One - to - Many (1 - N) and Many - to - Many (M-N).

- One to one relationship: Given two entity sets A and B, there is a one-to-one relationship between A and B if each entity in the set A is associated with at most one entity in the set B and vice versa each entity in the set B is associated with at most one entity in the set A.

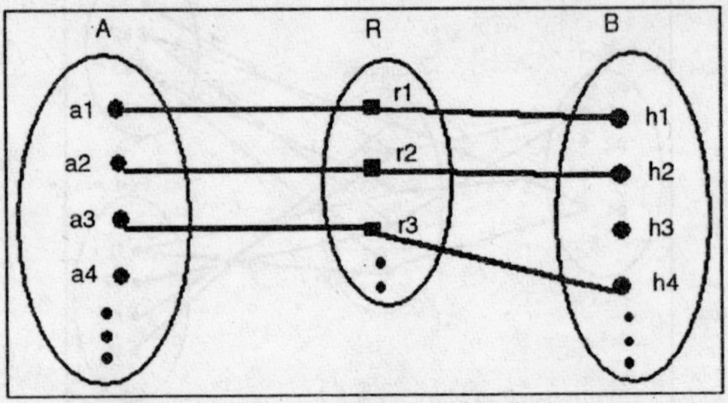

Fig. One-to-one Relationship Example

Example: An employee if is a manager then can manage one department and a department can have only one manager.

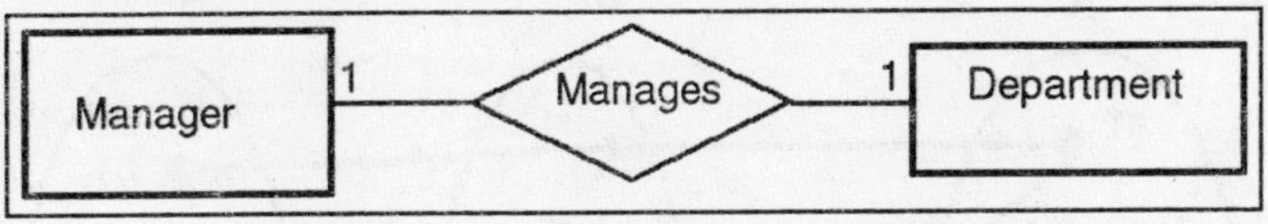

Fig. One-to-one Relationship Notation

- One to many relationship: There is a one to many relationship sets associates two entities sets A and B if each entity in A is associated with several entities in B however, each entity in B is associated with at most one entity in A.

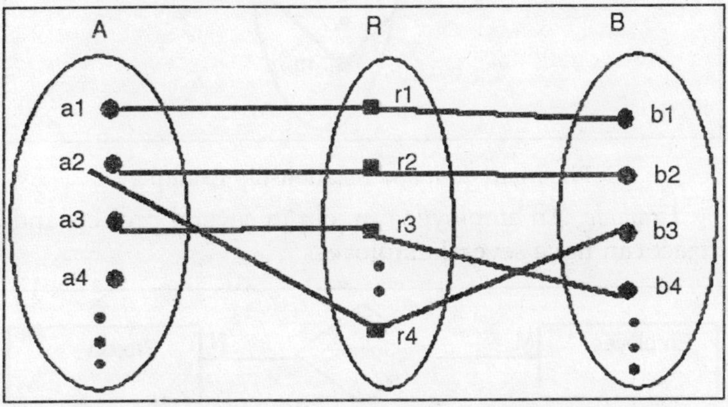

Fig. One-to-many Relationship Example

Example: There are many employees work in a department however, an employee can work for only one department.

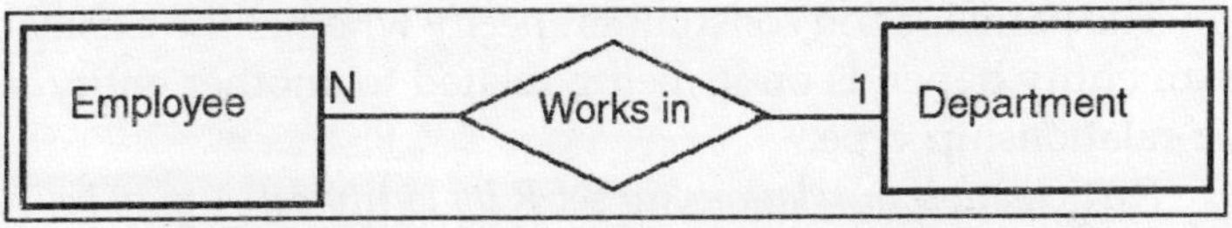

Fig. One-to-many Relationship Notation

- Many to many relationship : There is a many to many relationship sets associates two entities sets A and B if each entity in A is associated with several entities in B however, each entity in B is associated with several entities in A.

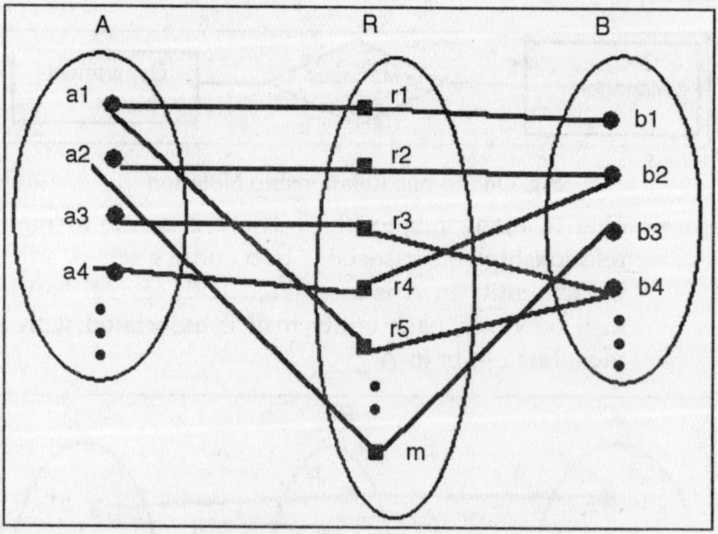

Fig. Many-to-many Relationship Example

Example: An employee can join in several projects and a project can have several employees

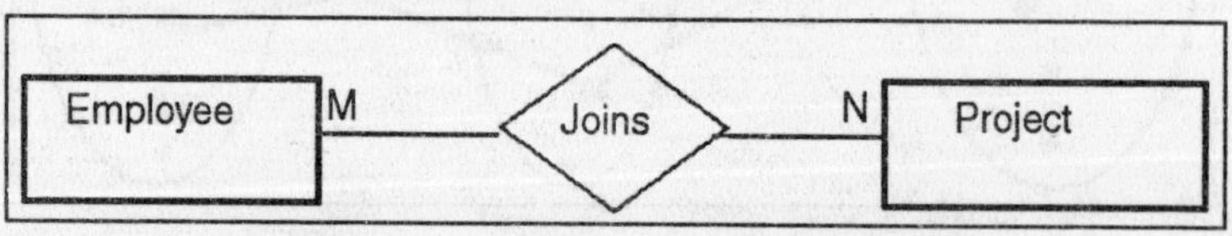

Fig. Many-to-many relationship notation

PARTICIPATION

The participation constraints specify whether the existence of an entity depends on its being related to another entity via the relationship type.

Participation in relationship set R by entity set A may be:

- *Total* : It means every entity a in A participates in at least 1 relationship in R
- *Partial*: It means only some a in A participate in relationships in R

Example: Every project have at least 1 employee joined in it. Not every employee in the company join in a project

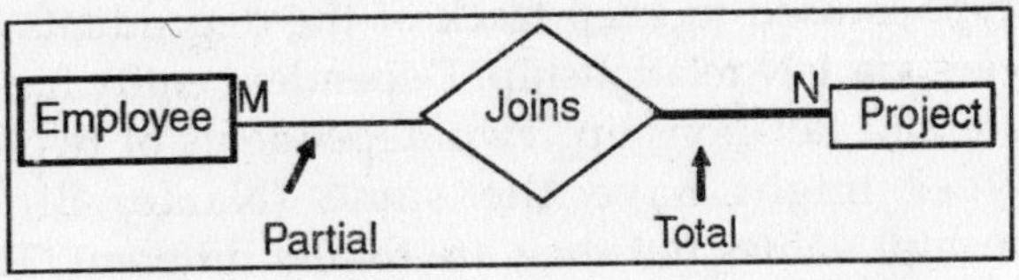

Fig. Participation in Relationship Notation

Attributes of Relationship Types

The relationship types can have attributes like entity types. For 1-1 and 1-N relationship types, attributes of the relationship can be migrated to one of the participating entity types. However, for M-N relationship types, attributes must be specified as the relationship attribute.

Example: The Start Date attribute records the date on which an employee joins in a project

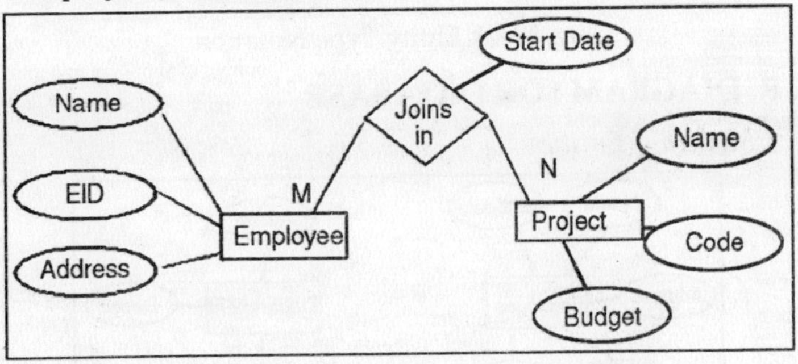

Fig. Attribute in Relationship Example

Weak Entity Type

Weak entity types are those whose existence depends on the existence of other entity type. Entities belongs to weak entity type are identified by being related to specific entities from another entity type which is called strong entity types.

The weak entity type does not have key attributes of their own. The keys of this type os partially or totally derived from strong entity types. In ER diagram, weak entity and strong/

weak relationship are denoted by double box/diamond. Example: Entity type Dependent related to Employee. This entity type is used to keep track of the dependents of each employees via 1-N relationship. Dependent entity has Name, Birthdate and Relationship. Two dependents of two distinct employees might have the same {Name, Birthdate, Relationship} values but they are totally different. They are identified as distinct only after consider the association with particular employee entities to which the dependents relates. So the key of the Dependent might be {EID, Name} in which EID is the attribute from the strong entity type Employee.

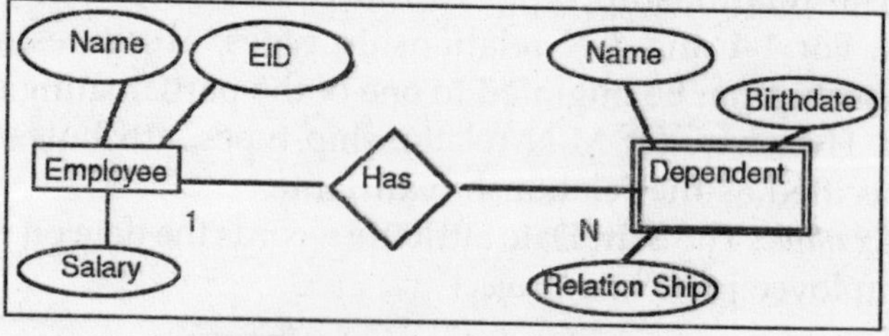

Fig. Weak Entity Type Notation

E. R. DIAGRAM FOR DATABASE

Modeling Entities:

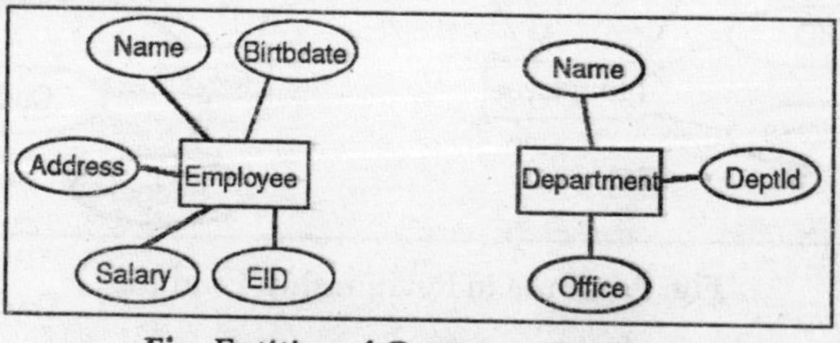

Fig. Entities of Company Database

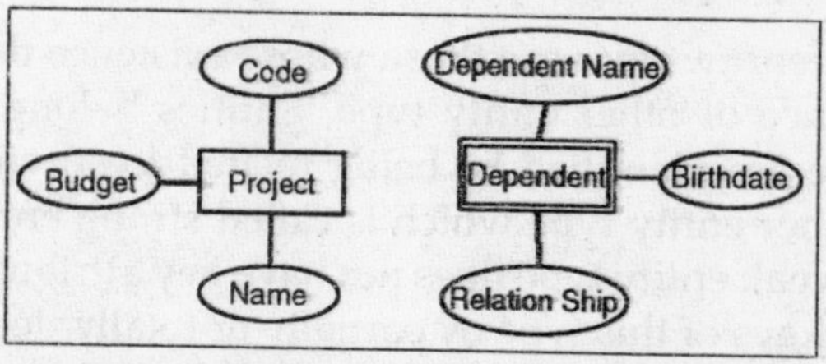

Fig. Entities of Company Database

Modeling Relationships

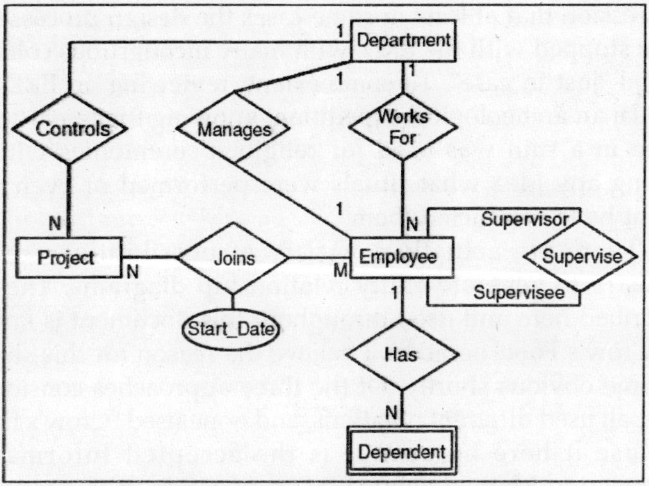

Fig. Relationships of Company Database

NOTATION FOR ER DIAGRAM

INTRODUCTION

Entity relationship diagrams, or ERDs as they are fondly known in the field, contain a wealth of information on the architecture of a relational database. Unfortunately, those not actively working on database design issues are likely to find them confusing, intimidating, and sometimes aggravating. In this brief tutorial I will try to dispel some of this miasma. Like so many things, it turns out that understanding a few key concepts is all that is required. This section is meant as a broad, rather high level introduction to the major concepts surrounding relational databases. This is a very broad and rapidly growing field, so that it is only possible to just barely scratch the surface. Fortunately there are now a great number of well written books on the subject.

An entity relationship diagram at best can only be considered a static picture of the "structure" of a database. Nothing is revealed regarding the flow of data, or anything else that relates to how the data changes. However, exploring an entity relationship diagram is often a first step in understanding a databases design. Unfortunately, one gets the impression that at least in some cases the design process may have stopped with the ERD, with many incongruous columns added "just in case". To some extent, reviewing an ERD is a bit like an archeological expedition, knowing that a particular room in a ruin was used for religious ceremonies without having any idea what rituals were performed or even who might have conducted them.

There are actually a variety of possibilities used in industry to generate entity relationship diagrams. The one described here and used throughout this document is known as "Crow's Foot" notation. I believe the reason for this should become obvious shortly. Of the three approaches considered here, all used different notations, and none used "Crow's Foot". We use it here because it is the accepted Information Engineering Methodology (IEM) convention, it is supported by the Visio ® drafting programme, and it is ubiquitous in articles and books describing Oracle ® applications. Also, once one convention is understood, it is not difficult to read diagrams using the others. For purposes of the comparisons in this document, I found it conventient to recast the three approaches into the same notational convention.

TABLES

There are two basic components comprising an entity relationship diagram, entities and relationships. Entities can be invisioned as tables with columns and rows somewhat like a spreadsheet. Each column has a name and contains some certain type of information such as the latitude of a hypocenter, or the arrival time of some seismic phase. The table itself also has a name by which it is referenced. Rows represent a particular instance of what the table represents. For example, an origin table might contain one row for each location that has been calculated. In the old days, columns were referred to as attributes, and rows were called tuples. It may be helpful to think of a relational database as a set of related spread sheets of varying dimensionality. On the other hand, maybe it won't.

In general a database contains only one or at most a few tables containing the same kinds of data. For example, one would expect to find a table containing one row for each entry in a local earthquake catalog. You wouldn't find a separate table for different regions or periods of time (months or years). Instead, tables contain all of the data of a particular kind and columns designated as keys uniquely identify a given row. Frequently a key will be represented by a single column, although sometimes a few columns might be required.

As an example, consider the local Id used in the CUSP system. For a local database, this number is sufficient to uniquely identifiy any earthquake in the database. However, a database containing hypocenters from multiple networks might require two columns, one identifying the source network in addition to the CUSP Id. Sometimes, although not frequently, there are two or more sets of columns that independently identify the rows in a table and where either could serve as keys. Of these, one set is designated the "primary key", and all others are termed "alternate keys". There is one other kind of key called a "foreign key". Although these are generally not unique within a given table, they do uniquely identify the row of some other table or collection of tables.

They are, in fact, identical to the primary keys in these tables. Foreign keys are used to form "relationships" between the table that contains them, and the table for which they are the primary key. For the earthquake catalog example, there might be a column designated as a region code, whose values would be primary keys in some "region information" table containing one row for each possible region. There are generally several columns in a table that are not part of any keys. These are simply data columns, and might contain such information as an earthquakes magnitude estimate, or the number of phases used to locate it.

RELATIONSHIPS

The lines with symbolized ends connecting database entities represent the relationship between two tables. Each line describe both directions of the relationship. There are four basic relationships that can be used to describe the relationship of one table to another.

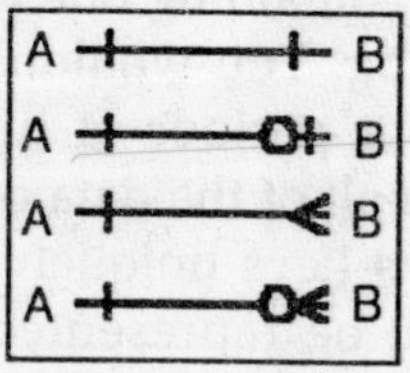

Fig. KEY: Key to ERD Relationships.

The diagram on the right shows these four possibilities by discussing the relationship of some entity B with another entity A. The first relationship shown is that of a one to one relationship between the two tables. Specifically this means that for every row in table A there is one and only one corresponding row in table B.

This requires that the number of rows in A must be the same as the number of rows in B. Such relationships represent a kind of a choice, in that it would be possible to merge two tables related in this manner into a single table sharing all of the columns of both.

Alternatively, and particularly for seismic applications, it might be better to keep two tables distinct, with B containing information of a specialized and possibly site specific nature, while A might contain information of a much more general nature. Generally one to one relationships are uncommon in database design.

The second relationship shown is much more common, and will help to understand the bidirectional nature of this notation. Simply put, the symbol is to be interpreted that every row of B is uniquely related to specific row of A, while every row of A is related to at most one row of B. As a pneumonic, I sometimes think of the symbol near the B entity as reading "0 or 1", since that is what it looks like.

One thing that is difficult to keep sorted out, speaking for myself, is the directionality of the relationship. One can think of the terminal symbol as an arrow head, defining how one entity, A in the example, is related to another, B. Apparently some of the rows in A do not relate to any rows in B, and the corresponding "foreign key" is said to be null. On the other hand, every row of B is related to exactly one row of A. One can see, that table Amust contain at least as many rows as table B, and possibly considerably more.With the third relationship shown in diagram KEY, things get quite a bit more interesting.

This notation reads that a given row of A is related to one or more rows in B. To accomplish this, particular values of some foreign key in B, which is also the primary key of A, might be duplicated one or more times.

For example, a column in a table holding information on the arrival times of particular seismic phases might have a column (foreign key) containing an ID, which is the primary key of a table of hypocenters.

In this example, the phase table is B, and the hypocenter list is A. In this way multiple phase arrivals can be "assocated" with a given hypocenter. The simple example below, however, shows that the situation is generally a bit more tricky than this for real applications. Note that every row of A must be associated with at least one row of B. The situation where a row of A corresponds to no row in B is shown in the fourth symbol.

This reads that rows of A are associated with zero or more rows of B. For the phase arrival example, this would mean that there could be a location for which no phase data was available. The location, perhaps, was simply typed in without supporting data. So far the discussion has been limited to the symbol on the right side of the connector.

In each example, the left hand symbol is shown as a unique connection. In fact the situation is a bit more tense than this, so that symbols can occur on each end in various combinations. For the most part this is not a concern, as the relationships in alternating directions can be considered independant. The exception to this is that of having any kind of "crow's feet" on both ends.

The problem is that such relationships cannot be represented in a normalized database, and thus cannot occur without introducing an additional linking table. This leaves 12 permit table permutations, or only 7 if reflexive pairs are taken as one. How this works out in a realistic example is shown in the following .

Simple Seismic Example

For the purposes of this tutorial I have chosen a familiar set of four entities directly related to the storage of earthquake data and summary information. This diagram demonstrates all of the important concepts required to understand the discussions in other sections of this document. The titles across the top show how I have classified the basic entities into four categories, Data, Link, Summary, and Catalog.

From left to right, these categories reflect increasing degrees of processing and analysis. The Data category contains information directly related to observations, for example pointers to waveform data, or tables of parameters directly extracted from waveforms, such as arrival times and amplitudes.

The Summary category contains tables that generalize information from the Data category such as earthquake hypocenters and magnitude estimates. For example an earthquake hypocenter requires at least 4 arrival times from the Data layer. Which arrival times are associated to a particular hypocenter, for example, is contained in the Link layer. Finally, on the far right, the Catalog layer contains the general index into the database. For seismic network applications, this is typically an earthquake catalog containing one entry for each significant event.

Generally, especially immediately following a significant event, several trial locations might exist, with only one eventually evolving into the definitive solution. In each of the four entities in diagram ERD below the name of the table appears in the upper rectangle, and key column names are shown in the lower rectangle. The basic idea is that there is an "origin" table and an "event" table. The "event" table can be thought of as the "gold standard" earthquake catalog, in that it has one and only one entry for each cataloged significant event. Its primary key, "evid", is a simple unique serial number with no other information content.

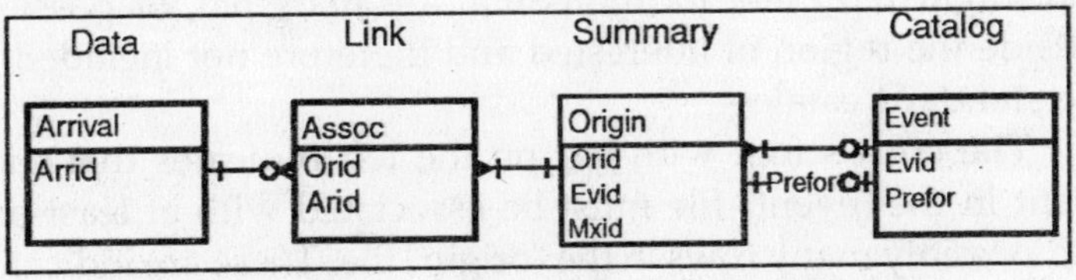

Fig. ERD: Fragment of the IDC Operational Schema Showing the Tables Related to Arrivals.

The basic idea is that there is an "origin" table and an "event" table. The "event" table can be thought of as the "gold standard" earthquake catalog, in that it has one and only one entry for each cataloged significant event. Its primary key, "evid", is a simple unique serial number with no other information content.

The "origin" table is similar, but contains possibly multiple locations for each event. This table has a primary key, "orid", which is also a vanilla identifier. Such could arise in a network that has both automated and manual processing, or when combining locations from adjacent regional seismic networks. Depending upon some factor such as the region of occurrence, one or another of these would be determined to be the "correct" location.

This would be the preferred origin referenced in the "event" table by setting its "prefer" foreign key to the "orid" of the appropriate entry in the "origin" table. This relationship is carried by the connector labelled "prefor" in the figure.

All rows in the "event" table must reference an entry in the origin table through the "prefer" foreign key. Each row in the "origin" table is referenced by no more than one row in the "event" table via its "prefor" foreign key. The upper connector reflects the contents of the "evid" foreign key in the "origin" table.

When the column names of both the foreign keys and the primary keys they reference are the same, the relations are unnamed to prevent clutter. The open circle and bar on the right end of this connector indicates that there can be rows in the "origin" table that are not represented at all in the "event" table. These would have null values in their "evid" column, and might represent locations that are marginal, or possibly outside the region of interested and therefore not included in the standard catalog.

The crow's foot with bar on the left indicates that each event in the "event" file must be associated with at least one and possibly many rows in the "origin" file. These are indicated by setting "evid" in the "origin" table to the value of the "evid" primary key in the "event" table.

This is typical of the manner inwhich the one to many relationship arises in relational databases. Note that a row cannot exist in the "event" table unless at least one row in the "origin" table references it.

Maintaining this condition during updates is within the purview of the processing application and are known generally as "business rules". The relationship between phase arrival and calculated origins is expressed by the three relations on the left. The "assoc" table is the critical link between rows in the "origin" table and the phase arrival data in the "arrival" table that supports it.

Such a table is required whenever a many to many relationship must be expressed. Each row of the "assoc" table contains exactly two columns, which together are unique and can be taken as a primary key. Each pair can also be thought of as two foreign keys, "arid" connects the "arrival" table, and "orid" connects to a particular row of the "origin" table.

Those rows of the "assoc" table with a common "orid" represent all of the data supporting a particular location in the "origin" table. Similarly, those rows in the "assoc" table with a common value of "arid" represents the list of all locations that a particular phase arrival was used as a datum. Similar link tables are used to associated amplitudes with magnitudes and so forth.

Notice that the the connectors on either side of the "assoc" table have different symbols. The one or many notation on the left (bar with a crow's foot) shows that all locations require at least one arrival. The none or many symbol on the right (circle with crow's foot) indicates that some phase arrivals might not be associated with any locations.

They might arise in a real-time transaction system when a noise burst is misidentified as a seismic arrival, or perhaps they are true arrivals for an event that is too small to provide enough arrivals to support a location. In either case, such orphans could eventually be expunged from the database.

ONE-TO-ONE OR ONE-TO-MANY RELATIONSHIP

The parent and child entities can either have an one-to-one relationship:

or an one-to-many relationship:

To express a many-to-many relationship in SchemaBank, you have to use a bridge entity to break it into two one-to-many relationships like this:

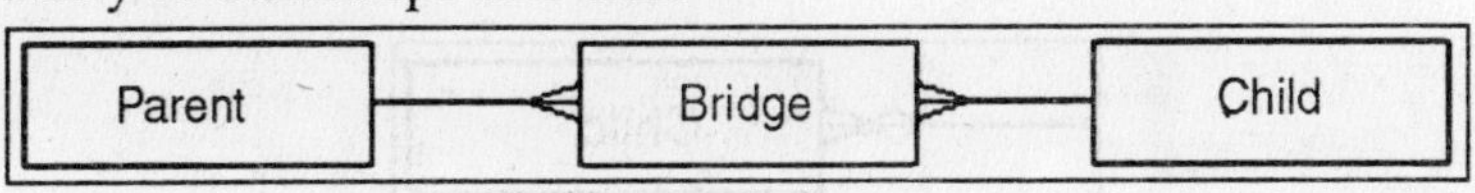

SELF-RELATIONSHIP

An entity can be related to itself to create a self-relationship:

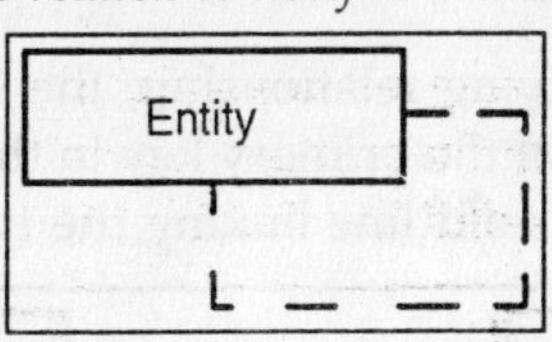

PARENT OPTIONALLY

If every record in the child entity must reference to a record in the parent entity, the parent optionally is mandatory and is expressed by adding a stroke beside the parent entity:

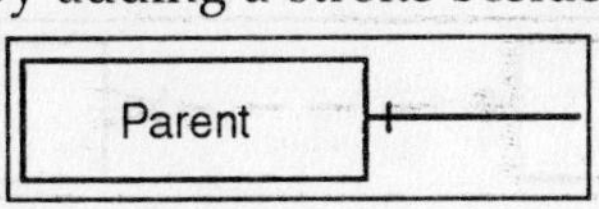

Otherwise, the parent optionality is optional and is expressed by adding a circle beside the parent entity:

When parent optionality is mandatory, the foreign keys (in the child entity) cannot be null. The foreign keys can be null if and only if the parent is optional.

CHILD OPTIONALITY

If every record in the parent entity must be referenced from a record in the child entity, the child optionality is mandatory and is expressed by adding a stroke beside the child entity:

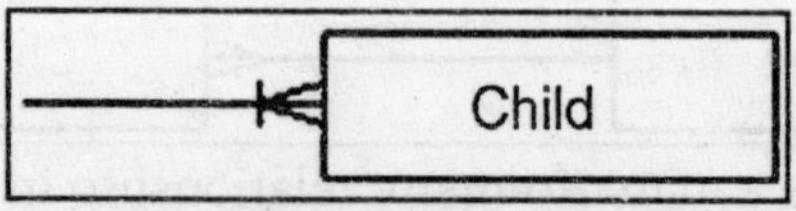

Otherwise, the child optionally is optional and is expressed by adding a circle beside the child entity:

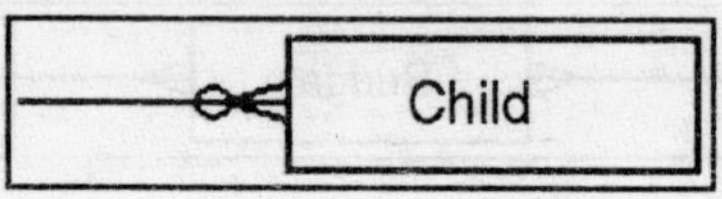

IDENTIFYING AND NON-IDENTIFYING RELATIONSHIPS

With an identifying relationship, the foreign keys in the child table are part of the primary key in the child entity. This is represented by a solid line linking the two entities:

On the contrary, the relationship would be a non-identifying one, represented by a dashed line:

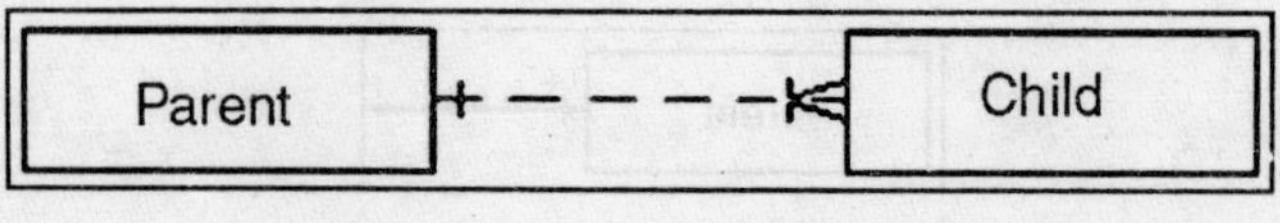

A SAMPLE MODEL

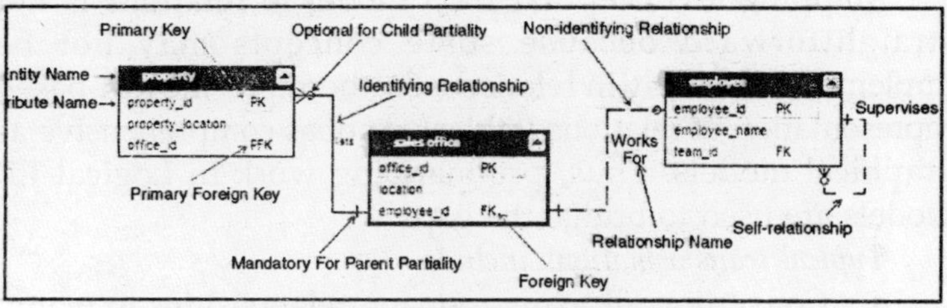

MAPPING CONSTRAINTS

An E-R Diagram scheme may define certain constraints to which the contents of a database must conform.

MAPPING CARDINALITIES:

Express the number of entities to which another entity can be associated via a relationship. For binary relationship sets between entity sets A and B, the mapping cardinality must be one of:

- *One-to-one*: An entity in A is associated with at most one entity in B, and an entity in B is associated with at most one entity in A.
- *One-to-many*: An entity in A is associated with any number in B. An entity in B is associated with at most one entity in A.
- *Many-to-one*: An entity in A is associated with at most one entity in B. An entity in B is associated with any number in A.
- *Many-to-many*: Entities in A and B are associated with any number from each other.

The appropriate mapping cardinality for a particular relationship set depends on the real world being modeled.

- *Existence Dependencies*: if the existence of entity X depends on the existence of entity Y, then X is said to be existence dependent on Y

MAPPING ER-DIAGRAM TO TABLES

A database conforming to an E-R diagram can be represented by a collection of tables.

Pre-mapping Preparation Work

Mapping a conceptual ERD model to relations is not straightforward because some concepts may not be implemented directly in relations. Furthermore, the text-based representation of relations (tables) is not as comprehensive as graphical models. Thus, pre-mapping work in Logical ER models are used to bridge the gap.

Typical transformations include:

- Converting all many-to-many relationships to many-to-one relationships
- Turning all weak entities into regular entities
- Separating multivalve attributes (repeating values) separate entities
- Converting all n-ary (n > 2) relationships into binary relationships
- Implementing all relationships by adding appropriate foreign keys to the connected entities

After the logical model is validated, the logical model is then mapped to relations in a rather straightforward way.

Mapping Logical ER-Diagram models to Relational Tables

For each entity set and relationship set, there is a unique table which is assigned the name of the corresponding set. Each table has a number of columns with unique names.

STEP 1: For regular entity type E in ER schema, create a relation R that includes all the simple attributes, and component attributes of composite attributes. Select the primary key.

STEP 2: For weak entity type W in ER schema, with owner entity type E, create a relation R, include all simple attributes (or component attributes of composite attributes) of W as attributes of R. In addition, include the primary key attributes of the relation Q for the owner entity type E. Primary key is the combination of primary key of Q and partial key of R.

STEP 3: For 1:1 relationship X, suppose S and T are the relations for the entity types participating in it. Include primary key of T as foreign key of S. Include other attributes of the relationship X as attributes of S.

STEP 4: For 1:N relationship Y, suppose S relation corresponds to the entity type at the N-side, and T relation corresponds to the entity type at the other side. Include primary key of T as foreign key of S.

STEP 5: For M:N relationship Z, create a new relation R to represent Z. Include simple attributes of Z in R. Include the primary keys of S and T as foreign keys of R, their combination forms the primary key of R.

STEP 6: For multivalued attribute A, create a new relation R that includes an attribute corresponding to A. Include primary key of the relation of the entity type having A as an attribute. Primary key is their combination.

STEP 7: For n-ary relationship type X, and n>2, create a new relation R. Include primary key of each participating entity type's relation as foreign key of R. Include attributes of X as simple attributes of R.

Relations Obtained Form ERD Above:

Teacher (Index no, first_name, Last_name, email, phone, paper, paper_de, Seq_no)

Conference (Time, Location, Descript Seq No)

Example above is the table obtained from ER Diagram for the Michigan Conference Management System.

KEYS

An entity is defined by its attributes. Furthermore, each entity occurrence can be uniquely identified, by using an attribute or a combination of attributes as a key.

The primary key is the attribute (or group of attributes) that serve to uniquely identify each entity occurrence. Consider the problem that might arise if the name and address of an individual were used as the primary key for identifying the patients within a hospital.

Take the example of a patient called David Smith living at 23 Acacia Avenue. He has a son also called David Smith living at the same address.

Name and Address would not necessarily provide a unique identifier and confusion could easily arise, potentially creating a mix up with the patient records.

For this reason, in a hospital system patients each have a Patient Number as their primary key.

If two or more data items are used as the unique identifier, then this represents a compound key. For example, a compound key used to identify a book could be 'Title' together with 'Author'.

There may be occasions of authors using a previously used title but not of an author using the same title for more than one of their own books.

Where several possible primary keys exist they are called candidate keys.

For example, a book could be identified, either by 'Title' together with 'Author' or by the widely used unique identifier for books - the ISBN number.

Where an attribute of one entity is a candidate key for another entity, it is termed a foreign key.

For example, the attribute 'Author' belonging to the entity Book is a foreign key within the entity Author. You may be able to think of some shortcomings to the use of this attribute as the primary key, for example two authors having the same name.

It is worth noting that entity relationships are often indicated by the presence of foreign keys.

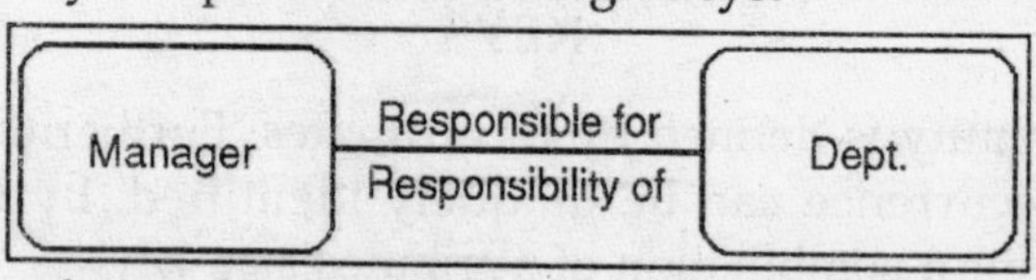

The relationship is the association between two entities to which all of the occurrences of those entities must conform. The diagram shown represents the beginnings of a data model where the relationship between a manager and a department needs to be defined.

The entities on data models are linked by relationship lines and together these are the only two components that make up a data model diagram. A relationship is an association between two entities to which all of the occurrences of those entities must conform.

Every relationship line shows two reciprocal relationships: That of the first entity with respect to the second and that of the second entity with respect to the first. In this example a manager is responsible for a department and a department is the responsibility of a manager.

Each relationship line has three distinct properties: Firstly the relationship link phrase, secondly the degree or cardinality of the relationship and thirdly the participation or optionality of the relationship. These three properties combine to form the relationship statement.

CONCEPTS OF SUPER KEY

A super key is a set of one or more attributes which; taken collectively, allow us to identify uniquely an entity in the entity set. * A super key may contain extraneous attributes, and we are often interested in the smallest super key.

A super key for which no subset is a super key is called a candidate key. A superkey is a set of one or more attributes which, taken collectively, allow us to identify uniquely an entity in the entity set.

Ecxample: In the entity set customer, customer-name and personal-number is a superkey. Note that customer-name alone is not a superkey, as two customers could have the same name. A superkey is defined in the relational model as a set of attributes of a relation variable (relvar) for which it holds that in all relations assigned to that variable there are no two distinct tuples (rows) that have the same values for the attributes in this set. Equivalently a superkey can also be defined as a set of attributes of a relvar upon which all attributes of the relvar are functionally dependent.

Note that if attribute set K is a superkey of relvar R, then at all times it is the case that the projection of R over K has the same cardinality as R itself.

Informally, a superkey is a set of columns within a table whose values can be used to uniquely identify a row. A candidate key is a minimal set of columns necessary to identify a row, this is also called a minimal superkey. For example, given an employee table, consisting of the columns employeeID, name, job, and departmentID, we could use the employeeID in combination with any or all other columns of this table to uniquely identify a row in the table. Examples of superkeys in this table would be {employeeID, Name}, {employeeID, Name, job}, and {employeeID, Name, job, departmentID}.

In a real database we don't need values for all of those columns to identify a row. We only need, per our example, the set {employeeID}. This is a minimal superkey-that is, a minimal set of columns that can be used to identify a single row. So, employee is a candidate key.

CANDIDATE KEY

A candidate key is a super key containing the minimum number of columns to uniquely identify each record in a table. Not every candidate key is a good primary key.

There are three fundamental demands on the candidate keys that we must never deviate from, if it is to become the subject for a primary key:

1. The candidate key must be unique within its domain (the entity it represents, and beyond, if you also intend to access external entities).
2. The candidate key can not hold NULL values (NULL is not zero. Zero is a number. NULL is 'nonexistent value').
3. The candidate key can never change. It must hold the same value for a given occurrence of an entity for the lifetime of that entity.

In 1., we say that the main purpose of the candidate key is to help us to identify one single row in a table, regardless of whether there exists billions of row. This sets high demands on the flexibility in terms of delivering uniqueness.

In 2., we say that a candidate key always, without exception, must hold a value. Without it, we break post 1.

In 3., we say that no matter what happens, inside our business or outside of it, we are not allowed to change the value of the candidate key. Adding an attribute (expanding) the candidate key, would pose a change. Some say that you should be able to change the primary key, and do a 'cascade update' to all underlying tables.

A candidate key is a set of attributes, taken from the header of a relational table; with the property that no two records/tuples/rows in the table may have the same Candidate Key. In other words, were a table to be projected by any of its candidate keys, the resulting table would always have the same cardinality. A table may have multiple candidate keys; but it must have at least one (consisting of all attributes in the header); otherwise it would be a bag and not a set.

PRIMARY KEY

INTRODUCTION

A primary key, also called a primary keyword, is a key in a relational database that is unique for each record. It is a unique identifier, such as a driver license number, telephone number (including area code), or vehicle identification number (VIN). A relational database must always have one and only one primary key. Primary keys typically appear as columns in relational database tables.

The choice of a primary key in a relational database often depends on the preference of the administrator. It is possible to change the primary key for a given database when the specific needs of the users changes. For example, the people in a town might be uniquely identified according to their driver license numbers in one application, but in another situation it might be more convenient to identify them according to their telephone numbers.

A non-empty set of columns (an ordered set in some RDBMS products) that contain non-null values and whose values uniquely identify a row (record). A table cannot have more than one Primary Key, and should not have zero primary keys (this is usually but not always enforced in RDBMS systems). Often the term Primary Key is used to refer to a set of columns which is a strict subset of all of the columns in the table; and in many cases it is assumed that the Primary Key consists of a single column.

Primary keys are useful and necessary because:

- They uniquely identify the record
- They are needed to implement Foreign Keys (though any Candidate Key will suffice).

  The ideal primary key would be
- A Candidate Key
- *Mandatory*: It is never possible to not have one (do All employees have SSN's?)
- *Immutable*: Can never be updated
- *And minimal*: As small as possible

Primary keys are distinguished from other Candidate Keys? in that their values are used by other tables to refer to rows in the (primary key's) table. A primary key also may capture the notion of Object Identity (e.g., I'm still the same person even though my name, weight, age, first and last name have changed). In a normalized database, primary key values are the only values that should appear multiple times in the database.

Whenever a row is inserted into a table, you need to provide (or generate) a primary key for it. Uh, no you don't... the entire record could be a Candidate Key, in which case it comes for free. Key Generation is done when there is no column or set of columns which meets the uniqueness constraint, account numbers are typical examples of generated Primary Keys.

DEFINITION

The primary key of a relational table uniquely identifies each record in the table. It can either be a normal attribute that is guaranteed to be unique (such as Social Security Number in a table with no more than one record per person) or it can be generated by the DBMS (such as a globally unique identifier, or GUID, in Microsoft SQL Server). Primary keys may consist of a single attribute or multiple attributes in combination.

Imagine we have a STUDENTS table that contains a record for each student at a university. The student's unique student

ID number would be a good choice for a primary key in the STUDENTS table. The student's first and last name would not be a good choice, as there is always the chance that more than one student might have the same name.

CONSTRAINTS

A table typically has a column or combination of columns that contain values that uniquely identify each row in the table. This column, or columns, is called the primary key (PK) of the table and enforces the entity integrity of the table. You can create a primary key by defining a Primary Ket constraint when you create or modify a table.

A table can have only one Primary Ket constraint, and a column that participates in the Primary Ket constraint cannot accept null values. Because Primary Ket constraints guarantee unique data, they are frequently defined on an identity column.

When you specify a Primary Ket constraint for a table, the Database Engine enforces data uniqueness by creating a unique index for the primary key columns. This index also permits fast access to data when the primary key is used in queries. Therefore, the primary keys that are chosen must follow the rules for creating unique indexes.

If aPrimary Ket constraint is defined on more than one column, values may be duplicated within one column, but each combination of values from all the columns in the Primary Ket constraint definition must be unique. As shown in the following illustration, the ProductID and VendorID columns in the Purchasing. Product Vendor table form a composite Primary Ket constraint for this table. This makes sure that that the combination of ProductID and VendorID is unique.

Primary Key

Product ID	Vendor ID	Averagelead Time	Standarddprice	Lest Receiptcost
1	1	17	47.8700	50.2635
2	104	19	39.9200	41.9160
7	4	17	54.3100	57.0255
609	7	17	25.7700	27.0585
609	100	19	28.1700	29.5785

Productvendor Table

When you work with joins, Primary Ket constraints relate one table to another. For example, to determine which vendors supply which products, you can use a three-way join between the Purchasing.Vendor table, the Production.Product table, and the Purchasing.ProductVendor table.

Because ProductVendorcontains both the ProductID and VendorID columns, both the Product table and the Vendor table can be accessed by their relationship to ProductVendor.

REDUCTION OF ER DIAGRAMS TO TABLES

Primary keys allow entity sets and relationship sets to be expressed uniformly as tables which represent the contents of the database. A database which conforms to an E-R diagram can be represented by a collection of tables.

For each entity set and relationship set there is a unique table which is assigned the name of the corresponding entity set or relationship set. Each table has a number of columns (generally corresponding to attributes), which have unique names. Converting an E-R diagram to a table format is the basis for deriving a relational database design from an E-R diagram.

REPRESENTING ENTITY SETS AS TABLES

A strong entity set reduces to a table with the same attributes:

Table. The Customer

Customer-name	Social-Security	C-Street	C-City
Jones	321-12-3123	Main	Harrison
Smith	019-28-3746	North	Rye
Hayes	677-89-9011	Main	Harrison

A weak entity set becomes a table that includes a column for the primary key of the identifying strong entity set.

Table. The Payment

Loan-Number	Payment- Number	Payment-Date	Payment-amount
L-17	5	10 May 1996	50
L-23	11	17 May 1996	75
L-15	22	23 May 1996	300

REPRESENTING RELATIONSHIP SETS AS TABLES

A many-to-many relationship set is represented as a table with columns for the primary keys of the two participating entity sets, and any descriptive attributes of the relationship set.

Table. The Depositor

Social-Security	Account-number	Access-Date
...	...	...

The table corresponding to a relationship set linking a weak entity set to its identifying strong entity set is redundant. The payment table already contains the information that would appear in the loan-payment table.

GENERALIZATION AS TABLES

Method 1: Form a table for the generalized entity account Form a table for each entity set that is generalized (include primary key of generalized entity set)

Table	Table Attributes
Account	Account-number, blance, account-type
Savings-account	Account-number, interest-rate
Checking-account	Account-number, Overdraft-amount

Method 2: Form a table for each entity set that is generalized Table

RELATIONS CORRESPONDS TO AGGREGATION

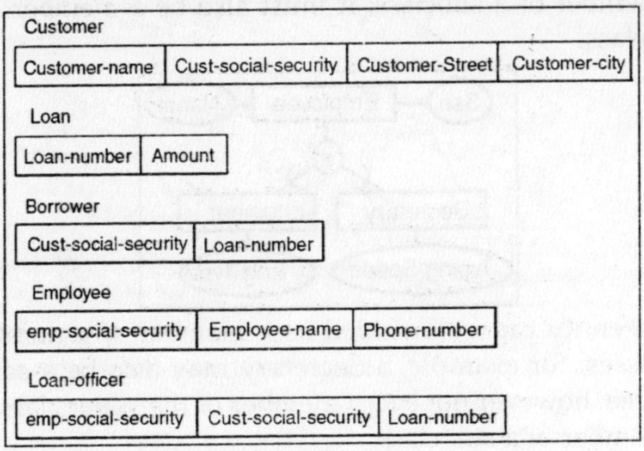

EXTENDED ER MODEL

- Contain all the basic modeling concepts of an ER Diagram
- Adds additional concepts:
  - Specialization/generalization
  - Subclass/super class
  - Categories Attribute inheritance

Extended ER diagrams use some object-oriented concepts such as inheritance. EER is used to model concepts more accurately than the ER diagram.

SUB CLASSES AND SUPER CLASSES

- In some cases, and entity type has numerous sub-groupings of its entities that are meaningful, and need to be explicitly represented, because of their importance.
- For example, members of entity Employee can be grouped further into Secretary, Engineer, Manager, Technician, Salaried Employee.
- The set listed is a subset of the entities that belong to the Employee entity, which means that every entity that belongs to one of the sub sets is also an Employee.

Each of these sub-groupings is called a subclass, and the Employee entity is called the super-class. An entity cannot only be a member of a subclass; it must also be a member of the super-class.

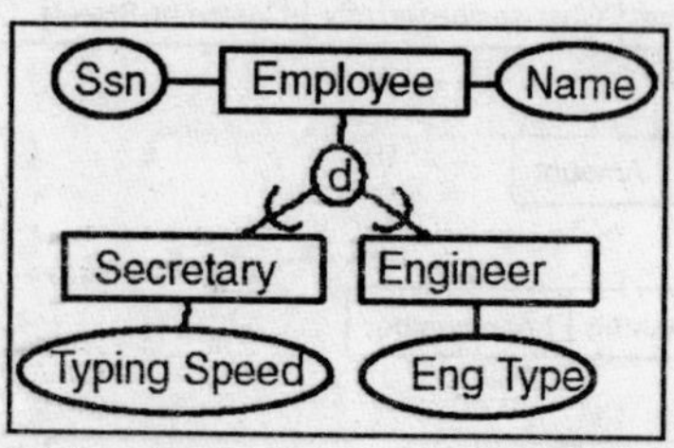

An entity can be included as a member of a number of sub classes, for example, a Secretary may also be a salaried employee, however not every member of the super class must be a member of a sub class.

TYPE INHERITANCE

Specialization

The process of defining a set of subclasses of a super class. Specialization is the top-down refinement into (super) classes and subclasses. The set of sub classes is based on some distinguishing characteristic of the super class.

For example, the set of sub classes for Employee, Secretary, Engineer, Technician, differentiates among employee based on job type.

There may be several specializations of an entity type based on different distinguishing characteristics. Another example is the specialization, Salaried_Employee and Hourly_Employee, which distinguish employees based on their method of pay.

Notation for Specialization

- To represent a specialization, the subclasses that define a specialization are attached by lines to a circle that represents the specialization, and is connected to the super class.
- The subset symbol (half-circle) is shown on each line connecting a subclass to a super class, indicates the direction of the super class/subclass relationship.

  Attributes that only apply to the sub class are attached to the rectangle representing the subclass. They are called specific attributes.
- A sub class can also participate in specific relationship types.

See Example:

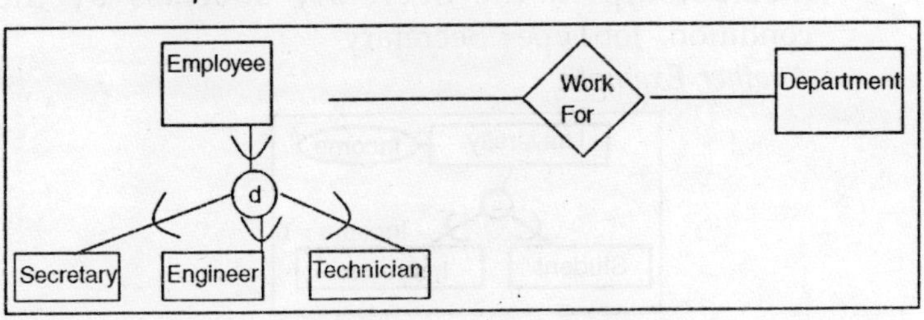

Reasons for Specialization

- Certain attributes may apply to some but not all entities of a super class. A subclass is defined in order to group the entities to which the attribute Apply.
- The second reason for using subclasses is that some relationship types may be participated in only by entities that are members of the subclass.

GENERALIZATION

The reverse of specialization is generalization. Several classes with common features are generalized into a super class. For example, the entity types Car and Truck share common attributes License_PlateNo, VehicleID and Price, therefore they can be generalized into the super class Vehicle.

CONSTRAINTS ON SPECIALIZATION

- Several specializations can be defined on an entity type.
- Entities may belong to subclasses in each of the specializations.
- The specialization may also consist of a single subclass, such as the manager specialization, in this case we don't use the circle notation.

TYPES OF SPECIALIZATIONS

Predicate or Condition-defined Specialization

- Occurs in cases where we can determine exactly the entities of each sub class by placing a condition of the value of an attribute in the super class.

  An example is where the Employee entity has an attribute, Job Type. We can specify the condition of membership in the Secretary subclass by the condition, JobType="Secretary"

  Another Example:

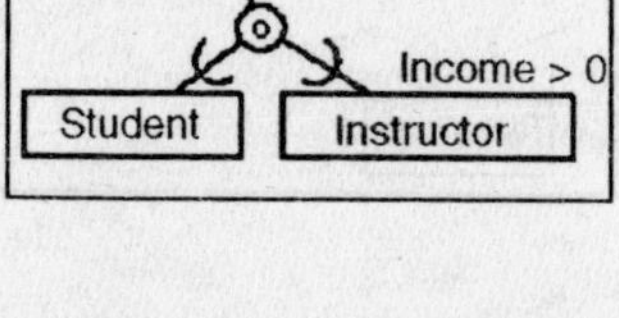

- The condition is called the defining predicate of the sub class.
- The condition is a constraint specifying exactly those entities of the Employee entity type whose attribute value for Job Type is Secretary belong to the subclass.
- Predicate defined subclasses are displayed by writing the predicate condition next to the line that connects the subclass to the specialization circle.

Attribute-defined Specialization

- If all subclasses in a specialization have their membership condition on the same attribute of the super class, the specialization is called an attribute-defined specialization, and the attribute is called the defining attribute.
- Attribute-defined specializations are displayed by placing the defining attribute name next to the arc from the circle to the super class.

User-defined Specialization

When we do not have a condition for determining membership in a subclass the subclass is called user-defined. Membership to a subclass is determined by the database users when they add an entity to the s bclass.

Disjointness/Overlap Constraint

- Specifies that the subclass of the specialization must be disjoint, which means that an entity can be a member of, at most, one subclass of the specialization.
- The d in the specialization circle stands for disjoint.
- If the subclasses are not constrained to be disjoint, they overlap.

Overlap means that an entity can be a member of more than one subclass of the specialization. Overlap constraint is shown by placing an o in the specialization circle.

Completeness Constraint

The completeness constraint may be either total or partial.

A total specialization constraint specifies that every entity in the superclass must be a member of at least one subclass of the specialization. Total specialization is shown by using a double line to connect the super class to the circle. A single line is used to display a partial specialization, meaning that an entity does not have to belong to any of the subclasses.

Disjointness vs. Completeness

- Disjoint constraints and completeness constraints are independent.

The following possible constraints on specializations are possible:

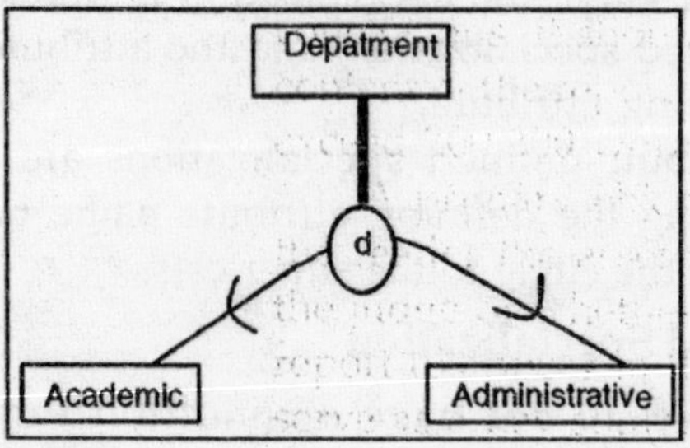

Disjoint, partial

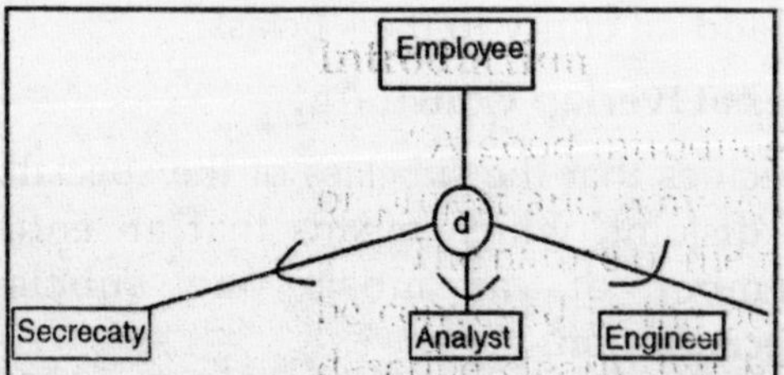

Overlapping, total

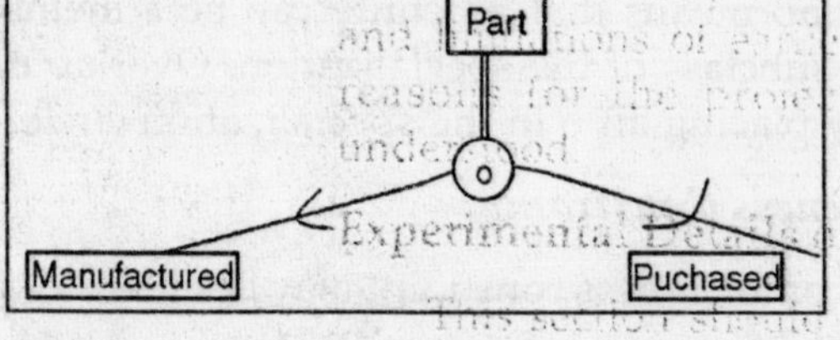

Overlapping, partial

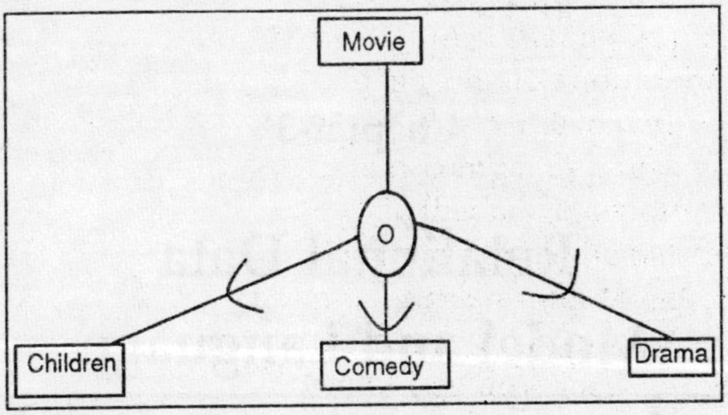

Chapter-3

Relational Data Model and Language

RELATIONAL DATA MODEL

CONCEPTS

Domain

A domain D is the original sets of atomic values used to model data. By atomic, we mean that each value in the domain is indivisible as far as the relational model is concerned.

For example:

- The domain of day shift is the set of all possible days : {Mon, Tue, Wed…}
- The domain of salary is the set of all floating-point numbers greater than 0 and less than 200,000 (say).
- The domain of name is the set of character strings that represents names of person

Relation (Relation state)

A relation is a subset of the Cartesian product of a list of domains characterised by a name. Given n domains denoted by D1, D2, …, Dn , r is a relation defined on these domains if $rD1 \times D2 \times ... \times Dn$. Relation can be viewed as a "table". In that table, each row represents a tuple of data values and each column represents an attribute.

Attribute

A column of a relation designated by name. The name associated should be meaningful.

Each attributes associates with a domain.

A relation schema denoted by R is a list of attributes (A1, A2, ..., An)

The degree of the relation is the number of attributes of its relation schema.

The cardinality of the relation is the number of tuples in the relation.

Example of relation, relation schema and attribute:

EMPLOYEE is Relation Name

Eid, Name, Birthdate, Salary, Department are called Attributes (column)

Each row of the tables is called Tuple (or Row/Record)

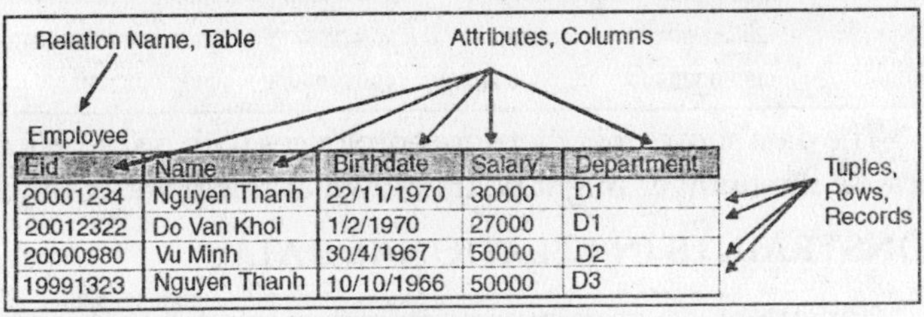

Fig. Sample Relation

Characteristic of Relations

- *Ordering of Tuples in a relation*: A tuple is a set of values. A relation is a set of tuples. Since a relation is a set, there is no ordering on rows.
- *Ordering of Values within a tuple*: The order of attributes and their values within a relation is not important as long as the correspondence between attributes and values is maintained. Thus the following is a different representation of the above EMPLOYEE relation

Employee

Department	**Eid**	**Name**	**Birthdate**	**Salary**
D1	20001234	Nguyen Thanh	22/11/1970	30000
D1	20012322	Do Van Khôi	1/2/1978	27000
D2	20000980	Vu Minh	30/4/1967	50000
D3	19991323	Nguyen Thành	10/10/1966	50000

- Values and NULL values in the tuple: Each value in a tuple is atomic. That means each value cannot be divided into smaller components. Hence, the composite and multivalued attributes are not allowed in a relation.

In a relation, there can be several value of attributes that may be unknown or currently not applicable. The following table contains some NULL values in it:

Employee Department	Eid	Name	Birthdate	Salary	CellPhone
D1	20001234	Nguyen Thành	22/11/1970	30000	0912304101
D1	20012322	Do Van Khôi	1/2/1978	27000	NULL
D2	20000980	Vu Minh	30/4/1967	50000	0903132123
D3	19991323	Nguyen Thành	10/10/1966	50000	NULL

The data shows that there are employees with no cell phone because the number might be unknown at this point of time.

CONSTRAINTS IN RELATIONAL DATA

Constraint is a very important feature in relational model. In fact, relational model support a well-defined theory of constraint on attributes or tables. Constraint is useful because it allows designer to specify the semantics of data in database and it is the rules to enforce DBMSs to check that new data satisfies the semantics.

Integrity Constraint

Relation allows us to represent data and association. Domain restrict the values of attributes in the relation and it is a constraint of relational model. However, there are real - world semantics on data that cannot specifies if use only domain. We need more specific way to state what data values are/are not allows, what format is suitable for an attributes. For example, employee number must be unique, employees' age is in the range [23, 65]. Such information is provided in logical statements called integrity constraints.

There are several kinds of integrity constraints:

- *Key constraint*: A relation is a set of tuples. By

definition, all elements in a set are distinct hence all tuple in a relation must be distinct.

In relational model, tuples have no identity like object - identification. Tuple identity is totally value-based. Therefore, we need key constraint that is the way of uniquely identify a tuple. Given a relation schema R with U is the list of attributes, there are a set K which is a subset of U. If in a relation r of E with any two distinct tuples t1 and t_2 we have the constraint that $t_1[K] \neq t_2[K]$ then K is called a superkey of the relation schema R.

A superkey can have redundant attributes. A superkey that have no such attributes is called a candidate key. Formally, we can define a candidate key as following.

Given a relation schema R, K' is called a candidate key of R if K' satisfies two constraint:

- K' is a superkey of R
- There is no such proper subset of K' that is also a superkey of R or K' is the minimum superkey)

Since a relation schema may have more than one candidate key thus there is a chosen candidate key whose values are used to identify tuples in the relation. Such key is primary key. Primary key is usually the most simple candidate key (i.e. key with single attribute or small number of attributes) In relational database, key are often implemented by introducing an attributes specially designed for being key.

Table. Employee

Department	Eid	Name	Birthdate	Salary	CellPhone
D1	20001234	Nguyen Thành	22/11/1970	30000	0912304101
D1	20012322	Do Van Khôi	1/2/1978	27000	NULL
D2	20000980	Vu Minh	30/4/1967	50000	0903132123
D3	19991323	Nguyen Thành	10/10/1966	50000	NULL

Superkey: {Name, Salary} , {Eid}, {Name, Birthdate}
Candidate key: {Eid} Primary key: {Eid}

- *Entity constraint*: No attribute in the primary key can be NULL. This is because, NULL values for the primary key means we cannot identify some tuples. For example, in the EMPLOYEE relation showed above, CellPhone cannot be a key since we cannot use this attribute to identify employees 20012322 and employee.

- *Refer·ntial constraint*: The constraint that is specified between two relations and maintain the correspondence between tuples in these relations. It means the reference from a tuple in one relation to other relation must be valid.

Examples of Referential integrity constraint

- *In the Bank Database (From Data Modelling lecture)*: The ACCOUNT relation need to take note the BRANCH where each account is held so in implementation, in each tuple of ACCOUNT relation, there is an attribute such as branchname to identify the associate BRANCH . The referential integrity constraint must state that the branchname attribute in the ACCOUNT relation refer to a valid branch (i.e. existing branch)
- *In the Company Database*: In the EMPLOYEE relation, we need to store the information about the department where each employee works in. The attribute Department in EMPLOYEE relation is used for that purpose so the values appears in the columns Department must be taken from set of values identify the Department number in the relation DEPARTMENT if this relation exists.

Referential constraint in relational model relates to notation of foreign key. A set of attributes FK in a relation schema R1 is foreign key if.

- The attributes in FK correspond to the attributes in the primary key of another relation schema R2
- The value for FK in each tuple of R1 either occur as values of primary key of a tuple in R2 or is entirely NULL

In a database of many relations, there are usually many foreign keys. They provide the "glue" that links individual relations into a cohesive database structure. The following figure describes an example of referential integrity constraint in a part of the BANK database

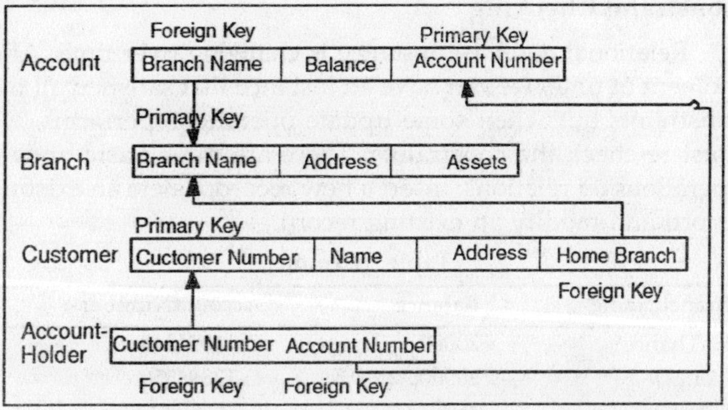

Fig. Referential Integrity Constraints in Part of BANK Database.

- *Semantic constraints*: This is a special kind of constraints that may have to enforced in relational database. Such constraints describe the semantics of data in the database or sometimes called the rules on data. For example, in the COMPANY database, we have the rule " An employee cannot take a part in more than 5 projects" or "Salary of an employee cannot exceed the salary of the employee's manager"
- *Functional Dependency constraints*: This constraints establishes a functional relationship among two sets of attributes.

RELATIONAL DATABASE

Relations, keys, foreign keys and integrity constraints provide a complete toolkit for building relational databases. A relational database consists of many relations and tuples in relations are related in various ways. Here, we will define relational database schema and relational database instance.

A relational database schema is:

- A set of relation schemas S = {R1, R2, … , Rn} , and
- A set of integrity constraints

A relational database instance is:

- A set of relations {r1(R1) , r2(R2) , … , rn(Rn) } where all of the integrity constraints are satisfied.

Constraint Checking

Relational database instance is changing over time. At a moment of time, we can have an instance that satisfied all the constraints but when some update operations performs, we must re-check the constraints. There are three basic update operations on relations: insert a new record, delete an existing record and modify an existing record.

Table. Account

BranchName	Balance	AccountNumber
HaThanh	20000	C-12894349
DongD–	20000	C-12894350
DongD–	3500	S-141510751
HaThanh	50000	S-520522620
BRANCH		
branchName	address	assets
HaThanh	Hai Ba Trung	900000000
DongD–	Dong Da	400000000
ThangLong	Hoan Kiem	500000000

Table. Customer

CustomerNumber	Name	Address	HomeBranch
111111	Anh	Hai Ba Trung	HaThanh
121314	Van Anh	Hai Ba Trung	Dong Do
515016	Son	Hoan Kiem	HaThanh

Table. Account-Holder

CustomerNumber	AccountNumber
111111	C-12894349
121314	C-12894350
121314	S-141510751
515016	S-520522620
111111	C-12894350

Domain constraint checking:

- For insert operation, it is need to check attribute value for type and other domain restrictions.
- For delete operation, it is no need to check any domain constraints

- For update operation, it is also need to check attribute value for type and other domain restrictions.

The following changes satisfy domain constraints:

- Insert Account(HaThanh, 50000, S-20071280)
- Insert Account(HaThan, 20000, C-20072242) (it is looks ok but actually the data value is not correct)
- Update Account(HaThanh, 50000, S-20071280) to Account(HaThanh, 60000, S-20071280)

The changes that do not satisfy domain constraints:

- Insert Account(HaThanh, 5000USD, S-20071280)
- Insert Account(DongDo, -20, C-12894349)
- Update Account(HaThanh, 50000, S-34252525) to Account(60000, HaThanh, S-34252525)

Key constraint checking:

- For insert operation, it is need to check the key value does not occur in any existing tuple in the relation.
- For delete operation, it is no need to check any domain key constraints
- For update operation, if the key value is modified then need the same check as for insertion.

Changes that satisfy key constraints:

- Insert Account(DongDo, 20000, C-12894350) (there is no account with that account number in the current relation)
- Insert Account-Holder(12334, C-12894350) (ok, but no such customer with number 12334)
- Update Account(HaThanh, 50000, S-34252525) to Account(60000, HaThanh, S-34252525) (key is not modified)

Changes that do not satisfied key constraints:

- Insert Account(DongDo, 50000, C-12894350) (key is alredy there in the relation)
- Update Account(DongDo, 20000, C-12894350) to Account(DongDo, 20000, C-12894349) (the account C-12894349 is already in the relation)

Referential integrity constraint checking:

- For insert operation, it is need to check the foreign keys occur as primary keys in the referenced relation.

- For delete operation, check all relations that have foreign keys refering to this relation
- An update need to treat as delete - then - insert for referential constraints checking.

Changes that satisfy referential constraint:

- Insert Account(ThangLong, 5000, C-12891230)
- Insert Account-Holder(111111, C-12891230)
- Update Customer(515016, Son, Hoan Kiem, HaThanh) to Customer(515016, Son, Hoan Kiem, ThangLong)
- Delete Account-Holder(111111, C-12894350)

Changes that does not satisty referential constraint:

- Insert Account-Holder(12334, C-12894350) (no such customer)
- Insert Customer(222222, Nha, DongDa, An Binh) (no such branch)
- Delete Customer with customerNumber = '111111' (this is not acceptable since there are tuples in Account-Holder relation refer to this customer)

Deletion can violate referential constraint when the tuple being deleted is referenced by the foreign keys from others tuples in a different relation. Several approaches are consider to handle this kind of violation.

- The first approach is simply disallow the deletion.
- The second approach: User must find the refering tuple then either delete them manually or change their foreign key to an acceptable value or NULL value (not possible if the foreign key also forms part of the primary key such as in the Account-Holder relation)
- The third approach: attempt to remove all refering tuple automatically (cascade)

When the referential constraint is specified in the database during the creation phase, the DBMSs will allow user to specify which of the above approach applies when a violation occur.

MAPPING ER DESIGNS RELATIONAL SCHEME

One useful stategy of database design is: Firstly, performing data modelling using conceptual model (ER model or Object-Oriented Model) then transform this conceptual to relational model. This section will introduce some "rule" to map an ER diagram in to a relational database schema.

1. *Mapping Regular Entity Types*: An entity type E with atomic attributes A1, A2, ... An maps to a relation R with attributes (columns) A1, A2, ... An . In addition, one of the keys of the entity type E will be chosen as the primary key for R. If the chosen keys is composite then the primary keys of R is made up of several attributes.

   Example:

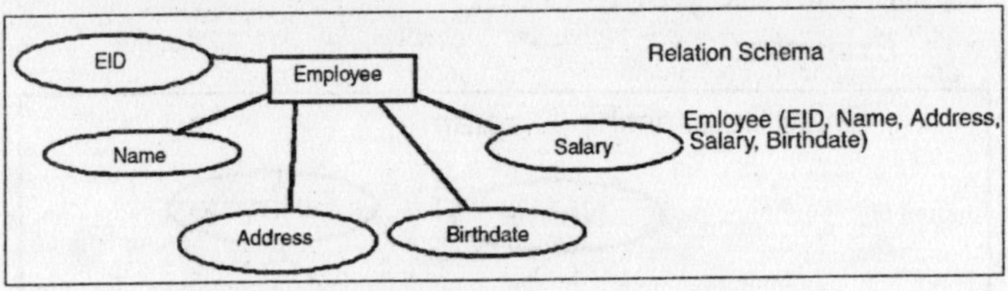

Fig. Mapping of Regular Entity Types

- Composite attributes are mapped by concatenation or flattering. Concatenating means we keep the composite attributes only, ignore the components of it. Flaterring, on the other hands, means including only the simple component attributes of a composite attribute.

  Example:

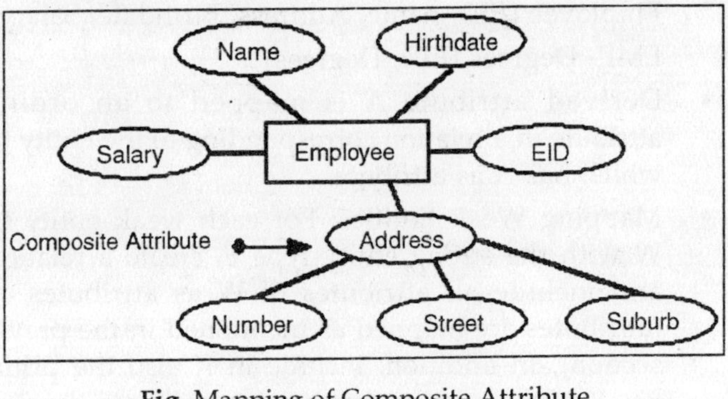

Fig. Mapping of Composite Attribute

Relational Scheama (Version 1-Concatenating)
Employee (Name, Address, Birthdate, Salary)
Relational Schema (Version 2-Fattering)
Employee (Name, Number, Sreet, Suburb, Birthdate, Salary)

- Multi-valued attributes are mapped by using additional relation schema. For each multi-valued attribute A, create a new relation R. This relation will include attribute corresponding to A plus the primary key K of the entity type or relationship type that has A as attribute. Combination of A and K becomes primary key of R.

Example:

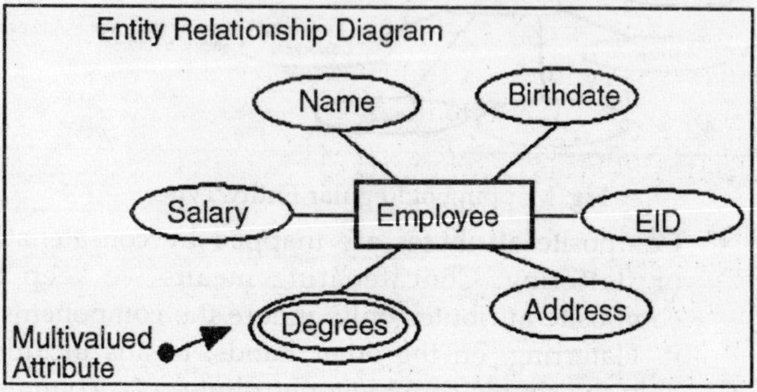

Fig. Mapping of Multivalues Attribute

Relational Schemas
Employee (EID, name, Address, Birthdate, Salary,)
EMP- Degrees (EID, Degrees)

- Derived attribute A is mapped to an ordinary attribute in a relation corresponding to the entity type which has A as attribute.
- Mapping Weak Entities: For each weak entity type W with the strong entity type E, create a relation R and include all attributes of W as attributes of R (attributes are mapped as mentioned in the previous section). In addition, include in R also the primary key K of the relation that corresponding to the strong

entity E. Keys of the relation R is the combination of K and the partial key of the weak entity type (if any)

Example: Consider the below entity relationship diagram, weak entity type DEPENDENT is mapped into relation EMP-DEPENTDENT. Primary key of this relation is {EID,Name} because Name can be considered as partial key of DEPENDENT.

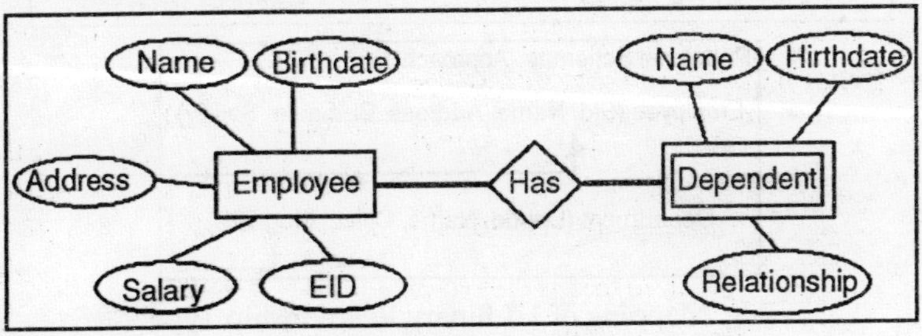

Fig. Mapping of Week Entities

Relational Schemas

Employee (Eid, Name, Address, Birthdate, Salary, Emp-Relationship)

Mapping Binary Relationship Type: For each 1-1 Binary Relationship Type R, identify relation A and B that correspond to the entity types participating in R. The relationship itself can be mapped using one of the following approaches.

- *Using foreign key*: This is the most popular approach. Choose one of the participating relation, say A (usually one with total participation); include in A as the foreign key the primary key of B. If R has attributes then put them in the relation A as well.
- *Merged relation*: If both participations of two related entity type are total then we can merge two entity types and the relationship into a relation.
- *Defining relationship relation*: Define a relation R to represent the relationship. All attributes of relationship is included in R. In addition, put the primary keys of two relations A , B into R. The primary keys of R is combination of primary keys of A and B.

  Example: Consider the relationship Manages between

EMPLOYEE and DEPARTMENT, in this relationship the participation of DEPARTMENT is total.

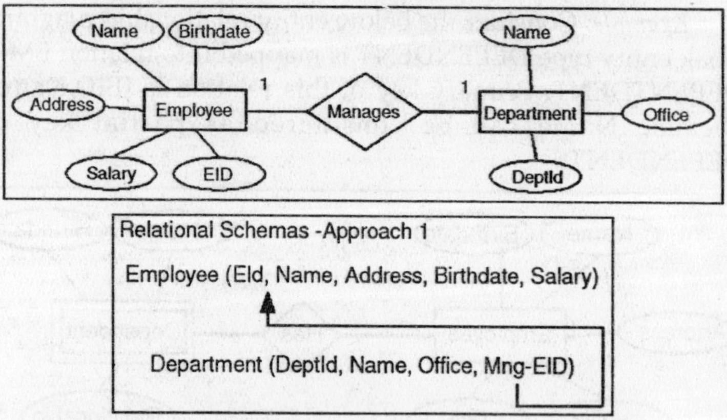

Fig. Mapping of 1-1 Binary Relationship Type

Relational Schemas-Approach 3
Employee (Eid, Name, Address, Birthdate, Salary)
Department (DeptId, Name, office)
Manages (EID, Deptid)

Mapping 1-N Binary Relationship Type: For each 1-N Binary Relationship Type R, identify two relations A and B correspond to two entity types participating in R.

A represents the entity type at 1-side and B represents the entity type at N-side. Include the primary key of A as the foreign key in B. This foreign key represent the relationship type R.

Example:

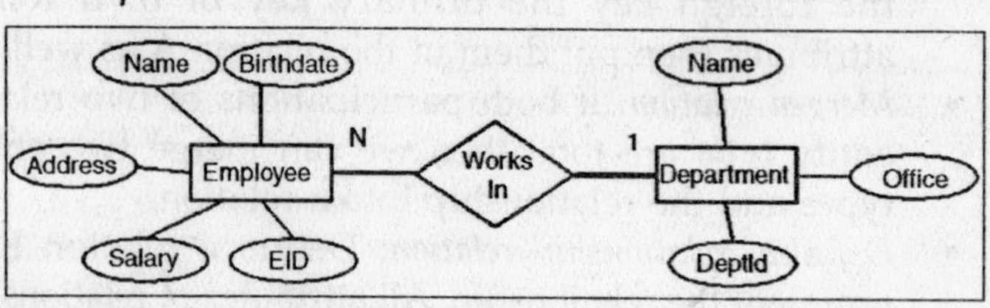

Fig. Mapping of 1-N Binary Relationship Type

Relational Schemas
Employee (Eid, name, Address, Birthdate, Salary, Deptid)
Department (DeptId, Name, Office)

- Mapping M-N Binary Relationship Type: For each M-N Binary Relationship Type R, identify two relation A, B represent two entity type participating in R. Create a new relation S to represent R. Include in S as foreign keys the primary keys of A and B and all the simple attributes of R. The combination of primary keys of A and B will make the primary key of S.
  Example:

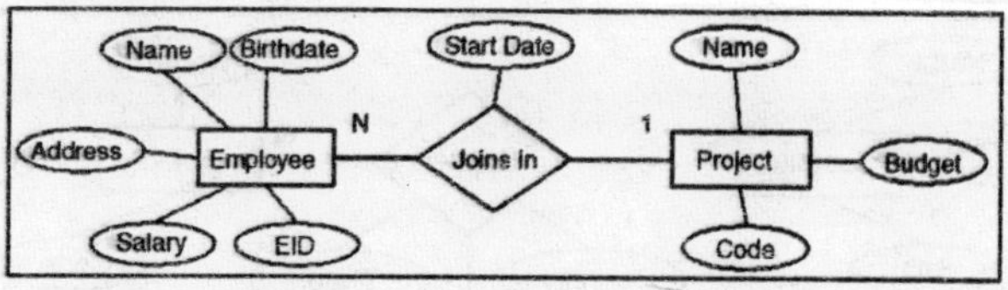

Fig. Mapping of M-N Binary Relationship Type

Relational Schema
Employee (Eid, Name, Address, Birthdate, Salary)
Project (Code, Name, Budget)
Join (Eid, Code, Start, Date)

Mapping Unary Relationship Type: For each Unary Relationship Type R, we identify the relation A represents the entity type involves in this relationship. Include in this relation one more time as foreign key the primary of itself. The two keys (primary key and foreign key) are the same but they represents two entities of different roles relate to this relationship.

Example

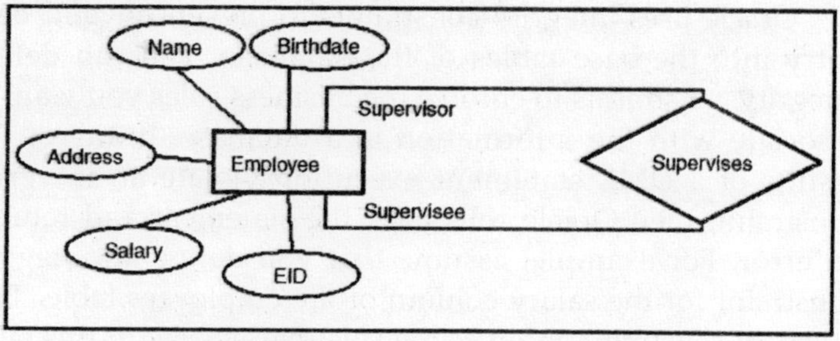

Fig. Mapping of Unary Relationship Type

Relational Schema

Employee (Eid, Name, Address, Birthdate, Salary, Salary super-EID)

Mapping Ternary Relationship Type: For each n-ary (> 2) Relationships create a new relation to represent the relationship. The primary key of the new relation is the combination of the primary keys of the participating entities that hold the N (many) side. In most cases of an n-ary relationship all the participating entities hold a many side.

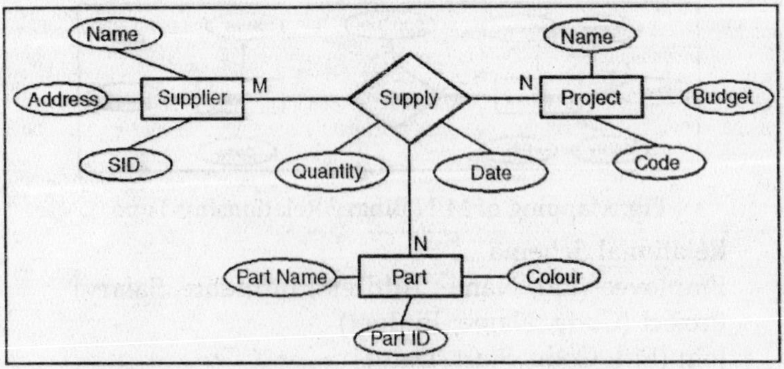

Relational Schema

Supplier (Sid, Name, Address)

Project (Code, Name, Budget)

Part, (Part ID, Part name, Colour)

Supply (SID, Code, partID, Quantity, Date)

INTEGRITY CONSTRAINTS

INTRODUCTION

Oracle uses integrity constraints to prevent invalid data entry into the base tables of the database. You can define integrity constraints to enforce the business rules you want to associate with the information in a database. If any of the results of a DML statement execution violate an integrity constraint, then Oracle rolls back the statement and returns an error. For example, assume that you define an integrity constraint for the salary column of the employees table. This integrity constraint enforces the rule that no row in this table can contain a numeric value greater than 10,000 in this column.

If anINSERT or UPDATE statement attempts to violate this integrity constraint, then Oracle rolls back the statement and returns an information error message. The integrity constraints implemented in Oracle fully comply with ANSI X3.135-1989 and ISO 9075-1989 standards.

ADVANTAGES OF INTEGRITY CONSTRAINTS

Some of the advantages that integrity constraints have over other alternatives, which include:

- Enforcing business rules in the code of a database application
- Using stored procedures to completely control access to data
- Enforcing business rules with triggered stored database procedures

Declarative Ease

Define integrity constraints using SQL statements. When you define or alter a table, no additional programming is required. The SQL statements are easy to write and eliminate programming errors. Oracle controls their functionality. For these reasons, declarative integrity constraints are preferable to application code and database triggers. The declarative approach is also better than using stored procedures, because the stored procedure solution to data integrity controls data access, but integrity constraints do not eliminate the flexibility of ad hoc data access.

Centralized Rules

Integrity constraints are defined for tables (not an application) and are stored in the data dictionary. Any data entered by any application must adhere to the same integrity constraints associated with the table. By moving business rules from application code to centralized integrity constraints, the tables of a database are guaranteed to contain valid data, no matter which database application manipulates the information. Stored procedures cannot provide the same advantage of centralized rules stored with a table. Database triggers can provide this benefit, but the complexity of implementation is far greater than the declarative approach used for integrity constraints.

Maximum Application Development Productivity

If a business rule enforced by an integrity constraint changes, then the administrator need only change that integrity constraint and all applications automatically adhere to the modified constraint. In contrast, if the business rule were enforced by the code of each database application, developers would have to modify all application source code and recompile, debug, and test the modified applications.

Immediate User Feedback

Oracle stores specific information about each integrity constraint in the data dictionary. You can design database applications to use this information to provide immediate user feedback about integrity constraint violations, even before Oracle executes and checks the SQL statement. For example, a SQL*Forms application can use integrity constraint definitions stored in the data dictionary to check for violations as values are entered into the fields of a form, even before the application issues a statement.

Superior Performance

The semantics of integrity constraint declarations are clearly defined, and performance optimizations are implemented for each specific declarative rule. The Oracle query optimizer can use declarations to learn more about data to improve overall query performance. (Also, taking integrity rules out of application code and database triggers guarantees that checks are only made when necessary.)

Flexibility for Data Loads and Identification of Violations

You can disable integrity constraints temporarily so that large amounts of data can be loaded without the overhead of constraint checking. When the data load is complete, you can easily enable the integrity constraints, and you can automatically report any new rows that violate integrity constraints to a separate exceptions table.

PERFORMANCE COST

The advantages of enforcing data integrity rules come with some loss in performance. In general, the cost of including an integrity constraint is, at most, the same as executing a SQL statement that evaluates the constraint.

TYPES OF INTEGRITY CONSTRAINTS

You can use the following integrity constraints to impose restrictions on the input of column values:

NOT NULL Integrity Constraints

By default, all columns in a table allow nulls. Null means the absence of a value. A NOT NULL constraint requires a column of a table contain no null values. For example, you can define a NOT NULL constraint to require that a value be input in the last_name column for every row of the employees table.

Table EMP

EMPNO	Ename	Job	Mgr	Hiredate	SAL	Comm	Deptno
7329	Smith	CEO		17-Dec-95	9,000.00		20
7499	Allen	VP_Sales	7329	20-Feb-95	7,500.00	100.00	30
7521	Ward	Manager	7499	22-Feb-90	5,000.00	200.00	30
7566	Jones	Salesman	7521	02-Apr-90	2,975.00	400.00	30

Not Null Constraint (No Row May Contain a Null Value for this Column)

Absence of Not Null Constraint (Any Row can Contain Null for this column)

Fig. Not Null Integrity Constraints

UNIQUE Key Integrity Constraints

A UNIQUE key integrity constraint requires that every value in a column or set of columns (key) be unique--that is, no two rows of a table have duplicate values in a specified column or set of columns. For example, in Figure a UNIQUE key constraint is defined on the DNAME column of the departments table to disallow rows with duplicate department names.

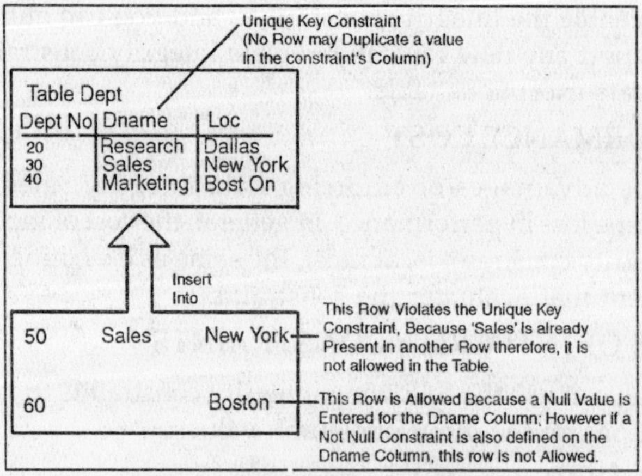

Fig. A UNIQUE Key Constraint

Unique Keys

The columns included in the definition of the UNIQUE key constraint are called the unique key. Unique key is often incorrectly used as a synonym for the terms UNIQUE key constraint or UNIQUE index. However, note that key refers only to the column or set of columns used in the definition of the integrity constraint. If the UNIQUE key consists of more than one column, that group of columns is said to be a composite unique key. For example, in Figure the customer table has a UNIQUE key constraint defined on the composite unique key: the area and phone columns.

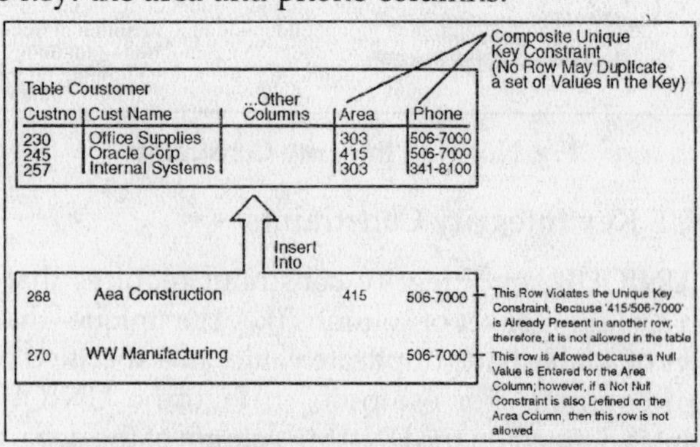

Fig. A Composite UNIQUE Key Constraint

This UNIQUE key constraint lets you enter an area code and telephone number any number of times, but the combination of a given area code and given telephone number cannot be duplicated in the table. This eliminates unintentional duplication of a telephone number.

UNIQUE Key Constraints and Indexes

Oracle enforces unique integrity constraints with indexes. For example, in Figure, Oracle enforces the UNIQUE key constraint by implicitly creating a unique index on the composite unique key. Therefore, composite UNIQUE key constraints have the same limitations imposed on composite indexes: up to 32 columns can constitute a composite unique key.

If a usable index exists when a unique key constraint is created, the constraint uses that index rather than implicitly creating a new one.

Combine UNIQUE Key and NOT NULL Integrity Constraints

In Figures , UNIQUE key constraints allow the input of nulls unless you also define NOT NULL constraints for the same columns. In fact, any number of rows can include nulls for columns without NOT NULL constraints because nulls are not considered equal to anything. A null in a column (or in all columns of a composite UNIQUE key) always satisfies a UNIQUE key constraint.

Columns with both unique keys and NOT NULL integrity constraints are common. This combination forces the user to enter values in the unique key and also eliminates the possibility that any new row's data will ever conflict with an existing row's data.

PRIMARY KEY Integrity Constraints

Each table in the database can have at most one PRIMARY KEY constraint. The values in the group of one or more columns subject to this constraint constitute the unique identifier of the row. In effect, each row is named by its primary key values. The Oracle implementation of the PRIMARY KEY integrity constraint guarantees that both of the following are true.

- No two rows of a table have duplicate values in the specified column or set of columns.
- The primary key columns do not allow nulls. That is, a value must exist for the primary key columns in each row.

Primary Keys

The columns included in the definition of a table's PRIMARY KEY integrity constraint are called the primary key. Although it is not required, every table should have a primary key so that.

- Each row in the table can be uniquely identified
- No duplicate rows exist in the table

Figure illustrates a PRIMARY KEY constraint in the departments table and examples of rows that violate the constraint.

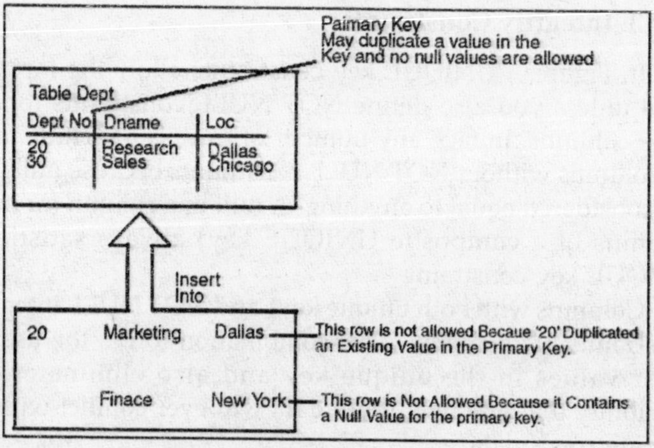

Fig. A Primary Key Constraint

Primary Key Constraints and Indexes

Oracle enforces all PRIMARY KEY constraints using indexes. In Figure, the primary key constraint created for the department_id column is enforced by the implicit creation of:

- A unique index on that column
- A NOT NULL constraint for that column

Oracle enforces primary key constraints using indexes, and composite primary key constraints are limited to 32 columns, which is the same limitation imposed on composite indexes. The name of the index is the same as the name of the constraint. Also, you can specify the storage options for the index by including the ENABLE clause in the CREATE TABLE or ALTER TABLE statement used to create the constraint. If a usable index exists when a primary key constraint is created, then the primary key constraint uses that index rather than implicitly creating a new one.

Referential Integrity Constraints

Different tables in a relational database can be related by common columns, and the rules that govern the relationship of the columns must be maintained. Referential integrity rules guarantee that these relationships are preserved. The following terms are associated with referential integrity constraints.

Term	Definition
Foreign key	The column or set of columns included in the definition of the referential integrity constraint that reference a referenced key.
Referenced key	The unique key or primary key of the same or different table that is referenced by a foreign key.
Dependent or child table	The table that includes the foreign key. Therefore, it is the table that is dependent on the values present in the referenced unique or primary key.
Referenced or parent table	The table that is referenced by the child table's foreign key. It is this table's referenced key that determines whether specific inserts or updates are allowed in the child table.

A referential integrity constraint requires that for each row of a table, the value in the foreign key matches a value in a parent key. Figure shows a foreign key defined on the department_id column of the employees table. It guarantees that every value in this column must match a value in the primary key of the departments table (also the department_id column). Therefore, no erroneous department numbers can exist in the department_idcolumn of the employees table. Foreign keys can be defined as multiple columns.

However, a composite foreign key must reference a composite primary or unique key with the same number of columns and the same datatypes. Because composite primary and unique keys are limited to 32 columns, a composite foreign key is also limited to 32 columns.

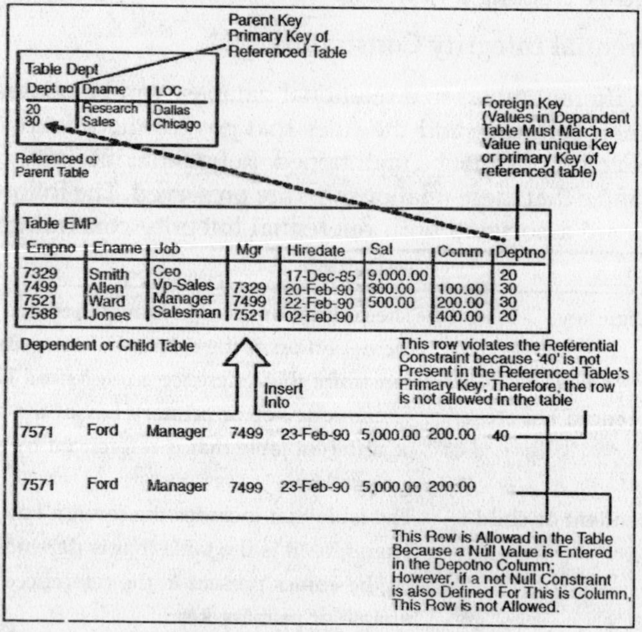

Fig. Referential Integrity Constraints

Self-Referential Integrity Constraints

Another type of referential integrity constraint, shown in Figure, is called a self-referential integrity constraint. This type of foreign key references a parent key in the same table. In Figure, the referential integrity constraint ensures that every value in the manager_id column of the employees table corresponds to a value that currently exists in the employee_id column of the same table, but not necessarily in the same row, because every manager must also be an employee. This integrity constraint eliminates the possibility of erroneous employee numbers in the manager_id column.

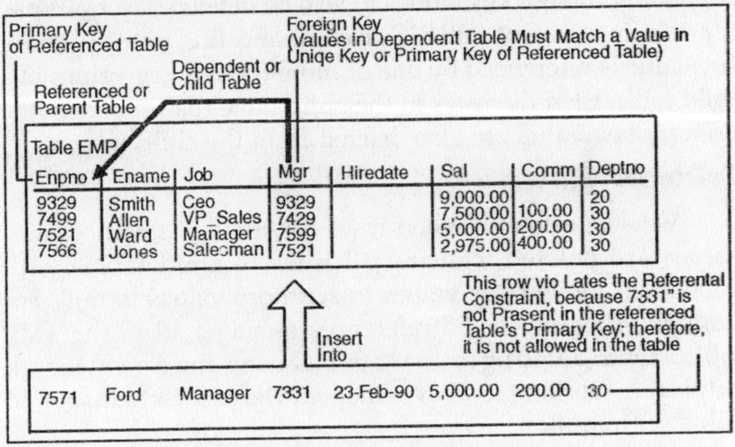

Fig. Single Table Referential Constraints

Nulls and Foreign Keys

The relational model permits the value of foreign keys either to match the referenced primary or unique key value, or be null. If any column of a composite foreign key is null, then the non-null portions of the key do not have to match any corresponding portion of a parent key.

Actions Defined by Referential Integrity Constraints

Referential integrity constraints can specify particular actions to be performed on the dependent rows in a child table if a referenced parent key value is modified.

Update and Delete No Action

The No Action (default) option specifies that referenced key values cannot be updated or deleted if the resulting data would violate a referential integrity constraint. For example, if a primary key value is referenced by a value in the foreign key, then the referenced primary key value cannot be deleted because of the dependent data.

Delete Cascade

A delete cascades when rows containing referenced key values are deleted, causing all rows in child tables with dependent foreign key values to also be deleted. For example, if a row in a parent table is deleted, and this row's primary key value is referenced by one or more foreign key values in a child table, then the rows in the child table that reference the primary key valuė are also deleted from the child table.

Delete Set Null

A delete sets null when rows containing referenced key values are deleted, causing all rows in child tables with dependent foreign key values to set those values to null. For example, if employee_id references manager_id in the TMP table, then deleting a manager causes the rows for all employees working for that manager to have their manager_id value set to null.

DML Restrictions with Referential Actions

Table outlines the DML statements allowed by the different referential actions on the primary/unique key values in the parent table, and the foreign key values in the child table.

Table. DML Statements

DML Statement	Issued Against Parent Table	Issued Against Child Table
INSERT	Always OK if the parent key value is unique.	OK only if the foreign key value exists in the parent key or is partially or all null.
UPDATE NoAction	Allowed if the statement does not leave any rows in the child table without a referenced parent key value.	Allowed if the new foreign key value still references a referenced key value.
DELETE NoAction	Allowed if no rows in the child table reference the parent key value.	Always OK.
DELETE Cascade	Always OK.	Always OK.
DELETE SetNull	Always OK.	Always OK.

Concurrency Control, Indexes, and Foreign Keys

You almost always index foreign keys. The only exception is when the matching unique or primary key is never updated or deleted. Oracle maximizes the concurrency control of parent keys in relation to dependent foreign key values.

You can control what concurrency mechanisms are used to maintain these relationships, and, depending on the situation, this can be highly beneficial. The following sections explain the possible situations and give recommendations for each.

No Index on the Foreign Key

Figure illustrates the locking mechanisms used by Oracle when no index is defined on the foreign key and when rows are being updated or deleted in the parent table. Inserts into the parent table do not require any locks on the child table. Oracle no longer requires a share lock on unindexed foreign keys when doing an update or delete on the primary key.

It still obtains the table-level share lock, but then releases it immediately after obtaining it. If multiple primary keys are update or deleted, the lock is obtained and released once for each row. In previous releases, a share lock of the entire child table was required until the transaction containing the DELETE statement for the parent table was committed.

If the foreign key specifies ON DELETE CASCADE, then the DELETE statement resulted in a table-level share-subexclusive lock on the child table. A share lock of the entire child table was also required for an UPDATE statement on the parent table that affected any columns referenced by the child table. Share locks allow reading only.

Therefore, no INSERT, UPDATE, or DELETE statements could be issued on the child table until the transaction containing the UPDATE or DELETE was committed. Queries were allowed on the child table.

INSERT, UPDATE, and DELETE statements on the child table do not acquire any locks on the parent table, although INSERT and UPDATE statements wait for a row-lock on the index of the parent table to clear.

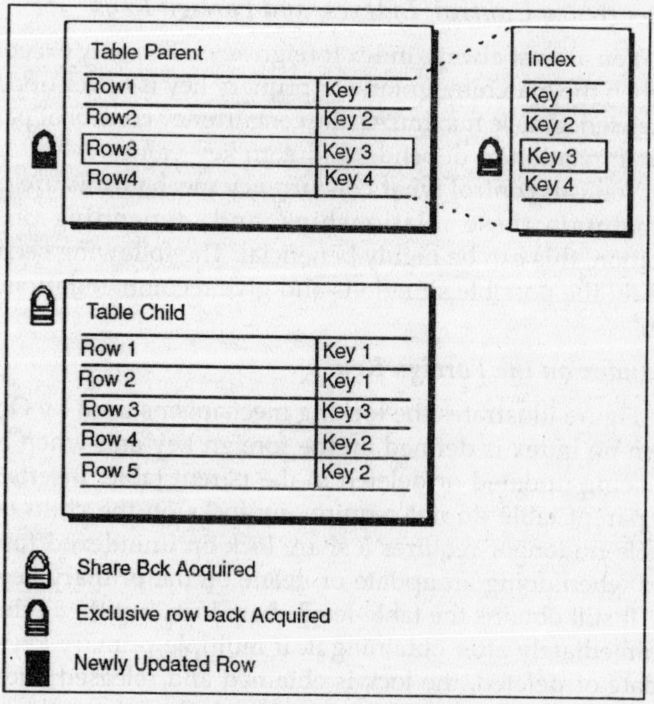

Fig. Locking Mechanisms

Index on the Foreign Key

Figure illustrates the locking mechanisms used by Oracle when an index is defined on the foreign key, and new rows are inserted, updated, or deleted in the child table.

Notice that no table locks of any kind are acquired on the parent table or any of its indexes as a result of the insert, update, or delete. Therefore, any type of DML statement can be issued on the parent table, including inserts, updates, deletes, and queries.

This situation is preferable if there is any update or delete activity on the parent table while update activity is taking place on the child table. Inserts, updates, and deletes on the parent table do not require any locks on the child table, although updates and deletes will wait for row-level locks on the indexes of the child table to clear.

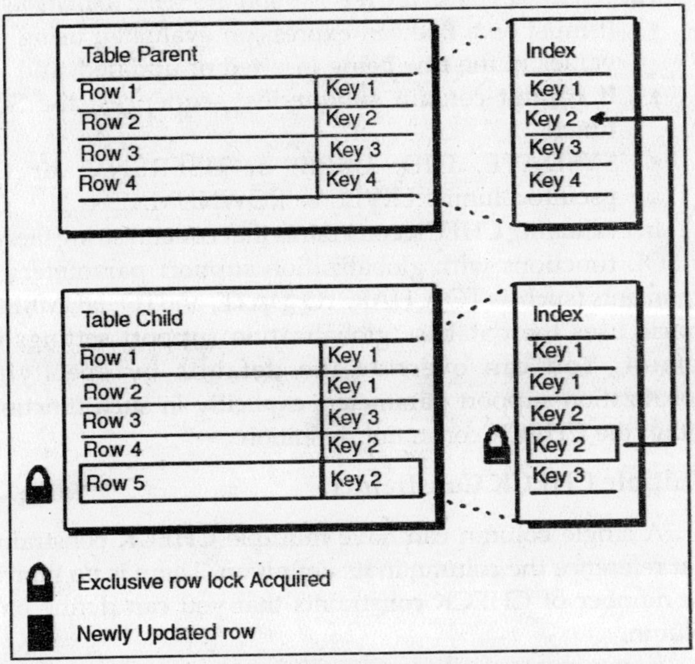

Fig. Locking Mechanisms When Index is Defined on the Foreign Key

If the child table specifies ON DELETE CASCADE, then deletes from the parent table can result in deletes from the child table. In this case, waiting and locking rules are the same as if you deleted yourself from the child table after performing the delete from the parent table.

Check Integrity Constraints

A CHECK integrity constraint on a column or set of columns requires that a specified condition be true or unknown for every row of the table. If a DML statement results in the condition of the CHECK constraint evaluating to false, then the statement is rolled back.

The Check Condition

CHECK constraints enable you to enforce very specific integrity rules by specifying a check condition.

The condition of a CHECK constraint has some limitations:

- It must be a Boolean expression evaluated using the values in the row being inserted or updated, and
- It cannot contain subqueries; sequences; the SQL functi
- SYSDATE, UID, USER, or USERENV; or the pseudocolumns LEVEL or ROWNUM.

In evaluating CHECK constraints that contain string literals or SQL functions with globalization support parameters as arguments (such as TO_CHAR, TO_DATE, andTO_NUMBER), Oracle uses the database globalization support settings by default. You can override the defaults by specifying globalization support parameters explicitly in such functions within the CHECK constraint definition.

Multiple CHECK Constraints

A single column can have multiple CHECK constraints that reference the column in its definition. There is no limit to the number of CHECK constraints that you can define on a column.

If you create multiple CHECK constraints for a column, design them carefully so their purposes do not conflict. Do not assume any particular order of evaluation of the conditions. Oracle does not verify that CHECK conditions are not mutually exclusive.

ENTITY INTEGRITY

Entity integrity ensures that each row in a table is uniquely identified. The concept is basic to database design. The primary key of a table is one or more columns that are used to uniquely identify each row of the table.

The primary key enforces entity integrity. A table can only have one primary key. The primary key constraint does not allow duplicate values and does not allow NULL.

Entity integrity is the most basic level of data integrity provided in the relational database model. Entity integrity is a property that ensures that no component of the primary key of any base relation can be null. That is, a single-attribute primary key cannot accept null values; neither can any of the attributes in a composite primary key. Entity integrity forms one of the two implicit integrity constraints (a constraint is implicit if the user need not explicitly define it) in the relational model, the other one being referential integrity.

Most relational database management systems (RDBMSs) support entity integrity by rejecting operations (INSERT or UPDATE) that produce an invalid primary key. However, no major RDBMS system forces that primary keys be specified for any relation (i.e. table). It is up to the user to specify a primary key for every new table that he/she creates.

It is incorrect to say that entity integrity states that primary key values should be unique. The reason behind the uniqueness of primary key values arises from the definition of the primary key concept itself and not from entity integrity.

REFERENTIAL INTEGRITY

Referential integrity is concerned with the maintenance of relationships between tables. A referential constraint defines a foreign key relationship between the referencing table and another table in the database.

The foreign key is defined in the referencing table as a relationship either the primary key or one of the unique keys in the referenced table. For example, you cannot insert into the referencing table a foreign key value that does not exist in the referenced table.

This rule of referential integrity ensures that a non-NULL value of a foreign key must be within the domain of the related primary or unique key. Rules can be defines in references that specify the action to be taken on the affected rows of the referencing table when a DELETE operation is performed on the referenced table.

These rules can define one of the following triggered actions: CASCADE, the affected rows are also deleted; SET NULL, the appropriate foreign key columns are set to NULL; SET DEFAULT, the appropriate foreign key columns are set to their default value; and NO ACTION, which raises an error because the referential constraint would be violated.

Referential integrity is a database concept that ensures that relationships between tables remain consistent. When one table has a foreign key to another table, the concept of referential integrity states that you may not add a record to the table that contains the foreign key unless there is a corresponding record in the linked table.

It also includes the techniques known as cascading update and cascading delete, which ensure that changes made to the linked table are reflected in the primary table. Consider the situation where we have two tables: Employees and Managers. The Employees table has a foreign key attribute entitled ManagedBy which points to the record for that employee's manager in the Managers table.

Referential integrity enforces the following three rules:

- We may not add a record to the Employees table unless the ManagedBy attribute points to a valid record in the Managers table.
- If the primary key for a record in the Managers table changes, all corresponding records in the Employees table must be modified using a cascading update.
- If a record in the Managers table is deleted, all corresponding records in the Employees table must be deleted using a cascading delete.

LOAD AND INSERT OPERATIONS

During a load or insert operation, if a row is to be added to a table and that row contains a value in a foreign key column that is not present in the table referenced by the foreign key, adding the row would violate referential integrity, so the row is discarded.

On load operations, these discarded records can be saved to a file and reloaded later, after a new row containing the missing foreign key value is inserted into the referenced table or after the file is edited to correct data conversion or content errors.

An alternative to discarding rows that violate referential integrity is generating a row with the new value and adding it to the referenced table, thereby preserving referential integrity. The new row is filled in with default values defined when the table was created. This alternative behaviour is implemented by a TMU option named Automatic Row Generation.

DELETE OPERATIONS AND CASCADEDS

During a delete operation, if a row to be deleted contains a value that is referenced by a foreign key in another table, a referential integrity violation is avoided by either:

- Deleting the original row and also deleting the referencing row from the other table. This action is called a cascaded delete and can cascade through a series of referencing tables.
- Deleting neither row--that is, taking no action. This lack of action is called a restricted delete.

During the delete operation, the system must lock not only the table from which the row is being deleted but other tables as well. To determine which tables to lock and whether a read or write lock is needed, the concept of an immediate and complete family for a table is used:

- An immediate family is the set of all tables that reference the table with a FOREIGN KEY reference clause.
- A complete family is the immediate family, plus all tables that reference the immediate family tables, and so on.

For the complete family, only one type of delete action is permitted, and a restricted delete (NO ACTION) anywhere in the complete family for a table overrides any cascaded delete conditions.

WARNING

An option to the DELETE statement (OVERRIDE REFCHECK) can be used to omit any checks for referential integrity but should be used only with great caution and a clear understanding of its actions.

Assume a database has two fact tables named Fact1 and Fact2; three dimension tables named Product, Market, and

Period; and two outboard tables named Brand and Monthname, with references as illustrated by the following figure.

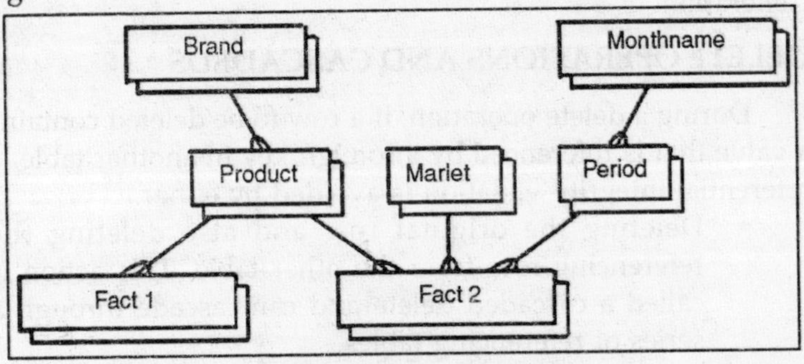

Fig. Schema Example

The following table defines the relationships among these tables in terms of immediate and complete families for delete locks.

Table name	Immediate family	Complete family
Fact1	None	None
Fact2	None	None
Product	Fact1, Fact2	Fact1, Fact2
Market	Fact2	Fact2
Period	Fact2	Fact2
Brand	Product	Product, Fact1, Fact2
Monthname	Period	Period, Fact2

A delete operation (and the FOR DELETE option to the LOCK TABLE statement) uses a special delete lock that provides necessary and sufficient access to all involved tables. A delete lock locks the named table for write (exclusive) access. The delete lock also locks all tables in the immediate family for either read or write access, depending on the referential action specified when the tables were created.

It then locks all tables in the immediate family of these tables in a similar manner. The complete family is locked for write access only if all ON DELETEactions are CASCADE. Otherwise, only the tables in the immediate family are locked for read access. The following examples illustrate how tables are locked and referential integrity is preserved during delete operations.

EXAMPLE

This example illustrates a delete operation in which all table references are defined for cascaded deletes. Assume the Brand table is referenced from the Product table as follows:

```
brandkey char(3) not null,
...
foreign key brandkey references brand (brandkey)
 on delete cascade
```

Assume the Product table is referenced from the Fact table as follows:

```
prodkey char(5) not null,
...
foreign key prodkey references product (prodkey)
on delete cascade
```

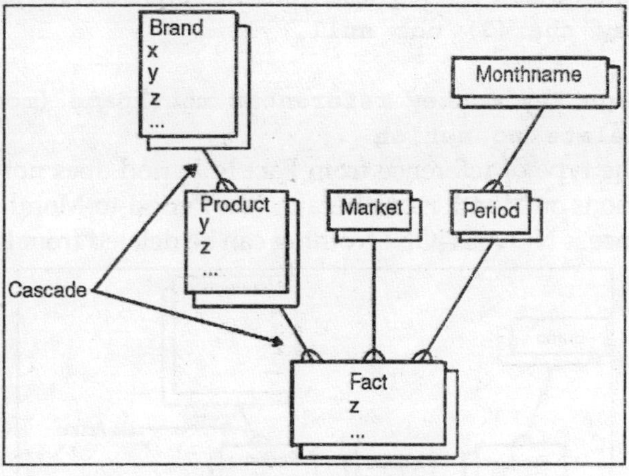

Fig. Delete Cascade

If a row is to be deleted from the Brand table, any row in Product that references (has a foreign key value that matches the primary key of) the deleted row in Brand is also deleted. Any row in Fact that references a deleted row in Productis also deleted. The following table illustrates how cascaded deletes work in this case.

From Brand, delete row containing:	Rows deleted from: Brand	Product	Fact
X	Yes	Not present	Not present
Y	Yes	Yes	Not present
Z	Yes	Yes	Yes

When the delete lock is applied to the Brand table for this operation, Brand and all tables in its complete family are locked for write access because rows might be deleted from any of those tables. This lock denies access by other users to any tables in the complete family until the delete lock is released.

EXAMPLE

This example illustrates the effect of a restricted (NO ACTION) delete on a family of tables. Delete operations are treated as if all references were restricted. Assume the Monthname table is referenced from the Period table as follows:

```
monkey char(3) not null,
...
foreign key monkey references monthname (monkey)
on delete no action
```

The type of reference from Fact to Period does not affect operations on Month name because the Period-to-Month name reference is NO ACTION. Nothing can be deleted from Period.

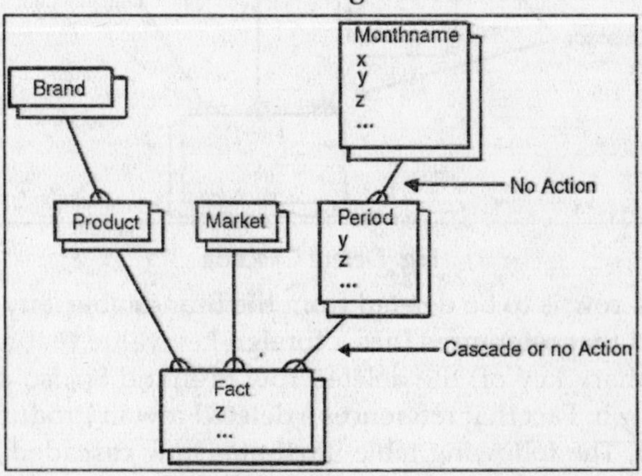

Fig. Delete No Action

If a row to be deleted from the Month name table is referenced by a row in Period, the row is not deleted from Month name.

If it is not referenced by a row in Period, it is deleted. Because no rows can be deleted from Period, it is not necessary to access the Fact table to check for referencing rows. The following table illustrates how restricted deletes work in this case.

From Monthname, delete row containing:	Rows deleted from:		
	Monthname	Period	Fact
x	Yes	No rows deleted from Period	No rows deleted from Fact
y	No		
z	No		

When the delete lock is applied to Month name for this operation, the Monthname table is locked for write access, and Period--the only table in its immediate family--is locked for read access. No lock is applied to Fact.

EXAMPLE

This example illustrates a delete operation with a restricted delete not in the immediate family but somewhere in the complete family, which includes both restricted and cascaded references.

Delete operations are treated as if all references were restricted. Assume the Brand table is referenced from the Product table as follows:

```
brandkey char(3) not null,
...
foreign key brandkey references brand (brandkey)
  on delete cascade
```

Assume the Product table is referenced from the Fact1 table with a cascaded delete as follows:

```
prodkey char(5) not null,
...
foreign key prodkey references product (prodkey)
  on delete cascade
```

Assume the Product table is referenced from the Fact2 table with a restricted delete as follows:

```
prodkey char(5) not null,
```

```
...
foreign key prodkey references product (prodkey)
 on delete no action
```

Even though the reference from Product to Brand is cascade, because another reference in the complete family is restricted, it is just as if Brand were referenced from Product with a restricted delete.

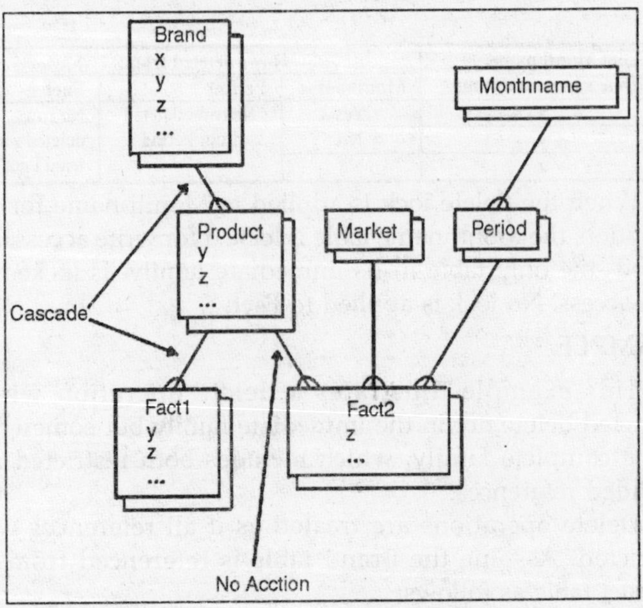

Fig. Restricted Delete

If a row to be deleted from Brand is referenced by Product, that row in Brand is not deleted. The following table illustrates how the combination of restricted and cascaded deletes works in this case.

From Brand, delete row containing:	**Rows deleted from:**			
	Brand	**Product**	**Fact1**	**Fact2**
x	Yes	Not present	No rows deleted from Fact1	No rows deleted from Fact2
y	No	No		
z	No	No		

This example does not indicate what happens in Fact2 when a row is to be deleted from Market, Period, or Month name. The relationships defined for the complete families of each of those tables determine the behaviour in those families. For example, if the Market table is referenced by Fact2 with a cascaded delete, a row deleted from the Market table can cause any corresponding referencing rows to be deleted from Fact2. The NO ACTION reference between Product and Fact2 does not affect references between Fact2 and other tables.

When the delete lock is applied to Brand for this operation, Brand is locked for write access. Product, the only table in its immediate family, is locked for read access. The Fact1 and Fact2 tables are not locked. Even though y is not referenced by Fact2, it is not deleted from Brand, Product, or Fact1. For more examples that illustrate how the ON DELETE clause and DELETE FROM statement affect referential integrity, see the DELETE statement in the SQL

KEYS CONSTRAINTS

CONSTRAINT ENFORCEMENT

Operations in a data base management system, such operations including manipulating multiple records of data,

- The improvement characterized by steps performed by a computer of manipulating each record and enforcing referential constraints respecting such record before another record is manipulated by a same operation.
- The method of claim 1, wherein at least one of the operations comprises the steps of:
  - Inserting a record;
  - Identifying any violation of a referential constraint respecting such record;
  - Aborting such insertion if any such violation is identified.
- The method of claim 2, wherein the step (a) of inserting the record is done before the step (b) of identifying any violation.
- The method of claim 1, wherein at least one of the operations comprises the steps of:

- Identifying any referential constraint violation respecting an updated primary key of a record;
- Updating the record;
- Identifying any referential constraint violation respecting any foreign key of the updated record; and
- Aborting such update if either type of violation is identified.

- The method of claim 4, wherein the step (b) of updating the record is performed after the step (a) of identifying any primary key constraint violation and before the step (c) of identifying any foreign key constraint violation.
- The method of claim 5, wherein such update is aborted immediately after either type of violation is identified.
- The method of claim 1, wherein at least one of the operations comprises the steps of:
  - Deleting a record;
  - Identifying any referential constraint violation respecting such deletion; and
  - Aborting such deletion if any such violation is identified.
- The method of claim 7, wherein the step (a) of deleting the record includes a cascade delete of any records dependent on the record.
- The method of claim 7, wherein the step (a) of deleting the record is done before the step (b) of identifying any violation.
- In a relational data base management system having tables consisting of rows of data, a method of manipulating rows and enforcing referential constraints comprising the steps performed by a computer of:

  (a) Executing an operation which manipulates at least two rows;

  (b) If the operation includes inserting a row,

  (b1) Inserting such row, and

(b2) Identifying any referential constraint violation resulting from such insertion;

(c) If the operation includes updating a row,

(c1) Identifying any referential constraint violation resulting from updating any primary key of the row,

(c2) Updating the row, and

(c3) Identifying any referential constraint violation Resulting from updating any foreign key of the row;

(d) If the operation includes the deletion of a row, performing in order the steps of:

(d1) Deleting the row, and

(d2) Identifying any referential constraint violation resulting from such deletion; and

(e) If any such referential constraint violation is identified, aborting the operation.

As you may already know, databases use tables to organize information. (If you don't have a basic familiarity with database concepts, read What is a Database?) Each table consists of a number of rows, each of which corresponds to a single database record. So, how do databases keep all of these records straight? It's through the use of keys.

Primary Keys

The first type of key we'll discuss is the primary key. Every database table should have one or more columns designated as the primary key. The value this key holds should be unique for each record in the database. For example, assume we have a table called Employees that contains personnel information for every employee in our firm. We'd need to select an appropriate primary key that would uniquely identify each employee. Your first thought might be to use the employee's name.

This wouldn't work out very well because it's conceivable that you'd hire two employees with the same name. A better choice might be to use a unique employee ID number that you assign to each employee when they're hired. Some organizations choose to use Social Security Numbers (or similar government identifiers) for this task because each employee already has one and they're guaranteed to be unique. However, the use of Social Security Numbers for this purpose is highly controversial due to privacy concerns. (If you work for a government organization, the use of a Social Security Number may even be illegal under the Privacy Act of 1974.) For this reason, most organizations have shifted to the use of unique identifiers (employee ID, student ID, etc.) that don't share these privacy concerns.

Once you decide upon a primary key and set it up in the database, the database management system will enforce the uniqueness of the key. If you try to insert a record into a table with a primary key that duplicates an existing record, the insert will fail. Most databases are also capable of generating their own primary keys. Microsoft Access, for example, may be configured to use the AutoNumber data type to assign a unique ID to each record in the table. While effective, this is a bad design practice because it leaves you with a meaningless value in each record in the table. Why not use that space to store something useful?

Foreign Keys

The other type of key that we'll discuss in this course is the foreign key. These keys are used to create relationships between tables. Natural relationships exist between tables in most database structures. Returning to our employees database, let's imagine that we wanted to add a table containing departmental information to the database. This new table might be called Departments and would contain a large amount of information about the department as a whole. We'd also want to include information about the employees in the department, but it would be redundant to have the same information in two tables (Employees and Departments). Instead, we can create a relationship between the two tables.

Let's assume that the Departments table uses the Department Name column as the primary key. To create a relationship between the two tables, we add a new column to the Employees table called Department. We then fill in the name of the department to which each employee belongs. We also inform the database management system that the Department column in the Employees table is a foreign key that references the Departments table. The database will then enforce referential integrity by ensuring that all of the values in the Departments column of the Employees table have corresponding entries in the Departments table.

Note that there is no uniqueness constraint for a foreign key. We may (and most likely do!) have more than one employee belonging to a single department. Similarly, there's no requirement that an entry in the Departments table have any corresponding entry in the Employees table. It is possible that we'd have a department with no employees.

DOMAIN CONSTRAINTS

Domain constraints allows us to test the values inserted into the database and to test the queries to make sure comparisons made are appropriate.

EXAMPLES

Create domain wage numeric (5,2) constraint wage-value-test check (value ⇐ 4.0)

- A domain of possible values should be associated with every attribute. These domain constraints are the most basic form of integrity constraint.
  They are easy to test for when data is entered.
- Domain types
  - Attributes may have the same domain, e.g. cname and employee-name.
  - It is not as clear whether bname and cname domains ought to be distinct.
  - At the implementation level, they are both character strings.
  - At the conceptual level, we do not expect customers to have the same names as branches, in general.
  - Strong typing of domains allows us to test for

values inserted, and whether queries make sense. Newer systems, particularly object-oriented database systems, offer a rich set of domain types that can be extended easily.

- The check clause in SQL-92 permits domains to be restricted in powerful ways that most programming language type systems do not permit.
  - The check clause permits schema designer to specify a predicate that must be satisfied by any value assigned to a variable whose type is the domain.

Examples:

```
Create domain hourly-wage numeric(5,2)
constraint wage-value-test check(value >= 4.00)
```

Note that ``constraint wage-value-test" is optional (to give a name to the test to signal which constraint is violated).

```
create domain account-number char(10)
constraint account-number-null-test
check(value not null)
create domain account-type char(10)
constraint account-type-test
check(value in (``Checking'', ``Saving''))
```

RELATIONAL ALGEBRA

RELATIONAL ALGEBRA

- A basic expression consists of either
  - A relation in the database.
  - A constant relation.
- General expressions are formed out of smaller subexpressions using
  - $\sigma_p(E_1)$ select (p a predicate)
  - $\prod_s(E_1)$ project (s a list of attributes)
  - $\rho_x(E_1)$ rename (x a relation name)
  - $E_1 \cup (E_2)$ union
  - $E_1 - E_2$ set difference
  - $E_1 \times E_2$ cartesian product

WHAT? WHY

- Similar to normal algebra (as in 2+3*x-y), except we use relations as values instead of numbers, and the operations and operators are different.
- Not used as a query language in actual DBMSs. (SQL instead.)
- The inner, lower-level operations of a relational DBMS are, or are similar to, relational algebra operations. We need to know about relational algebra to understand query execution and optimization in a relational DBMS.
- Some advanced SQL queries requires explicit relational algebra operations, most commonly outer join.
- Relations are seen as sets of tuples, which means that no duplicates are allowed. SQL behaves differently in some cases. Remember the SQL keyworddistinct.
- SQL is declarative, which means that you tell the DBMS what you want, but not how it is to be calculated. A C++ or Java programme is procedural, which means that you have to state, step by step, exactly how the result should be calculated. Relational algebra is (more) procedural than SQL. (Actually, relational algebra is mathematical expressions.)

SET OPERATIONS

Relations in relational algebra are seen as sets of tuples, so we can use basic set operations.

Review of Concepts and Operations from Set Theory

- Set
- Element
- No duplicate elements (but: multiset = bag)
- No order among the elements (but: ordered set)
- Subset
- Proper subset (with fewer elements)
- Superset
- Union

- Intersection
- Set difference
- Cartesian product

PROJECTION

Example: The Table E (for EMPLOYEE)

nr	name	salary
1	John	100
5	Sarah	300
7	Tom	100

SQL	Result		Relational algebra
Select nr, salary from E	select salary salary 100 300		$PROJECT_{salary}(E)$
	nr	salary	
PROJECTnr, salary(E) from E	1 5 7	100 300 100	$PROJECT_{nr, salary}(E)$

Note that there are no duplicate rows in the result.

Selection

The same Table E (for EMPLOYEE) as above.

SQL	Result			Relational algebra
Select * from E where salary < 200	Nr 1 7	Name John Tom	Salary 100 100	$Select_{salary < 200}(E)$
Select * from E where salary < 200 and nr >= 7	Nr 7	Name Tom	Salary 100	$Select_{salary < 200 \text{ and } nr >= 7}(E)$

Note that the select operation in relational algebra has nothing to do with the SQL keyword select. Selection in relational algebra returns those tuples in a relation that fulfil a condition, while the SQL keyword select means "here comes an SQL statement".

Relational Algebra Expressions

SQL	Result	Relational algebra
select name, salary from E where salary ← 200	Name salary John 100 Tom 100	PROJECT$_{name, salary}$ (SELECT$_{salary < 200}$(E)) or, step by step, using an intermediate result
		Temp ← Select$_{salary < 200}$(E) Result ← Project$_{name, salary}$(Temp)

Notation

The operations have their own symbols. The symbols are hard to write in HTML that works with all browsers, so I'm writing PROJECT etc here. The real symbols:

Operation	My HTML	Symbol
Projection	Project	π
Selection	Select	σ
Renaming	Rename	ρ
Union	Union	∪
Intersection	Intersection	∩
Assignment	←	←

Operation	My HTML	Symbol
Cartesian product	X	X
Join	Join	********
Left outer join	Left Outher Join	********
Right outer join	Right Outer Join	********
Full outer join	Full Outer Join	********
Semijoin	Semijoin	********

Example: The relational algebra expression which I would here write as PROJECTNamn (SELECTMedlemsnummer < 3 (Medlem)) should actually be written

π Namn (σ medlemsnummer < 3 (Medlem))

Cartesian Product

The cartesian product of two tables combines each row in one table with each row in the other table.

Example: The table E (for EMPLOYEE)

enr	ename	dept
1	Bill	A
2	Sarah	C
3	John	A

Example: The Table D (for DEPARTMENT)

dnr	dname
A	Marketing
B	Sales
C	Legal

	SQL	Result			Relational algebra
select * from E, D	enr	ename	dept	dnr	dname E X D
	1	Bill	A	A	Marketing
	1	Bill	A	B	Sales
	1	Bill	A	C	Legal
	2	Sarah	C	A	Marketing
	2	Sarah	C	B	Sales
	2	Sarah	C	C	Legal
	3	John	A	A	Marketing
	3	John	A	B	Sales
	3	John	A	C	Legal

- Seldom useful in practice.
- Usually an error.
- Can give a huge result.

The cartesian product example above combined each employee with each department. If we only keep those lines where the dept attribute for the employee is equal to the dnr (the department number) of the department, we get a nice list of the employees, and the department that each employee works for:

SQL	Result					Relational algebra
select *	enr	ename	dept	dnr	dname	Select$_{dept = dnr}$ (EXD)
from E, D	1	Bill	A	A	Marketing	or, using the
where dept	2	Sarah	C	C	Legal	equivalent join
= dnr	3	John	A	A	Marketing	operation
						Ejoin$_{dept = dnr}$ D

- A very common and useful operation.
- Equivalent to a cartesian product followed by a select.
- Inside a relational DBMS, it is usually much more efficient to calculate a join directly, instead of calculating a cartesian product and then throwing away most of the lines.
- Note that the same SQL query can be translated to several different relational algebra expressions, which all give the same result.
- If we assume that these relational algebra expressions are executed, inside a relational DBMS which uses relational algebra operations as its lower-level internal operations, different relational algebra expressions can take very different time (and memory) to execute.

Natural Join

A normal inner join, but using the join condition that columns with the same names should be equal. Duplicate columns are removed.

Renaming Tables and Columns

Example: The Table E (for EMPLOYEE)

nr	name	dept
1	Bill	A
2	Sarah	C
3	John	A

Example: The Table D (for DEPARTMENT)

nr	Name
A	Marketing
B	Sales
C	Legal

We want to join these tables, but:

- Several columns in the result will have the same name (nr and name).
- How do we express the join condition, when there are two columns called nr?

Solutions:

- Rename the attributes, using the rename operator.
- Keep the names, and prefix them with the table name, as is done in SQL.

SQL	Result	Relational algebra
select * from E as E(enr, dept = dnrename, dept), D as D(dnr, dname) where	enr ename dept dnr dname 1 Bill A A Marketing 2 Sarah C C Legal 3 John A A Marketing	$(\text{Rename}_{(enr,\ ename,\ dept)}(E))\ \text{Join}_{dept = dnr}\ (\text{Rename}_{(dnr,\ dname)}(D))$
select * from E, D where dept = D.nr	nr name dept nr Name 1 Bill A A Marketing 2 Sarah C C Legal 3 John A A Marketing	$E\ \text{JOIN}_{dept = D.nr}\ D$

You can use another variant of the renaming operator to change the name of a table, for example to change the name of E to R. This is necessary when joining a table with itself.

$\text{RENAME}_R(E)$

A third variant lets you rename both the table and the columns:

$\text{RENAME}_{R(enr,\ ename,\ dept)}(E)$

AGGREGATE FUNCTIONS

Example: The Table E (for EMPLOYEE)

nr	Name	Salary	dept
1	John	100	A
5	Sarah	300	C
7	Tom	100	A
12	Anne	null	C

SQL	Result	Relational algebra
select sum(salary) from E	sum 500	Fsum(salary)(E)

Note: Duplicates are not eliminated, Null values are ignored.

SQL	Result	Relational algebra
select count(salary) from E	Result: Count 3	$F_{count(salary)}(E)$
select count(distinct salary) from E	Result: Count 2	$F_{count(salary)}(\text{Project}_{salary}(E))$

You can calculate aggregates "grouped by" something:

SQL	Result	Relational algebra
select sum(salary) from E group by dept	dept sum A 200 C 300	${}_{dept}F_{sum(salary)}(E)$

Several aggregates simultaneously:

SQL	Result	Relational algebra
select sum(salary), count(*)from E group by dept	dept sum count A 200 2 C 300 1	${}_{dept}F_{sum(salary), count(*)}(E)$

Standard aggregate functions: sum, count, avg, min, max

Hierarchies

nr	name	mgr
1	Gretchen	null
2	Bob	1
5	Anne	2
6	John	2
3	Hulda	1
4	Hjalmar	1
7	Usama	4

Going up in the hierarchy one level: What's the name of John's boss?

SQL	Result	Relational algebra
select b.name from E p, E b where p.mgr = b.nr and p.name = "John"	Name Bob	$Project_{bname}$ ([$SELECT_{pname = "John"}$($Rename_{P(pnr, pname, pmgr)}$(E))] $Join_{pmgr = bnr}$ [$Rename_{B(bnr, bname, bmgr)}$(E)]) or, in a less wide-spread notation $Project_{b.name}$ ([$SELECT_{name = "John"}$($Rename_P$(E))] $JOIN_{p.mgr = b.nr}$ [$Rename_B$(E)]) or, step by step P ← $Rename_{P(pnr, pname, pmgr)}$(E) B ← $Rename_{B(bnr, bname, bmgr)}$(E) J ← $Select_{name = "John"}$(P) C ← J $Join_{pmgr = bnr}$ B R ← $Project_{bname}$(C)

Notes about renaming:

- We are joining E with itself, both in the SQL query and in the relational algebra expression: it's like joining two tables with the same name and the same attribute names.
- Therefore, some renaming is required.
- Renamep(E) Join... Renameb(E) is a start, but then we still have the same attribute names.

Going up in the hierarchy two levels: What's the name of John's boss' boss?

SQL	Result	Relational algebra
select ob.name from E p, E b, E ob where b.mgr = ob.nr where p.mgr = b.nr and p.name = "John"	Name Gretchen	$PROJECT_{ob.name}$ (([$SELECT_{name = "John"}$($Rename_P$(E))] $JOIN_{p.mgr = b.nr}$ [$Rename_B$(E)]) $JOIN_{b.mgr = ob.nr}$[$Rename_{OB}$(E)]) or, step by step P ← $Rename_{P(pnr,\ pname,\ pmgr)}$(E) B ← $Rename_{B(bnr,\ bname,\ bmgr)}$(E) OB ← $Rename_{OB(obnr,\ obname,\ obmgr)}$(E) J ← $Select_{name = "John"}$(P) C1 ← J $Join_{pmgr = bnr}$ B C2 ← C1 $Join_{bmgr = bbnr}$ OB R ← $Project_{obname}$(C2)

Recursive Closure

Both one and two levels up: What's the name of John's boss, and of John's boss' boss?

SQL	Result	Relational Algebra
(select b.name ...) union (select ob.name ...)	Name Bob Gretchen	(...) UNION (...)

Recursively: What's the name of all John's bosses? (One, two, three, four or more levels.)

- Not possible in (conventional) relational algebra, but a special operation called transitive closure has been proposed.
- Not possible in (standard) SQL (SQL2), but in SQL3, and using SQL + a host language with loops or recursion.

Outer Join

Example: The Table E (for EMPLOYEE)

enr	**ename**	**dept**
1	Bill	A
2	Sarah	C
3	John	A

Example: The Table D (for DEPARTMENT)

dnr	**Dname**
A	Marketing
B	Sales
C	Legal

List each employee together with the department he or she works at:

SQL	Result	Relational algebra
select * from E, D where edept = dnr or, using an explicit join select * from (E join D on edept = dnr)	enr ename dept dnr dname 1 Bill A A Marketing 2 Sarah C C Legal 3 John A A Marketing	E $\text{JOIN}_{edept = dnr}$ D

No employee works at department B, Sales, so it is not present in the result. This is probably not a problem in this case. But what if we want to know the number of employees at each department?

SQL	Result	Relational algebra
select dnr, dname, count(*) from E, D where edept = dnr group by dnr, dname or, using an explicit join select dnr, dname, count(*) from (E join D on edept = dnr) group by dnr, dname	dnr dname count A Marketing 2 C Legal 1	$_{dnr, dname}F_{count(*)}$(E $\text{JOIN}_{edept = dnr}$ D)

No employee works at department B, Sales, so it is not present in the result. It disappeared already in the join, so the aggregate function never sees it. But what if we want it in the result, with the right number of employees (zero)? Use a right outer join, which keeps all the rows from the right table. If a row can't be connected to any of the rows from the left table according to the join condition, null values are used:

SQL	Result	Relational algebra
select * from (E right outer join D on edept = dnr)	enr ename dept dnr dname 1 Bill A A Marketing 2 Sarah C C Legal 3 John A A Marketing null null null B Sales	E RightOuter Join$_{edept = dnr}$ D
select dnr, dname, count(*) from (E right outer join D on edept = dnr) group by dnr, dname	dnr Dname count A Marketing 2 B Sales 1 C Legal 1	$_{dnr, dname}F_{count(*)}$(E Right Outer Join$_{edept = dnr}$ D)
select dnr, dname, count(enr) from (E right outer join D on edept = dnr) group by dnr, dname	dnr Dname count A Marketing 2 B Sales 0 C Legal 1	$_{dnr, dname}F_{count(enr)}$(E Right Outer Joined$_{edept = dnr}$ D)

- Join = "normal" join = Inner join
- Left Outer Join = Left outer join
- Right Outer Join = Right outer join
- Full Outer Join = Full outer join

Outer Union

Outer union can be used to calculate the union of two relations that are partially union compatible. Not very common.

Example: The Table R

A	B
1	2
3	4

Example: The Table S

B	C
4	5
6	7

The result of an outer union between R and S:

A	B	C
1	2	null
3	4	5
null	6	7

Division

Who works on (at least) all the projects that Bob works on?

Semi Join

A join where the result only contains the columns from one of the joined tables. Useful in distributed databases, so we don't have to send as much data over the network.

Update

To update a named relation, just give the variable a new value. To add all the rows in relation N to the relation R:

$$R \leftarrow R \text{ Union } N$$

FUNDAMENTAL OPERATIONS

The Select Operation

Select selects tuples that satisfy a given predicate. Select is denoted by a lowercase Greek sigma (σ), with the predicate appearing as a subscript. The argument relation is given in parentheses following the σ. For example, to select tuples (rows) of the borrow relation where the branch is ``SFU", we would write

$$\sigma b_n ame =^{\alpha} SFU^{\sigma}(borrow)$$

Let Figure be the borrow and branch relations in the banking example.

Table. The Borrow and Branch Relations

Bname	**Loan#**	**ename**	**amount**
Downtown	17	Joier	1000
Lougheed_Mall	23	Smith	2000
SFU	13	Hayer	1300

Bname	**assets**	**beity**
Downtown	9,000,000	Vaneouver
Lougheexd_Mall	21,000,000	Binnaby
SFU	17,000,000	Binnaby

The new relation created as the result of this operation consists of one tuple: We allow comparisons using =, ≠, <, ≤, > and ≥ in the selection predicate.

We also allow the logical connectives ∧ (or) and > (and). *For example*:

Table. The Client Relation.

Cname	**banker**
Hayer	Jonea
Johnaon	Johaon

Suppose there is one more relation, client, shown above with the scheme

Client_Scheme = (cnme, banker)

we might write

$$\sigma_{ename} = \text{banker (client)}$$

to find clients who have the same name as their banker.

The Project Operation

Project copies its argument relation for the specified attributes only. Since a relation is a set, duplicate rows are eliminated. Projection is denoted by the Greek capital letter pi (II). The attributes to be copied appear as subscripts. For example, to obtain a relation showing customers and branches, but ignoring amount and loan#, we write

$$\pi_{bname,\ ename} \text{ (Borrow)}$$

We can perform these operations on the relations resulting from other operations.

Cartesian Product Operation

The cartesian product of two relations is denoted by a cross (×), written

$r_1 \times r_2$ for rclations r_1 and r_2

The result of $r_1 \times r_2$ is a new relation with a tuple for each possible pairing of tuples from r_1 and r_2. In order to avoid ambiguity, the attribute names have attached to them the name of the relation from which they came. If no ambiguity will result, we drop the relation name.

The result client ×customer is a very large relation. If r_1 has n_1 tuples, and r_2 has n_2 tuples, then $r = r_1 \times r_2$ will have n_1 n_2 tuples. The resulting scheme is the concatenation of the schemes of r_1 and r_2, with relation names added as mentioned.

Rename Operation

The rename operation solves the problems that occurs with naming when performing the cartesian product of a relation with itself.

Suppose we want to find the names of all the customers who live on the same street and in the same city as Smith.

We can get the street and city of Smith by writing

$$II_{strest,eeity} \text{ (name=}^{\alpha}\text{Smith* (customer))}$$

To find other customers with the same information, we need to reference the customer relation again:

$$\text{sp(customer} \times (\pi_{\text{street, ecity}}(\sigma_{\text{ename} = \alpha\text{Smith}}{}^{*}\text{(customer))))}$$

where P is a selection predicate requiring street and ccity values to be equal.

Problem: how do we distinguish between the two street values appearing in the Cartesian product, as both come from a customer relation? Solution: use the rename operator, denoted by the Greek letter rho (ρ).

We write

$$\rho_x(r)$$

to get the relation r under the name of x.

Union Operation

The union operation is denoted ∪ as in set theory. It returns the union (set union) of two compatible relations.

For a union operation $r \cup s$ to be legal, we require that

- r and s must have the same number of attributes.
- The domains of the corresponding attributes must be the same.

To find all customers of the SFU branch, we must find everyone who has a loan or an account or both at the branch.

We need both borrow and deposit relations for this:

$$\pi\text{ename(abname} = {}^{\alpha}\text{SFU}^{\sigma}\text{ (borrow))} \cup \text{ IIename } (\sigma_{\text{bname} =} \alpha \text{ SFU* (dcposit))}$$

Set Difference Operation

Set difference is denoted by the minus sign (–). It finds tuples that are in one relation, but not in another. Thus r – s results in a relation containing tuples that are in r but not in s.

To find customers of the SFU branch who have an account there but no loan, we write

$$\pi_{name}(\sigma_{name} = \alpha SFU^{\alpha} (deposit)) - II_{name} (\sigma name = \alpha SFU^{*}(borrow))$$

The result is shown in Figure.We can do more with this operation. Suppose we want to find the largest account balance in the bank.

Strategy:

- Find a relation r containing the balances not the largest.
- Compute the set difference of r and the deposit relation.

Table. Find the Largest Account Balance in the Bank.

Halance	Halance
400	1300
300	
700	

ADDITIONAL OPERATIONS

1. Additional operations are defined in terms of the fundamental operations. They do not add power to the algebra, but are useful to simplify common queries.
2. *The Set Intersection Operation*: Set intersection is denoted by $\cap$, and returns a relation that contains tuples that are in both of its argument relations.

It does not add any power as

$$r \cap s = r - (r - s)$$

To find all customers having both a loan and an account at the SFU branch, we write

$$\pi_{ename}(\sigma_{bname=aSFU}\sigma(borrow)) \cap IIename(\sigma_{bname} = \alpha SFU^{\sigma}(deposit))$$

The Natural Join Operation

Often we want to simplify queries on a cartesian product. For example, to find all customers having a loan at the bank and the cities in which they live, we need borrow and customer relations:

$$\pi_{borrow.ename,\ ecity}\ (s_{borrow.\ ename=\ customer.\ ename}\ (borrow \times customer))$$

Our selection predicate obtains only those tuples pertaining to only one cname. Natural join combines a cartesian product and a selection into one operation. It performs a selection forcing equality on those attributes that appear in both relation schemes. Duplicates are removed as in all relation operations.

Table. Joining Borrow and Customer Relations

ename	ceity
Smith	Burnaby
Hayer	Burnaby
Joner	Vaneouver

We can now make a more formal definition of natural join.

- Consider R and S to be sets of attributes.
- We denote attributes appearing in both relations by $R \cap S$.
- We denote attributes in either or both relations by $R \cap S$.
- Consider two relations r(R) and s(S).
- The natural join of r and s, denoted by r *** s is a relation on scheme $R \cup S$.
- It is a projection onto $R \cup S$ of a selection on r $R \cup S$ r×s where the predicate requires $r.\Lambda = S.\Lambda$ for each attribute Λ in $R \cap S$.

Formally,

$$rs = IIRUS(\sigma_r A_1 = s.A_2 \wedge \ldots \wedge r.A_n = s.A_n (r \times s))$$

where $R \cap S = \{\Lambda_1, \Lambda_2, \ldots \Lambda_n\}$.

To find the assets and names of all branches which have depositors living in Stamford, we need customer, deposit and branch relations:

$$\pi_{banama,assets}\ (\sigma ecity = {}^{\alpha}Stamf \text{ or } d\ (cus))$$

To find all customers who have both an account and a loan at the SFU branch.

$$\pi ename(\sigma_{bname} = {}^{\alpha}SFU^{*})$$

This is equivalent to the set intersection version we wrote earlier. We see now that there can be several ways to write a query in the relational algebra.

If two relations r(R) and s(S) have no attributes in common, then $R \cap S = \theta$, and $r**S = r \times s$.

The Division Operation Division, denoted , is suited to queries that include the phrase ``for all". Suppose we want to find all the customers who have an account at all branches located in Brooklyn. Strategy: think of it as three steps.

We can obtain the names of all branches located in Brooklyn by

$$r_1 = \pi_{bname} \text{ (sbeity = "Brooklyn"(branch))}$$

Figure in the textbook shows the result.

We can also find all cname, bname pairs for which the customer has an account by

$$r_2 = \pi_{\text{ ename, bnams}} \text{ (deposit)}$$

Figure in the textbook shows the result. Now we need to find all customers who appear in r_2 with every branch name in r_1.

The divide operation provides exactly those customers:

$$\pi_{enams,bname}(\text{deposit}) \div \pi_{bname}(\sigma_{beity} =^{\alpha} \text{Brooklyn"(branch))}$$

which is simply $r_2 \div r_1$.

Formally,

- Let r(R) and s(S) be relations.
- Let $S \subseteq R$.
- The relation r ÷ s is a relation on scheme R–S.
- A tuple t is in r ÷ s if for every tuple t_s in s there is a tuple t_r in r satisfying both of the following:

$$t_r[S] = t_s[S]$$
$$t_r[R - S] = t[R - S]$$

- These conditions say that the R – S portion of a tuple t is in r ÷ s if and only if there are tuples with the S portion and the r portion in S for everyvalue of the S portion in relation S.

The division operation can be defined in terms of the fundamental operations.

$$r \div s = \pi_{n-s}(r) - (\pi_{n-s}(r) \times s) - r$$

Read the text for a more detailed explanation.

5. *The Assignment Operation*: Sometimes it is useful to be able to write a relational algebra expression in parts using a temporary relation variable (as we did with r_1 and r_2 in the division example).

The assignment operation, denoted ←, works like assignment in a programming language.

We could rewrite our division definition as

$$temp \leftarrow \pi_{n-s}(r)$$
$$temp \leftarrow \pi_{n-s}((temp \times s) - r)$$

No extra relation is added to the database, but the relation variable created can be used in subsequent expressions. Assignment to a permanent relation would constitute a modification to the database.

RELATIONAL ALGEBRA

- The formal description of how a relational database operates
- An interface to the data stored in the database itself
- The mathematics which underpin SQL operations

Operators in relational algebra are not necessarily the same as SQL operators, even if they have the same name. For example, the SELECT statement exists in SQL, and also exists in relational algebra. These two uses of SELECT are not the same. The DBMS must take whatever SQL statements the user types in and translate them into relational algebra operations before applying them to the database.

TERMINOLOGY

- *Relation*: A set of tuples.
- *Tuple*: A collection of attributes which describe some real world entity.
- *Attribute*: A real world role played by a named domain.
- *Domain*: A set of atomic values.
- *Set*: A mathematical definition for a collection of objects which contains no duplicates.

OPERATORS - WRITE

- *Insert*: provides a list of attribute values for a new tuple in a relation. This operator is the same as SQL.
- *Delete*: provides a condition on the attributes of a relation to determine which tuple(s) to remove from the relation. This operator is the same as SQL.
- *Modify*: changes the values of one or more attributes in one or more tuples of a relation, as identified by a condition operating on the attributes of the relation. This is equivalent to SQL Update.

OPERATORS - RETRIEVAL

There are two groups of operations:

- Mathematical set theory based relations.
  Union, Intersection, Difference, and Cartesian Product.
- Special database operations.
  Select (not the same as SQL Select), Project, and Join.

RELATIONAL SELECT

Select is used to obtain a subset of the tuples of a relation that satisfy a select condition. For example, find all employees born after 1st Jan 1990:

$\texttt{Selectdob}_{\texttt{'01/JAN/1950'}}\texttt{(employee)}$

RELATIONAL PROJECT

The Project operation is used to select a subset of the attributes of a relation by specifying the names of the required attributes. For example, to get a list of all employees surnames and employee numbers:

$\texttt{Project}_{\texttt{surname,empno}}\texttt{(employee)}$

SET OPERATIONS - SEMANTICS

Consider two relations R and S.

- Union of R and S the union of two relations is a relation that includes all the tuples that are either in R or in S or in both R and S. Duplicate tuples are eliminated.

- Intersection of R and S the intersection of R and S is a relation that includes all tuples that are both in R and S.
- Difference of R and S the difference of R and S is the relation that contains all the tuples that are in R but that are not in S.

SET OPERATIONS - REQUIREMENTS

For set operations to function correctly the relations R and S must be union compatible. Two relations are union compatible if

- They have the same number of attributes
- The domain of each attribute in column order is the same in both R and S.

Union Example

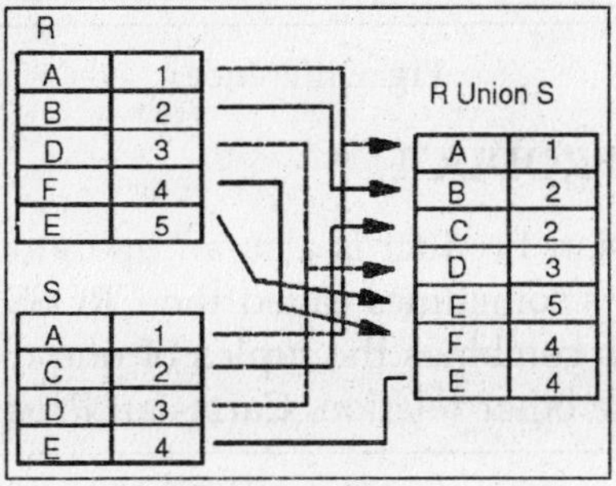

Fig. Union

Intersection Example

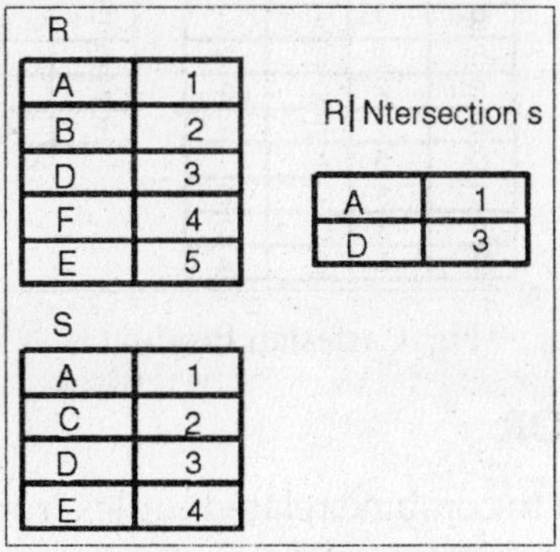

Fig. Intersection

Difference Example

R

A	1
B	2
D	3
F	4
E	5

S

A	1
C	2
D	3
E	4

R Difference S

B	2
F	4
E	5

S Difference R

C	2
E	4

Fig. Difference

CARTESIAN PRODUCT

The Cartesian Product is also an operator which works on two sets. It is sometimes called the CROSS PRODUCT or CROSS JOIN. It combines the tuples of one relation with all the tuples of the other relation. Cartesian Product example

R

A	1
B	2
D	3
F	4
E	5

S

A	1
C	2
D	3
E	4

R Cross s

A	1	A	1
A	1	C	2
A	1	D	3
A	1	E	4
B	2	A	1
B	2	C	2
B	2	D	3
B	2	E	4
D	3	A	1
D	3	C	2
D	3	D	3
D	3	E	4

F	4	A	1
F	4	C	2
F	4	D	3
F	4	E	4
E	5	A	1
E	5	C	2
E	5	D	3
E	5	E	4

Fig. Cartesian Product

JOIN OPERATOR

JOIN is used to combine related tuples from two relations:

- In its simplest form the Join operator is just the cross product of the two relations.

- As the join becomes more complex, tuples are removed within the cross product to make the result of the join more meaningful.
- Join allows you to evaluate a join condition between the attributes of the relations on which the join is undertaken.

Join Example

R

ColA	ColB
A	1
B	2
D	3
F	4
E	5

R Join $_{R.ColA}$ = S.SColA S

A	1	A	1
D	3	D	3
E	5	E	4

S

SColA	SColB
A	1
C	2
D	3
E	4

R Join $_{R.ColB}$ = S.SColB S

A	1	A	1
B	2	C	2
D	3	D	3
F	4	E	4

Fig. Join

Natural Join

Invariably the JOIN involves an equality test, and thus is often described as an equi-join. Such joins result in two attributes in the resulting relation having exactly the same value. A `natural join' will remove the duplicate attribute(s).

- In most systems a natural join will require that the attributes have the same name to identify the attribute(s) to be used in the join. This may require a renaming mechanism.
- If you do use natural joins make sure that the relations do not have two attributes with the same name by accident.

OUTER JOIN

Notice that much of the data is lost when applying a join

to two relations. In some cases this lost data might hold useful information. An outer join retains the information that would have been lost from the tables, replacing missing data with nulls.

There are three forms of the outer join, depending on which data is to be kept.

- *Left Outer Join*: Keep data from the left-hand table
- *Right Outer Join*: Keep data from the right-hand table
- Full Outer Join: Keep data from both tables

Outer Join Example

R

Col A	Col B
A	1
B	2
D	3
F	4
E	5

S

SCol A	SCol B
A	1
C	2
D	3
E	4

R Left Outer Join R.Col A = S. SCol A

A	1	A	1
D	3	D	3
E	5	E	4
B	2	–	–
F	4	–	–

R Right Outer Join R.Col A = S. SCol A

A	1	A	1
D	3	D	3
E	5	E	4
–	–	C	2

Fig. Outer Join (Left/Right)

Example:

Col A	Col B
A	1
B	2
D	3
F	4
E	5

SCol A	SCol B
A	1
C	2
D	3
E	4

R Full Outer Join R. ColA = S.ColA

A	1	A	1
D	3	D	3
E	5	E	4
B	2	–	–
F	4	–	–
–	–	C	2

Fig. Outer Join (full)

Consider the following SQL to find which departments have had employees on the `Further Accounting' course.

```
SELECT DISTINCT dname
FROM department, course, empcourse, employee
WHERE cname = `Further Accounting'
AND course.courseno = empcourse.courseno
AND empcourse.empno = employee.empno
AND employee.depno = department.depno;
```

The equivalent relational algebra is

```
PROJECTdname (department JOINdepno = depno (
PROJECTdepno (employee JOINempno = empno (
PROJECTempno (empcourse JOINcourseno = courseno
(
 PROJECTcourseno (SELECTcname = `Further
Accounting' course)
))
))
))
```

SYMBOLIC NOTATION

From the example, one can see that for complicated cases a large amount of the answer is formed from operator names, such as PROJECT and JOIN. It is therefore commonplace to use symbolic notation to represent the operators.

- Select →σ (sigma)
- Project → π(pi)
- Product → ×(times)
- Join → |×| (bow-tie)
- Union → (cup)
- Intersection → ∩(cap)
- Difference → – (minus)
- Rename → ρ (rho)

Usage

The symbolic operators are used as with the verbal ones. So, to find all employees in department 1:

```
SELECTdepno = 1(employee)
becomes σdepno = 1(employee)
```

Conditions can be combined together using ^ (AND) and v (OR). For example, all employees in department 1 called 'Smith':

```
SELECT depno = 1 ^ surname = 'Smith' (employee)
becomes σ depno = 1 ^ surname = 'Smith' (employee)
```

The use of the symbolic notation can lend itself to brevity. Even better, when the JOIN is a natural join, the JOIN condition may be omitted from |×|.

The earlier example resulted in:

```
PROJECT dname (department JOIN depno = depno (
PROJECT depno (employee JOIN empno = empno (
   PROJECT empno (empcourse JOIN courseno = courseno
   (
      PROJECTcourseno (SELECTcname = 'Further
Accounting' course))))))
```

becomes

```
πdname (department |×| (
 πdepno (employee |×| (
  πempno (empcourse |×| (
    πcourseno (?cname = 'Further Accounting'
 course)))))))
```

Rename Operator

The rename operator returns an existing relation under a new name. $\rho_A(B)$ is the relation B with its name changed to A. For example, find the employees in the same Department as employee 3.

```
 ρ emp2.surname,emp2.forenames (
σ employee.empno = 3 ^ employee.depno = emp2.depno (
 employee × (?emp2employee)
)
)
```

Derivable Operators

- Fundamental operators:σ, π, ×, □, -, ρ
- Derivable operators: |×|,∩

A ∩ B

□A – (A – B)

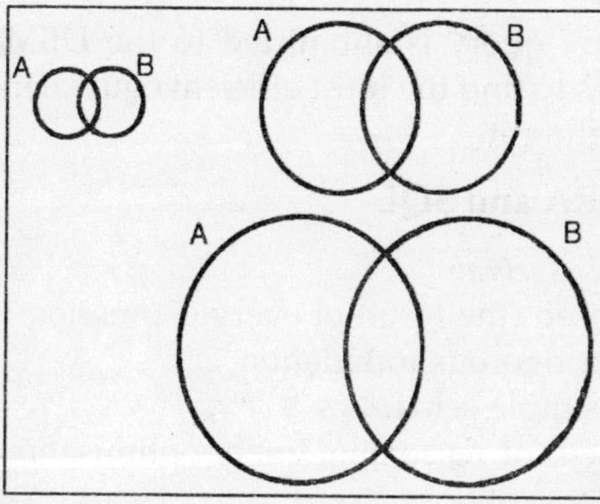

Equivalence

$A|\times|_c B$ ** $\pi a_1, a_2, ... a_N(\sigma_c(A \times B))$

- where c is the join condition (eg A.a1 = B.a1),
- and $a_1, a_2, ... a_N$ are all the attributes of A and B without repetition.

c is called the join-condition, and is usually the comparison of primary and foreign key. Where there are N tables, there are usually N-1 join-conditions. In the case of a natural join, the conditions can be missed out, but otherwise missing out conditions results in a cartesian product (a common mistake to make).

Equivalences

The same relational algebraic expression can be written in many different ways. The order in which tuples appear in relations is never significant.

- $A \times B$? $B \times A$
- $A \cap B$? $B \cap A$
- $A \cap B$? $B \cap A$
- (A – B) is not the same as (B – A)
- $\sigma_{c1}(\sigma_{c2}(A))$? $\sigma_{c2}(\sigma_{c1}(A))$? $\sigma_{c1} \wedge {}_{c2}(A)$
- $\pi_{a1}(A)$? $\pi_{a1}(\pi_{a1}, etc(A))$

where etc represents any other attributes of A.

- Many other equivalences exist.

While equivalent expressions always give the same result, some may be much easier to evaluate that others.

When any query is submitted to the DBMS, its query optimiser tries to find the most efficient equivalent expression before evaluating it.

Comparing RA and SQL

Relational algebra:

- Is closed (the result of every expression is a relation)
- Has a rigorous foundation
- Has simple semantics
- Is used for reasoning, query optimisation, etc.

SQL:

- Is a superset of relational algebra
- Has convenient formatting features, etc.
- Provides aggregate functions
- Has complicated semantics
- Is an end-user language.

Comparing RA and SQL

Any relational language as powerful as relational algebra is called relationally complete.

A relationally complete language can perform all basic, meaningful operations on relations.

Since SQL is a superset of relational algebra, it is also relationally complete.

RELATIONAL CALCULUS

In Relational Calculus, we write a declarative expression to specify a retrieval request. Relational Calculus expression specifies what data to be retrieved rather than how to retrieve the expected data. Therefore, Relational Calculus is a non-procedural language.

The Relational Calculus comes in two flavors

- *Tuple Relational Calculus (TRC)*: Variables range over tuples of a relation
- *Domain Relational Calculus (DRC)*: Variables range over elements of a domain

The concepts used in Relational Calculus include : variables, constants, comparison operations, logical connectivities and quantifiers. Each query is specified in Relational Calculus as a formula. An answer tuple is an assignment of constants to variables that make formula evaluated to true. The following sections will cover in detail two type of Relational Calculus.

TUPLE AND DOMAIN CALCULUS

DEFINITION

Tuple calculus A form of relational calculus in which a variable's only permitted values are tuples of a given relation. Codd's unimplemented language ALPHA and the subsequent QUEL are examples of the tuple calculus.

The tuple calculus is a calculus that was introduced by Edgar F. Codd as part of the relational model in order to give a declarative database query language for this data model. It formed the inspiration for the database query languages QUEL and SQL of which the latter, although far less faithful to the original relational model and calculus, is now used in almost all relational database management systems as the ad-hoc query language. Along with the tuple calculus Codd also introduced the domain calculus which is closer to first-order logic and showed that these two calculi (and the relational algebra) are equivalent in expressive power.

CALCULUS

The fundamental assumption in this calculus is that variables range over tuples as they are defined in the relational model. (In what follows the term tuple is always used in that meaning) The atoms of our language are going to be statements about such variables and defined by the following context-free grammar:

B ::= (T.A = T.A) | (T.A = C) | R(T)

where T denotes the set of tuple variables, A denotes the set of attribute names, C denotes the set of constant values and Rdenotes the set of relation names. Examples of atoms are

- (t.name = "Codd") -- tuple t has a name attribute and its value is "Codd"

- (t.age = s.age) -- t has an age attribute and s has an age attrbute with the same value
- Book(t) -- tuple t is present in relation Book.

Note that the last formula states that all books that are written by C. J. Date have as their subject the relational model. As usual we omit brackets if this causes no ambiguity about the semantics of the formula.

We will assume that the quantifiers quantify over the universe of all tuples. It is easy to see that then a closed formula, i.e., a formula with no free variables, is either true or false for a certain database instance. This means that we can already use those to ask boolean queries, i.e., queries that result in either "yes" or "no". If it is not closed then given a database instance a formula defines a set of bindings, i.e., a function b of the free variables to tuples, such that the formula becomes true iff every free variable x in it is replaced with b(x). A query language should not only make statements about the contents of the database but it should also be able to construct new tuples that are not yet in the database. For this purpose the tuple constructor is introduced that can construct a tuple given a certain variable binding. Its syntax is defined as follows:

K::= (A:T.A, ..., A:T.A)

Examples of tuple constructors:

- () -- constructs the empty tuple
- (employee:t.name, manager:s.name) -- constructs a tuple with attributes names "employee" and "manager" and gives them resepectively the values of the "name" of t and the "name" of s.

The semantics of a tuple constructor is defined as a partial function that maps a variable binding, i.e., a partial function from tuple variables to tuples, to a tuple. In order for this function to be defined the variable binding should satisfy the following constraints:

- it must bind all the variables in the constructor, and
- if t.a appears in the konstructor then t should be bound to a tuple with an a attribute.

Finally we define what a query expression looks like:

Q ::= { K | F }

The result of a query { k | f } is the set of tuples that is constructed by the tuple constructor k from all the bindings that make the formula f true. Since the result of the tuple constructor is only defined for certain bindings we have to add certain restrictions such that the result of the tupel constructor is defined for all bindings generated by the formula. Fortunately we can decide this as follows.

We define P(f) and N(f) as functions that map a formula f to a set of pairs (t, a) with t a tuple variable and a an attribute name. The intended meaning of these functions is that P(f) contains a pair (t, a) if in all bindings that make f true the variable t is bound to a tuple with an attribute a, and for N(f) this holds if this is the case for all bindings that make f false.

We then call a query expression { k | f } well formed if for every occurrence of t.a in k it holds that (t, a) is in P(f). It will be clear that the result of every well formed query expression is well defined.

Discuss safeness to prevent that the result may be infinite. Actually we should also check if the comparisos are legal according to the schema, but this is not strictly necessary. In computer science, domain relational calculus is a calculus that was introduced by Edgar F. Coddas part of the relational model in order to give a declarative database query language for this data model.

TRC

Unlike SQL, the Domain Relational Calculus makes assumptions about the order of the attributes in the database's tables. For example, the objects that are quantified over are attributes, which are constrained to occur in certain positions in particular tables. In contrast, SQL's quantifiers range over tuples. We need nct know where a particular attribute appears in a tables: if we know that a tuple is from a certain table, then we can pick the appropriate attribute using a column name.

The expression:

```
{fval!name;fval:emp;
 exists(skf1:emp,
 exists(t1:boss,t1!mgr=skf1!name)&
```

```
exists(t2:boss,t2!name=fval!name&t2!mgr=skfl!name)
)}
```

is a representation of:

$$\{x.name \mid x \in cmp \mid \exists y \in cmp(\exists t_1 \in boss(t_1.mar=y.name) \& \exists t_2 \in boss(t_2.name=x.name \& t_2\ mar=y.name))\}$$

INTRODUCTION ON SQL

INTRODUCTION

Structured Query Language, commonly abbreviated to SQL and pronounced as sequel, is not a conventional computer programming language in the normal sense of the phrase. With SQL you don't write applications, utilities, batch processes, GUI interfaces or any of the other types of programme for which you'd use languages such as Visual Basic, C++, Java etc. Instead SQL is a language used exclusively to create, manipulate and interrogate databases. SQL is about data and results, each SQL statement returns a result, whether that result be a query, an update to a record or the creation of a database table.

The purpose of this tutorial is to give an introduction to the key concepts of SQL, and to provide sample code illustrating the use of the most common and useful of the SQL commands. The tutorial is structured around the building of a simple database of software and network users.

RELATIONAL DATABASES

Before looking at SQL itself it's worth looking more closely at what is meant by a database. Although some people talk about SQL databases, there is in fact no such thing.

SQL itself makes no references to the underlying databases which it can access, which means that it is possible to have a SQL engine which can address relational databases, non-relational (flat) databases, even spreadsheets. However, SQL is most often used to address a relational database, which is what some people refer to as a SQL database.

The relational model of a database was first defined by Dr E Codd in 1970, working at the IBM Research Labs at San Jose, and it describes a way of structuring data which is mathematically consistent and abstracted away from the physical implementation of the database.

The key concept of the relational model is that data sits in tables, and that data elements within different tables can be related in some way to provide meaningful information rather than just lists of data.

Each table in the database has a number of fields which define the content and a number of instances of that field - think of the fields as columns in a table and the instances as rows.

For example if we had a table of LAN users, then it might have fields of first name, surname and userID. The rows in such a table would contain the values which define each instance of user, for example the entry to define user John Smith might be: John, Smith, JSmith.

A single table of LAN users does not provide very much, even though it is more useful than no table at all. However the user table becomes immediately more useful when there are other tables to which it can be linked dynamically.

Imagine that there is also a table of software products, with fields of Product, Version, User Licence and Product Code. Again this is useful information, especially for inventory purposes, but its value is magnified when there is a relationship between the user table and the software table.

For example a link between these tables could be used to record which users are licensed for which software products. From this it would be possible to find out how many users are licensed to use product X, or which products user Y is using.

Add fields of department to the user table, for example, and it's possible to derive the relationship between departmental software requirements and the software that is licensed and so on. Obviously there is much more to the relational model then this, but as far as SQL is concerned it is the concept of tables, fields and relationships which is important.

DESIGNING A DATABASE

Finally, we're almost ready to start looking at some SQL code. The first place to start is in the creation of our sample database. In every kind of database project, the first step is to design the database on paper rather than jumping straight in with the code. One of the aims of this example database is to record the software that is installed on a network and to link this to users and to their departments. Additionally, building on the inventory side of things, it will also keep track of the PC hardware we have installed.

Based on these requirements four tables are required:

- *User*: To record users
- *Software*: Table for the installed software products
- *UserSoftware*: To record the Software used by each user (more on why we need this table later)
- *PC*: Table to record the PC details of each user

Designing each table is a fairly straightforward process of deciding what information is required for each element in the table. For the User we obviously need First Name, Last Name and Department, but we have to beware of having two users with the same name, so we need to be able to differentiate between them. One way to do this would be to use some kind of unique UserID, an email address or network login, for example. An alternative would be to either create a unique code for each user, or else to use some pre-existing unique identifier, such as an ID from a payroll application. In this example a field called EmpNo will be used to contain this unique identifier, which we shall also assume is an integer rather than a mix of alphanumerics. Finally, we want to record the type of PC for each user, so we'll add a field called PCType.

Our User table therefore looks like this:

- First Name - First Name - a text string
- Last Name - Last Name - a text string
- User ID - Network User ID - a text string

- Dept - Department - a text string
- Emp No - Employee Number from Payroll system - an integer
- PC Type - Unique identifier for type of PC - a text string

The Software table has the following fields:

- Product Name - Name of Product - a text string
- Vers - Product Version - a text string
- Product ID - Unique identifier for product - a text string
- Licenses - Number of users licensed - an integer
- DateOfPurchase - Purchase data from invoicing system - a date
- Cost - PPersecutors of product -a currency code

Our table of software used by each user we'll call UserSoftware. In the case of the User table a code for this was included for the PCType, why not do the same with the Software? Because each user is likely to have many pieces of software, and each piece of software is likely to have many different users. It therefore makes sense to create a separate table to record this many-to-many relationship. For this simple table we need fields only for EmpNo - to uniquely identify the user - and ProductID to uniquely identify the software. Our final table stores the data for the different PCs, and provides the value to enter into the PCType field of the User table.

- PC Type Name - A text string
- Processor - CPU Processor - A text string
- OpSys - Operating system name - A text string
- RAM - Mb of RAM - An integer
- Disk - Gb of hard disk - An floating point number
- ScreenSize - Screen size in inches - A text string
- Date Of Purchase - Purchase date from invoicing system - a date code
- Cost - Cost of purchase -a currency code

WORD ABOUT DATA TYPES

Many kinds of data can be stored in a database, from simple text to various types of number to Boolean flags to binary objects and graphics. This is one area where there are differences between different products.

Not just in the formats of data that can be stored, but also in how these formats are named. Boolean fields, for example, are called Yes/No fields in Microsoft Access, and BOOLEAN in the later releases of MySQL.

This is one of the areas where you have to refer to the documentation of whatever database platform you are using. In this tutorial datatypes (or column types as they are also known), will conform as closely as possible to those which are most commonly supported on the majority of platforms.

CREATING A DATABASE

Many database systems have graphical interfaces which allow developers (and users) to create, modify and otherwise interact with the underlying database management system (DBMS).

However, for the purposes of this tutorial all interactions with the DBMS will be via SQL commands rather than via menus, wizards or any of the other tools which sit between the developer and the database. This is, after all, a SQL tutorial...It is assumed, therefore, that you have access to a DBMS system that allows the use of SQL commands directly. SQL commands follow a number of basic rules.

SQL keywords are not normally case sensitive, though this in this tutorial all commands (SELECT, UPDATE etc) are upper-cased. Variable and parameter names are displayed here as lower-case. New-line characters are ignored in SQL, so a command may be all on one line or broken up across a number of lines for the sake of clarity. Many DBMS systems expect to have SQL commands terminated with a semi-colon character, a practice that is followed in this tutorial.

Finally, although there is a SQL standard, actual implementaions vary by vendor/system, so if in doubt always refer to the documentation that comes with your DBMS.

Creating a database is remarkably straightforward. The SQL command is just:

```
Create DataBase dbname;
```

In this example we'll call the database AssetReg, so the command is:

```
Create DataBase AssetReg;
```

Once the database is created it, is possible to start implementing the design sketched out previously.

CREATING TABLES WITH SQL

Having created the database it's time to use some SQL to create the tables required by the design. Note that all SQL keywords are shown in upper case, variable names in a mixture of upper and lower case.

The SQL statement to create a table has the basic form:

```
Create Table name( col1 datatype, col2 datatype,
...);
```

So, to create our User table we enter the following command:

```
Create Table User (FirstName Text, LastName Text,
UserID Text, Dept Text,
EmpNo Integer, PCType Text );
```

The TEXT datatype, supported by many of the most common DBMS, specifies a string of characters of any length. In practice there is often a default string length which varies by product. In some DBMS TEXT is not supported, and instead a specific string length has to be declared. Fixed length strings are often called CHAR(x), VCHAR(x) or VARCHAR(x), where x is the string length. In the case of INTEGER there are often multiple flavours of integer available. Remembering that larger integers require more bytes for data storage, the choice of int size is usually a design decision that ought to be made up front.

The commands to create the other tables are:

```
Create Table Software (ProductName Varchar(15),
Vers Varchar(10), ProductID Varchar(10),
Licenses Integer, DateOfPurchase Date, Cost
CURRENCY);
```

CURRENCY is another datatype that varies by vendor/product. Consult your documentation. Where an explicit CURRENCY type is not available, there is often a DECIMAL type which can be used as a replacement.

```
Create Table UserSoftware (EmpNo Integer,
```

```
ProductID Varchar(10));
Create Table PC (PCTypeName Varchar(20),
Processor Varchar(20), OpSys Varchar(10),
RAM Integer, Disk Float, ScreenSize Varchar(10),
DateOfPurchase DATE, Cost CURRENCY);
```

Float contains floating point numbers, a Double type often also exists for higher precision floating point numbers. Date also comes in various flavours and formats.

There is more to the Create Table command, just as there is more to database design then we have allowed for in this example. Principally we have ignored any considerations of indexing our tables or of any kinds of constraints or data validation rules. For example you would normally want to ensure that the EmpNo field in the User is unique, that is, no two users should have the same EmpNo. Additionally, you would normally decide in advance the size of various fields, especially for text strings. SQL can code for all of these design considerations, though the syntax is likely to vary between implementations to a greater extent than the basic Create Table command.

As an example let's refine our User design so that the first name and surname fields can be no longer than 20 characters each; the userID entry can be no longer than 12 characters and that the UserID and EmpNo fields should be unique (which is what the Unique keyword does for us). If you have already executed the original Create Table command your database will already contain a table called User, so let's get rid of that using the Drop command:

Drop Table User;

And now we'll recreate the User table we'll use throughout the rest of this tutorial:

Create Table User (FirstName VARCHAR (20), LastName VARCHAR (20),

UserID Varchar(12) Unique, Dept Varchar(20), EmpNo Integer Unique, PCType Varchar(20);

Once a table is created it's structure is not necessarily fixed in stone. In time requirements change and the structure of the database is likely to evolve to match these. SQL can be used to change the structure of a table, so, for example, if we need to add a new field to our

SQL (Structured Query Language) is a database sublanguage for querying and modifying relational databases. It was developed by IBM Research in the mid 70's and standardized by ANSI in 1986.

The Relational Model defines two root languages for accessing a relational database -- Relational Algebra and Relational Calculus. Relational Algebra is a low-level, operator-oriented language. Creating a query in Relational Algebra involves combining relational operators using algebraic notation. Relational Calculus is a high-level, declarative language. Creating a query in Relational Calculus involves describing what results are desired.

The SQL language and relational database systems based on it are one of the most important foundation technologies in the computer industry. Over the last two decades, SQL has grown from its first commercial use into a computer product and services market segment worth tens of billions of dollars per year, and SQL stands today as the standard computer database language. Literally hundreds of database products now support SQL, running on computer systems from mainframes to personal computers and even handheld devices.

An official international SQL standard has been adopted and expanded twice. Virtually every major enterprise software product relies on SQL for its data management, and SQL is at the core of the database products from Microsoft, Oracle, and IBM, the three largest software companies in the world. SQL is also at the heart of open-source database products that are helping to fuel the popularity of Linux and the open-source movement. From its obscure beginnings as an IBM research project, SQL has leaped to prominence as both an important computer technology and a powerful market force.

What, exactly, is SQL? Why is it important? What can it do, and how does it work? If SQL is really a standard, why are there so many different versions and dialects? How do popular SQL products like SQL Server, Oracle, Informix, Sybase, and DB2 compare? How does SQL relate to Microsoft standards, such as ODBC and COM? How does JDBC link SQL to the world of Java and object technology? What role does it play in the emerging "web services" architecture and the competing web services architectures from the Microsoft and Java-based camps? Does SQL really scale from mainframes to handheld devices? Has it really delivered the performance needed for high-volume transaction processing? How will SQL impact the way you use computers, and how can you get the most out of this important data management tool?

SQL is a special-purpose language used to define, access, and manipulate data. SQL is nonprocedural, meaning that it describes the necessary components (i.e., tables) and desired results without dictating exactly how those results should be computed. Every SQL implementation sits atop a database engine, whose job it is to interpret SQL statements and determine how the various data structures in the database should be accessed to accurately and efficiently produce the desired outcome.

The SQL language includes two distinct sets of commands: Data Definition Language (DDL) is the subset of SQL used to define and modify various data structures, while Data Manipulation Language (DML) is the subset of SQL used to access and manipulate data contained within the data structures previously defined via DDL. DDL includes numerous commands for handling such tasks as creating tables, indexes, views, and constraints, while DML is comprised of just five statements:

- *Insert*: Adds data to a database.
- *Update*: Modifies data in a database.
- *Delete*: Removes data from a database.
- *Merge*: Adds and/or modifies data in a database. Merge is part of the 2003 Aansi SQL standard.
- *Select*: Retrieves data from a database.

Some people feel that DDL is the sole property of database administrators, while database developers are responsible for writing DML statements, but the two are not so easily separated. It is difficult to efficiently access and manipulate data without an understanding of what data structures are available and how they are related; likewise, it is difficult to design appropriate data structures without knowledge of how the data will be accessed.That being said, this book deals almost exclusively with DML, except where DDL is presented to set the stage for one or more DML examples.

The reasons for focusing on just the DML portion of SQL include:

- DDL is well represented in various books on database design and administration as well as in SQL reference guides.
- Most database performance issues are the result of inefficient DML statements.
- Even with a paltry five statements, DML is a rich enough topic to warrant not just one book, but a whole series of books.

Anyone who writes SQL in an Oracle environment should be armed with the following three books: a reference guide to the SQL language, such as Oracle in a Nutshell (O'Reilly); a performance-tuning guide, such as Optimizing Oracle Performance (O'Reilly); and the book you are holding, which shows how to best utilize and combine the various features of Oracle's SQL implementation.

So why should you care about SQL? In this age of Internet computing and n-tier architectures, does anyone even care about data access anymore? Actually, efficient storage and retrieval of information is more important than ever:

- Many companies now offer services via the Internet. During peak hours, these services may need to handle thousands of concurrent requests, and unacceptable response times equate to lost revenue. For such systems, every SQL statement must be carefully crafted to ensure acceptable performance as data volumes increase.
- We can store a lot more data today than we could just a few years ago. A single disk array can hold tens of terabytes of data, and the ability to store hundreds of terabytes is just around the corner. Software used to load or analyse data in these environments must harness the full power of SQL to

process ever-increasing data volumes within constant (or shrinking) time windows.

Hopefully, you now have an appreciation for what SQL is and why it is important. The next section will explore the origins of the SQL language and the support for the SQL standard in Oracle's products.

CHARACTERISTICS OF SQL

WHAT ARE THE CHARACTERISTICS OF SQL DATABASE ENGINES

SQL databases tend to be mysterious when it comes to the information that is stored within them. It is likely that you have a number of applications that put information into your various SQL database engines. From this information set, you need to be able to retrieve meaningful information and that is where this course comes in. This hands-on class focuses on retrieving information from your systems in a way that is much more insightful in terms of getting

- What you need from the system,
- Working with multiple tables, and
- Doing it easily.

STATEMENT IN SQL

After you have a good understanding of what SQL can do, it's time to move on to more sophisticated queries. It's important to understand what your database engine is capable of, and what your requirements are for pulling information from your system. This module will introduce some new elements that you can use for your queries. These new clauses include grouping and filtering. You'll see how to make sure you skip duplicate information in the database, making the information more meaningful and easier to digest.

CHARACTERISTICS OF PL/SQL TABLES

A definition worth repeating: A PL/SQL table is a one-dimensional, unbounded, sparse collection of homogenous elements, indexed by integers. Let's examine each of these characteristics in detail.

One-dimensional

A PL/SQL table can have only one column. It is, in this way, similar to a one-dimensional array. You cannot define a PL/SQL table so that it can be referenced as follows:

```
my_table (10, 44)
```

This is a two-dimensional structure and not currently supported.

Unbounded or Unconstrained

There is no predefined limit to the number of rows in a PL/SQL table. The PL/SQL table grows dynamically as you add more rows to the table. The PL/SQL table is, in this way, very different from an array. Related to this definition, no rows for PL/SQL tables are allocated for this structure when it is defined.

Sparse

In a PL/SQL table, a row exists in the table only when a value is assigned to that row. Rows do not have to be defined sequentially. Instead you can assign a value to any row in the table. So row 15 could have a value of `Fox' and row 15446 a value of `Red', with no other rows defined in between. In contrast, an array is a dense data structure. When you declare an array, all cells in the array are allocated in memory and are ready to use.

Homogeneous Elements

Because a PL/SQL table can have only a single column, all rows in a PL/SQL table contain values of the same datatype. It is, therefore, homogeneous. With PL/SQL Release 2.3, you can have PL/SQL tables of records. The resulting table is still, however, homogeneous. Each row simply contains the same set of columns.

Indexed by Integers

PL/SQL tables currently support a single indexing mode. by BINARY_INTEGER. This number acts as the "primary key" of the PL/SQL table. The range of a BINARY_INTEGER is from –231–1 to 231–1, so you have an awful lot of rows with which to work. Notice that the index of a row in the table can even be negative. In the PL/SQL table, a negative row number is no different from a positive one; it's just another integer.

However, there are ways that you, the programmer, can take advantage of differences between positive and negative row numbers in your application. For example, the ps_global package, included on the companion disk, uses rows with positive numbers to store "globals-by-number" and uses negative row values to store "globals-by-name". Because the row number does not have to be used sequentially and has such enormous range, you can use this integer index in interesting ways. For example, the row number for a PL/SQL table could be the primary key of your company table, so that:

```
company_name (14055)
```

contains the name of the company whose company_id = 14055.

A PL/SQL table is a one-dimensional, unbounded, sparse collection of homogeneous elements, indexed by integers. In technical terms, it is like an array; it is like a SQL table; yet it is not precisely the same as either of those data structures. This chapter explains these characteristics of the PL/SQL table in detail, so that you will understand the differences between PL/SQL tables and traditional arrays and SQL tables, and so that you will know how to use PL/SQL tables in your Programmes. Like PL/SQL records, PL/SQL tables are composite data structures.

Table. The Single-column, One-dimensional PL/SQL

Table	Emp_Name
100	Smith
225	Feuerstein
226	Silva
300	Russell
340	Ziemba

Let's take a look at an example and then explore the characteristics of a table. The following procedure accepts a name and a row and assigns that name to the corresponding row in the PL/SQL table:

```
1 PROCEDURE set_name (name_in IN VARCHAR2, row_in
  in INTEGER)
2 IS
3
4 TYPE string_tabletype IS
5 TABLE OF VARCHAR2(30) INDEXED BY
  BINARY_INTEGER;
6
7 company_name_table string_tabletype;
8
9 BEGIN
10   company_name_table (row_in) := name_in;
11 END;
```

The TYPE statement in lines 4-5 defines the structure of a PL/SQL table: a collection of strings with a maximum length of 30 characters. The INDEXED BY BINARY_INTEGER clause defines the integer key for the data structure. The table declaration in line 7 declares a specific PL/SQL table based on that table structure. In line 10, traditional array syntax is used to assign a string to a specific row in that PL/SQL table.

PL/SQL TABLES AND OTHER COLLECTIONS

A PL/SQL table is one type of collection structure and, until Oracle8, it was the only one supported by PL/SQL. With Oracle8, there are now two additional types. This section briefly describes those types and includes information you need to know about using PL/SQL tables and other collections with different versions of PL/SQL. For detailed information about the new collection types,

PL/SQL Tables

PL/SQL tables are available only in releases of PL/SQL Version 2. PL/SQL tables reside in the private PL/SQL area of the Oracle Server database instance; they are not available as client-side structures at this time. As a result, you cannot declare and manipulate PL/SQL tables in your Oracle

Developer/2000 environment. You can, on the other hand, build stored procedures and packages which work with PL/SQL tables, but hide these structures behind their interface. You can then call this stored code from within Oracle Developer/2000 to take advantage of Version 2 features like PL/SQL tables.

Note that PL/SQL Release 2.3 offers several substantial enhancements to the PL/SQL tables, covered in Section 10.8, "PL/SQL Table Enhancements in PL/SQL Release 2.3". If you are using PL/SQL Release 2.3 (available with Oracle7 Server Release 7.3), make sure you read through this section and make use of these advanced features. All topics covered earlier in the chapter assume PL/SQL Release 2.2 or earlier and do not take advantage of these new features. (Where applicable, I will point you to the relevant Release 2.3 features.)

Nested Tables and VARRAYs

Like PL/SQL tables, the two collection types introduced under Oracle8 -- nested tables and variable arrays (VARRAYs) can be used in PL/SQL Programmes. But these collection types offer something new: they can be used as the datatypes of fields in conventional tables and attributes of objects.

ADVANTAGE OF SQL

ADVANTAGE SQL SERVER

"Since installing the Advantage SQL server we have noticed a significantly enhanced network performance. In specific, scheduling appointments, statements, and running recall labels & lists, are faster. "

When a PC database application is used by only a few users on a LAN and the database is small, the application usually provides good performance, is easy to maintain, and is relatively stable.

As more users and remote access capabilities are added, performance, data integrity and security begin to suffer. If your site has multi-user performance problems, suffers from frequent index corruption, and lacks database security, it is time to look for a client/server and DataBase Management solution. Compulink has partnered with Extended Systems to bring you the finest SQL client/server solution available.

WORKING

Increasing Users Increases the Problems

As the number of application users at the site increases, the size of the database doubles, then triples. Suddenly, performance has slowed to a crawl. The network is swamped with traffic and index corruption becomes commonplace. Accessing the database on the LAN is taking longer and the database is no longer stable or secure.

Why Performance Declines and Data Corrupts

With desktop database applications, most tasks are performed on the workstation. The file server only acts as a shared hard drive. When a workstation needs to access a piece of data, it must first attempt to provide database concurrency by locking the data it needs to access. With only a few users on the system, there is little contention for common data. However, as the number of users at a site increases, so does database access contention. The workstation data locking attempts will fail more frequently on initial and subsequent attempts; therefore causing a decline in the performance. If the workstation or network goes down at any time during the update operation, indexes will be corrupt and the database will be left in an unstable state.

Intelligent Processing

The Advantage Database Server provides client/server processing by intelligently dividing processing between the client and the server. The user interface and much of the business calculations are done by the client workstation. All database concurrency control, data movement, data searching, and data manipulation are performed by the Advantage Database Server on the file server. The Advantage Database Server becomes a central point of control for database access.

So unlike non-client/server desktop applications, Advantage moves the shared data processing operations to the file server where it makes sense and where the data is stored. Only the results of the database operation are returned to the client.

ADS Requirements

The Advantage Database Server does not require new dedicated server hardware. It runs on existing Windows NT/2000/2003. Advantage installs in minutes and is easy to maintain. It does not require a database administrator for maintenance like most other database systems. Compulink's support staff is fully trained to answer any technical support or installation questions on ADS and is committed to insure a smooth transition and continued hassle free operation for your office.

INDEPTH DETAILS

Initial Desktop Database Development

Desktop database applications developed with tools such as CA-Clipper, FoxPro,Visual Basic and Delphi have traditionally been popular because they are relatively inexpensive to implement and deploy. But as more users and Internet and remote access capabilities are added, performance, data integrity and security begin to suffer. When a PC database application is used by only a few users on a LAN, and the database is small, the application usually provides good performance, is easy to maintain, and is relatively stable. Very small user sites often acquire additional tools for use against their database, such as report generators and database browsers. Everything is running smoothly and all database tools are in place. Performance is good and the database is stable.

Increasing users increases the problems as the number of application users at the site increases, the size of the database doubles, then triples. Transaction loads skyrocket. A remote site is added that requires access to the home site data via a WAN. Suddenly, performance has slowed to a crawl. The network is swamped with traffic and index corruption becomes commonplace. When workstations or the network go down, the database becomes corrupt. With the addition of new users, there is now a need to limit access to key data. Database security becomes a larger issue. Performance is declining. Accessing the database on the LAN is taking longer, and performance of the WAN is even worse-it is unusable. The database is no longer stable or secure.

Users have lost their ability to do their work in a timely manner. why the performance declined With desktop database applications, the user interface, business logic, database concurrency control, data movement, data searching, and data manipulation are all performed on the workstation. The file server only acts as a shared hard drive. There is no central point of control to the data.

When a workstation needs to search for, read, write, or otherwise access data, it must first attempt to provide database concurrency by locking the data it needs to access. With only a few users on the system, there is little contention for common data. However, as the number of users at a site increases, so does database access contention. The workstation data locking attempts will fail more frequently on initial and subsequent attempts. Not only does the individual application performance suffer but other users' application performance suffers due to the additional network traffic generated by multiple database concurrency lock requests.

The performance problems have become a double-edged sword. The database concurrency locking requires multiple retries and the additional network traffic makes it tougher to make the lock requests.

Why there is more frequent index corruption The increased frequency of index corruption also has a simple explanation. Every time a table record is to be updated, one or more index files usually need to be changed to complete the update operation. Once an update operation begins, the database will only remain in a stable state if each and every table and index update is completed. Each individual index update operation requires a concurrency lock to be obtained, index page(s) to be read and written, the index header to be read and written, and finally an index "flush to disk" operation to occur.

This is for each and every index affected! If the workstation or network goes down at any time during the update operation, indexes will be corrupt, and the database will be left in an unstable state. Advantage Database Server brings you the benefits of client/server A move to client/server is in order. What is needed is a product that provides all the security and integrity benefits of client/server and all the performance benefits that should be available in a client/server environment-while allowing developers to keep all their existing applications, their existing hardware, and their years of accumulated expertise. The product that delivers is Advantage Database Server.

Intelligent Processing

The Advantage Database Server provides client/server processing by intelligently dividing processing between the client and the server. The user interface and much of the business logic are left to be done by the client workstation. All database concurrency control, data movement, data searching, and data manipulation are performed by the

Advantage Database Server on the file server. The Advantage Database Server becomes a central point of control for database access. Unlike non-client/server desktop applications, Advantage moves the shared data processing operations to the file server where it makes sense-where the data is stored. Only the results of the database operation are returned to the client. The superior architecture of Advantage leads to far better performance than non-client/server systems.

Eliminate Concurrency Contention Problems

Because the Advantage Database Server is the central point of control to the database, data concurrency contention issues are minimal. The intelligent lock management system of the Advantage Database Server allows multiple users to search through and read from shared files concurrently. This leads to drastically improved performance in multi-user systems. By performing all database concurrency control and data access on the server, network traffic is reduced significantly which also leads to drastically improved performance in multi-user environments. Reduced network traffic not only helps LAN performance, but it makes WAN database access feasible whereas before it was out of the question.

Eliminate Index Corruption

Advantage Database Server eliminates index corruption. Table and index updates are performed on the server. A table or index is never passed to the client to be updated.

When a table record and the associated indexes are updated by Advantage, the update operations do not occur until all necessary information has reached the Advantage Database Server on the file server. Even if a workstation or the network goes down, no index corruption will ever occur and the database integrity will always remain intact.

Transaction Processing

The Advantage Database Server also adds a complete Transaction Processing System (i.e., Begin, Commit, and Rollback Transaction) to your application. This allows application developers to define business transactions which usually involve multiple updates to one or more tables in the database. If one or more of these updates in the defined business transaction do not occur, the database is left in an unstable state. With the Advantage

Transaction Processing System, all of the updates necessary to complete the business transaction would be placed between the Begin and Commit Transaction statements.

If the workstation or network were to go down before the Commit Transaction was reached, all updates would be automatically rolled back. If the server were to go down before the Commit Transaction was reached, all updates would be automatically rolled back once the server was brought back up, and the Advantage Database re-started.

In either case, the database would be left as if the transaction did not even begin.

Referential Integrity and Database Constraints

Advantage Database Server provides Referential Integrity and Database Constraints to verify the validity of data in your database and maintain relationships between records in your database. Specifically, Advantage has support for Unique and Primary Keys, Referential Integrity, Field-level constraints, and Record-level constraints.

Security

The Advantage Database Server can be used to provide database security by allowing only Advantage-enabled applications to access the database. The system administrator can take away all desired network access rights to the directories that contain the database tables and index files, so that non-Advantage applications cannot gain access to the database. Unauthorized access to the database is eliminated. Advantage Database. Server provides further database security functionality by allowing creation of user accounts to control the access to tables, columns, views and stored procedures.

ADVANTAGES OF STATIC SQL

Programming using static SQL requires less effort than using embedded dynamic SQL. Static SQL statements are simply embedded into the host language source file, and the precompiler handles the necessary conversion to database manager run-time services API calls that the host language compiler can process.

Because the authorization of the person binding the application is used, the end user does not require direct privileges to execute the statements in the package. For example, an application could allow a user to update parts of a table without granting an update privilege on the entire table. This can be achieved by restricting the static SQL statements to allow updates only to certain columns or to a range of values. Static SQL statements are persistent, meaning that the statements last for as long as the package exists. Dynamic SQL statements are cached until they are either invalidated, freed for space management reasons, or the database is shut down. If required, the dynamic SQL statements are recompiled implicitly by the DB2(R) SQL compiler whenever a cached statement becomes invalid.

The key advantage of static SQL, with respect to persistence, is that the static statements exist after a particular database is shut down, whereas dynamic SQL statements cease to exist when this occurs. In addition, static SQL does not have to be compiled by the DB2 SQL compiler at run time, while dynamic SQL must be explicitly compiled at run time (for example, by using the PREPARE statement). Because DB2 caches dynamic SQL statements, the statements do not need to be compiled often by DB2, but they must be compiled at least once when you execute the application.

There can be performance advantages to static SQL. For simple, short-running SQL Programmes, a static SQL statement executes faster than the same statement processed dynamically because the overhead of preparing an executable form of the statement is done at precompile time instead of at run time.

The performance of static SQL depends on the statistics of the database the last time the application was bound. However, if these statistics change, the performance of equivalent dynamic SQL can be very different. If, for example, an index is added to a database at a later time, an application using static SQL cannot take advantage of the index unless it is rebound to the database. In addition, if you are using host variables in a static SQL statement, the optimizer will not be able to take advantage of any distribution statistics for the table.

SQL DATA TYPE AND LITERALS

DATA TYPES

Like all other computer languages, SQL deals with data.

So let's first look at how SQL defines data. *Data Type*: A group of data that shares some common characteristics and operations.

SQL defines the following data types:

- *Character String*: A sequence of characters from a predefined character set.
- *Bit String*: A sequence of bit values: 0 or 1.
  Exact Number: A numeric value who's precision and scale need to be preserved. Precision and scale can be counted at decimal level or binary level. The decimal precision of a numerical value is the total number of significant digits in decimal form. The decimal scale of a numerical value is the number of fractional digits in decimal form. For example, the number 123.45 has a precision of 5 and a scale of 2. The number 0.012345 has a precision of 6 and a scale of 6.
- Approximate Number: A numeric value who's precision needs to be preserved, and scale floated to its exponent. An approximate number is always expressed in scientific notation of "mantissa "E" exponent". *Note that an approximate number has two precisions*: mantissa precision and exponent precision. For example, the number 0.12345e1 has a mantissa precision of 5 and exponent precision of 1.
- *Date and Time*: A value to represent an instance of time. A date and time value can be divided into many portions and related them to a predefined calendar system as year, month, day, hour, minute, second, second fraction, and time zone. A date and time value also has a precision, which controls the number of digits of the second fraction portion. For example: 1999-1-1 1:1:1.001 has precision of 3 on the second fraction portion.

DATA BINARY REPRESENTATIONS

Now we know what types of data SQL must work with. The next step is to understand how different types of data are represented in binary forms. Since computers can only work with binary digits, we have to represent all data in computer memory in binary forms.

Character String

A character string is usually represented in memory as an array of characters. Each character is represented in 8 bits (one byte) or 16 bits (two bytes) based on the character set and the character encoding schema.

Bit String

The binary representation of a bit string should be easy. A bit string should be represented in memory as it is. Bit string "01000001" should be represented as "01000001". There might an issue with memory allocation, because computer allocates memory in units of bytes (8 bits per byte). If the length of a bit string is not multiples of 8 bits, the last allocated byte is not full. How to handle the empty space in the last byte? I guess different SQL implementation will have different rules.

Approximate Number

An approximate number is normally represented in binary form according to the IEEE 754 single-precision or double-precision standards in either 4 bytes or 8 bytes. The binary representation is divided into 3 components with different number of bits assigned to each components:

Code:

```
Sign Exponent Fraction Total
Single-Precision 1 8 23 32
Double-Precision 1 11 52 64
```

With the double precision standard, the mantissa precision can go up to 52 binary digits, about 15 decimal digits.

Data and Time: A date and time value is usually stored in memory as an exact integer number with 8 bytes representing an instance by measuring the time period between this instance and a reference time point in millisecond precision, second fraction precision of 3. How MySQL is store date and time values? We will try to find out later.

DATA LITERALS

Now we know the types of data, and how they are stored in memory. Next we need know how data can get in to the computer. One way is to enter it through the programme source code as a data literal.

Data Literal: An programme source element that represents a data value. Data literals can be divided into multiple groups depending the type of the data it is representing and how it is representing.

Character String Literals

Character String Literals are used to construct character strings, exact numbers, approximate numbers and data and time values.

The syntax rules of character string literals are pretty simple:

- A character string literal is a sequence of characters enclosed by quote characters.
- The quote character is the single quote character "'".
- If "'" is part of the sequence, it needs to be doubled it as "''".

Examples of character string literals:

Quote:

```
'Hello world!'
'Loews L''Enfant Plaza'
'123'
'0.123e-1'
'1999-01-01'
```

Hex String Literals

Hex String Literals are used to construct character strings and exact numbers.

The syntax rules for hex string literals are also very simple:

- A hex string literal is a sequence of hex digits enclosed by quote characters and prefixed with "x".
- The quote character is the single quote character "'".

Examples of hex string literals:

Code:

```
x'41424344'
x'31323334'
x'31323334'
```

```
x'01'
x'0001'
x'ff'
x'ffffffff'
x'ffffffffffffffff'
```

Numeric

Numeric Literals are used to construct exact numbers and approximate numbers. Syntax rules of numeric literals are:

- A numeric literal can be written in signed integer form, signed real numbers without exponents, or real numbers with exponents.

Examples of numeric literals:

Quote:

```
1
-22
33.3
-44.44
55.555e5
-666.666e-6
```

Date and Time

Date and Time Literals are used to construct date and time values.

The syntax of date and time literals are:

- A date literal is written in the form of "DATE 'yyyy-mm-dd'".

Examples of data and time literals:

Quote:

```
DATE '1999-01-01'
TIMESTAMP '1999-01-01 01:02:03'
```

SQL Server's datetime data type generates a lot of questions and confusion in the SQL Server community. Unlike some other major database platforms, SQL Server doesn't provide discrete date and time data types.

Instead, SQL Server's datetime data type does the work of both. Here are answers to six commonly asked questions about how to use SQL Server's datetime data type.

Questions

1. How does SQL Server store the datetime data type?

SQL Server uses 8 bytes to store the datetime data type. The first 4 bytes make up an integer value that represents the number of days since January 1, 1900. The second 4 bytes are an integer value that represents the number of milliseconds since midnight.

2. How to retrieve rows based on datetime values?

SQL Server recognizes date and time data enclosed in single quotes. You can couple date and time values together or use them independently. You can also combine character date formats ('May 15, 2004 4 am'), numeric date formats ('5/15/2004 04:30'), or contiguous string formats ('20040515') with standard <, >, or = operators, as the following example shows:
SELECT * FROM orders WHERE OrderDate < 'May 15, 2004'

3. How to retrieve only the date or time portion of the data?

You can use T-SQL's DATEPART() function to return a subset of the values that SQL Server's datetime columns store. The DATEPART() function uses two arguments. The first argument specifies the portion of the date that you want, and the second value specifies the datetime column:

```
Select  orderID,  Date  Part(MM,OrderDate)  AS
OrderMonth FROM Orders
```

4. How to insert a value into a datetime column?

To insert values into a datetime column, you need to enclose the values in single quotes, then use one of SQL Server's date formats to supply the date value that you want to insert. For example:

```
Declare @MyTable Table
  (MyDateTime DateTime)
INSERT INTO @MyTable VALUES ('May
  15, 2004 11:25am')
```

5. How do I find the day of the week?

Using the weekday argument as its first parameter, SQL Server's DATEPART() function returns the day of the week, returning 1 for Sunday, 2 for Monday, and so on. The following example uses the GETDATE() function combined with the DATEPART() function to retrieve the current day value:

```
Select DatePart(weekday, Getdate())
```

6. How to find the last day of the month?

You can combine T-SQL's DATEADD() and DATEDIFF() functions to calculate different date and time values. Subtract 5ms from the first day of the next month to find the last day of the current month:

Select Date Add (ms, -5, DATE ADD (mm, Date Diff (m,0, Get Date())+1, 0))

TYPES OF SQL COMMANDS

Abort: Aborts the current transaction

Alter Group: Add users to a group, remove users from a group

Alter Table: Modifies table properties

Alter User: Modifies user account information

Begin: Begins a transaction in chained mode

Checkpoint: Force transaction log checkpoint

Close: Close a cursor

Cluster: Gives storage clustering advice to the server

Comment: Add comment to an object

Commit: Commits the current transaction

Copy: Copies data between files and tables

Create Aggrate: Defines a new aggregate function

Create Constraint Trigger: Create a trigger to support a constraint

Create Data Base: Creates a new database

Create Function: Defines a new function

Create Group: Creates a new group

Create Index: Constructs a secondary index

Create Language: Defines a new language for functions

Create Operator: Defines a new user operator

Create Rule: Defines a new rule

Create Sequence: Creates a new sequence number generator

Create Table: Creates a new table

Create Table As: Creates a new table from the results of a

SELECT
Create Trigger: Creates a new trigger
Create Type: Defines a new base data type
Create User: Creates a new database user
Create View: Constructs a virtual table
Declare: Defines a cursor for table access
Delete: Removes rows from a table
Drop Aggregate: Removes the definition of an aggregate function
Drop Data Base: Removes an existing database
Drop Function: Removes a user-defined C function
Drop Group: Removes a group
Drop Index: Removes existing indexes from a database
Drop Language: Removes a user-defined procedural language
Drop Operator: Removes an operator from the database
Drop Rule: Removes existing rules from the database
Drop Sequence: Removes existing sequences from a database
Drop Table: Removes existing tables from a database
Drop Trigger: Removes an existing trigger
Drop Type: Removes user-defined types from the system catalogs
Drop User: Removes a user
Drop View: Removes existing views from a database
End: Commits the current transaction
Explain: Shows statement execution plan
Fetch: Gets rows using a cursor
Grant: Grants access privilege to a specific user, a specific group of users, or all users
Iinsert: Inserts new rows into a table
Lisen: Listen for a response on a notify condition
Load: Dynamically loads an object file
Lock: Explicitly lock a table inside a transaction
Move: Moves cursor position
Notify: Signals all frontends and backends listening on a notify condition
Reindex: Recover corrupted system indexes under stand-

alone PostgreSQL
Reset: Restores run-time parameters to default values
Revoke: Revokes access privilege from a specific user, a group of users, or all users.
Roll back: Aborts the current transaction
Select: Retrieves rows from a table or view
Set: Set run-time parameters
Set Constraints: Set the constraint mode of the current SQL transaction
SET Transaction: Set the characteristics of the current SQL-transaction
Show: Shows run-time parameters
Truncate: Empty a table
Unlisten: Stop listening for notification
Update: Replaces values of columns in a table
Vacuum: Clean and analyse a PostgreSQL database

Chapter 5

Data Definition Language

STATEMENT

Data definition language (DDL) statements let you to perform these tasks:

- Create, alter, and drop schema objects
- Grant and revoke privileges and roles
- Analyse information on a table, index, or cluster
- Establish auditing options
- Add comments to the data dictionary

The Create, Alter, and Drop commands require exclusive access to the specified object. For example, an Alter Table statement fails if another user has an open transaction on the specified table. The Grant, Revoke, Analyse, Audit, and Comment commands do not require exclusive access to the specified object. For example, you can analyse a table while other users are updating the table.

Oracle Database implicitly commits the current transaction before and after every DDL statement.

Many DDL statements may cause Oracle Database to recompile or reauthorize schema objects. For information on how Oracle Database recompiles and reauthorizes schema objects and the circumstances under which a DDL statement would cause this concept. DDL statements are supported by PL/SQL with the use of the DBMS_SQL package.

The DDL statements are:

ALTER ... (All statements beginning with ALTER, except ALTER SESSION and ALTER SYSTEM- "Session Control Statements"and "System Control Statement")

```
ANALYSE
ASSOCIATE STATISTICS
AUDIT
COMMENT
```

CREATE ... (All statements beginning with CREATE)
DISASSOCIATE STATISTICS
DROP ... (All statements beginning with DROP)
FLASHBACK ... (All statements beginning with FLASHBACK)

```
GRANT
NOAUDIT
PURGE
RENAME
REVOKE
TRUNCATE
```

DATA MANIPULATION LANGUAGE (DML)

Data manipulation language (DML) statements access and manipulate data in existing schema objects. These statements do not implicitly commit the current transaction. The data manipulation language statements are:

```
CALL
DELETE
EXPLAIN PLAN
INSERT
LOCK TABLE
MERGE
SELECT
UPDATE
```

The SELECT statement is a limited form of DML statement in that it can only access data in the database. It cannot manipulate data stored in the database, although it can manipulate the accessed data before returning the results of the query. The SELECT statement is supported in PL/SQL only when executed dynamically. However, you can use the similar PL/SQL statement SELECT INTO in PL/SQL code, and you do not have to execute it dynamically. The CALL and EXPLAIN PLANstatements are supported in PL/SQL only when executed dynamically. All other DML statements are fully supported in PL/SQL.

TRANSACTION CONTROL

Transaction control statements manage changes made by DML statements. The transaction control statements are:

```
COMMIT
ROLLBACK
SAVEPOINT
SET TRANSACTION
SET CONSTRAINT
```

All transaction control statements, except certain forms of the COMMIT and ROLLBACK commands, are supported in PL/SQL. For information on the restrictions, COMMIT and ROLLBACK.

SESSION CONTROL

Session control statements dynamically manage the properties of a user session. These statements do not implicitly commit the current transaction.

PL/SQL does not support session control statements. The session control statements are:

```
ALTER SESSION
SET ROLE
```

SYSTEM CONTROL

The single system control statement, ALTER SYSTEM, dynamically manages the properties of an Oracle Database instance. This statement does not implicitly commit the current transaction and is not supported in PL/SQL.

OPERATORS AND PROCEDURE

SQL OPERATORS

Operators come in three flavors: mathematical, logical, and equality. Mathematical operators add, subtract, multiply, and divide numbers. Logical operators include AND and OR.

Take note of the following tables for future reference. SQL operators are generally found inside of queries-- more specifically, in the conditional statements of the WHERE clause.

SQL Equality Operator Query

```
USE mydatabase;

SELECT customer,day_of_order
FROM orders
WHERE day_of_order > '7/31/08'
```

Sql Equality Operator

customer	day_of_order
Tizag	2008-08-01 00:00:00.000
Tizag	2008-08-01 00:00:00.000

In this case, we've used the equality operator greater than (>) to return orders from the orders table with a date greater than '7/31/08'.

SQL - EQUALITY OPERATOR TABLE

Equality involves comparing two values. To do so requires the use of the (<), (>), or (=) special characters. Does X = Y Is Y < X These are both questions that can be answered using a SQL Equality Operator expression.

SQL Equality Operators

Operator	Example	Defined	Result
=, IS	5 = 5	5 equal to 5?	True
!=, IS NOT	7 != 2	7 IS NOT (!=) equal to 2?	True
<	7 < 4	7 less than 4?	False
>	7 > 4	greater than 4?	True
⇐	7 ⇐ 11	Is 7 less than or equal to 11?	True
⇒	7⇒ 11	Is 7 greater than or equal to 11?	False

SQL - MATHEMATICAL OPERATORS

SQL mathematical operations are performed using mathematical operators (+, –, *, /, and %).

We can use SQL like a calculator to get a feel for how these operators work.

SQL Mathematical Operators

```
SELECT
15 + 4, --Addition
15 - 4, --Subtraction
15 * 4, --Multiplication
15 / 5, --Division
15 % 4; --Modulus
```

SQL Results

Addition	Subtraction	Multiplication	Division	Modulus
19	11	60	3	3

Modulus may be the only unfamiliar term on the chart. Modulus performs division, dividing the first digit by the second digit, but instead of returning a quotient, a "remainder" value is returned instead.

Modulus Example

```
USE mydatabase;
SELECT (5 / 2) -- = 2.5
SELECT (5 % 2) -- = 1 is the value that will
be returned
```

SQL - LOGICAL OPERATORS

These operators provide you with a way to specify exactly what you want SQL to go and fetch, and you may be as specific as you'd like! We'll discuss these a little later on and provide some real world scenarios as well. We cover these operators thoroughly in the SQL AND/OR lesson.

- *And*: Compares/Associates two values or expressions
- *Or* - Compares/Associates two values or expressions
- Use equal (=) to select rows for which a specified

column contains a specified value.

```
COL = value
```

- Use the IN predicate to select each row that has a column value equal to one of several listed values.

```
COL IN ('B01', 'C01', 'D01')
```

- Use LIKE to specify a character string that is similar to the column value of rows you want to select:
  - Use a per cent sign (%) to indicate any string of zero or more characters.

```
COL LIKE '%char'
```

  - Use an underscore (_) to indicate any single character.

```
COL LIKE '_char'
```

- Use BETWEEN to select rows in which a column has a value within two limits.

```
COL BETWEEN value1 AND value2
```

- Use IS NULL to retrieve rows that contain a null value in some column. A null value indicates the absence of a column value in a row. A null value is not the same as zero or all blanks.

```
COL IS NULL
```

- Use the NOT keyword to select all rows except the rows identified with the search condition.
  - Not equal (<>)

```
COL <> value
```

  - not in

```
COL NOT IN (list)
```

  - not like

```
COL NOT LIKE ' char'
```

  - not between

```
COL NOT BETWEEN value1 AND value2
```

  - is not null

```
COL IS NOT NULL
```

  - You can also use the symbols:

- ⇐
- <
- >
- ⇒

IN OPERATOR IN PROCEDURE

```
SQL>
SQL>
SQL>
SQL> -The IN operator used to test for long weekends.
SP2-0734: unknown command beginning "-The IN op..."- rest of line ignored.
SQL> SET SERVEROUTPUT ON
SQL> DECLARE
test_date DATE;
day_of_week VARCHAR2(3);
years_ahead INTEGER;
BEGIN
--Assign a date value to test_date.

test_date := TO_DATE('4-Jul-1997','dd-mon-yyyy');

FOR years_ahead IN 1..10 LOOP
day_of_week := TO_CHAR(test_date,'Dy');

IF day_of_week IN ('Mon','Fri','Sat','Sun') THEN
DBMS_OUTPUT.PUT_LINE(TO_CHAR(test_date,'dd-Mon-yyyy')|| ' A long weekend!');
ELSE
DBMS_OUTPUT.PUT_LINE(TO_CHAR(test_date,'dd-Mon-yyyy')|| ' Not a long weekend.');
END IF;
--Advance one year (12 months)
test_date := ADD_MONTHS(test_date,12);
END LOOP;
END;
/
04-Jul-1997 A long weekend!
04-Jul-1998 A long weekend!
```

```
04-Jul-1999 A long weekend!
04-Jul-2000 Not a long weekend.
04-Jul-2001 Not a long weekend.
04-Jul-2002 Not a long weekend.
04-Jul-2003 A long weekend!
04-Jul-2004 A long weekend!
04-Jul-2005 A long weekend!
04-Jul-2006 Not a long weekend.
PL/SQL procedure successfully completed.
SQL>
SQL>
SQL>
```

TABLES, VIEWS AND INDEXES

VIEWS AND INDEXES

Indexes are very important part of SQL Server database, indexes help database engine to find relevent rows faster. In SQL Server each table can have up to 249 nonclustered indexes. Up to 16 columns can be combined into a single index. All the columns in an index must be in the same table or view. The maximum allowable size of the combined index value can not exceed from 900 bytes. You can have only one clustered index on each table.

In SQL Server 2000 and 2005 you can query sysindexes and sys.sysindexes table and table view (in 2005 for backward compatibility) to get the list of all the indexes. Index keys are stored in sysindexkeys, many times you want to view indexes in your database. Here is a handy T-SQL scripts to find available indexes on each table.

Here is an easy way to find all the user defined indexes in a database.

```
Select
OBJECT_NAME( i.id ) AS [Table Name],

i.name AS [Index Name],

i.keycnt as [Total Keys],
```

```
i.rows as [Total Rows],
CASE INDEXPROPERTY( i.id , i.name , 'IsClustered')
WHEN 1 THEN 'YES' ELSE 'NO' END AS [Clustered Index],
Case Indexpoperty (i.id,i.name,'IsUnique') When 1 Then
'Yes' Else 'No' End As [Unique Index],
Stats_Date( i.id , i.indid ) AS [Date Last Updated]
FROM sysindexes AS i
Where Objectporperty ( i.id, 'IsMsshipped' ) = 0 And
Indexproperty ( i.id , i.name , 'IsStatistics') = 0 And
Indexproperty( i.id , i.name , 'IsAuto Statistics' ) = 0 And
Indexproperty( i.id , i.name , 'IsHypothetical') = 0 And
i.indid BETWEEN 1 And 250
Order By [Table Name], [Index Name]
```

To view clustered indexes or non-clustered indexes only you can change the query by adding another filter in WHERE clause. The following query will only display clustered indexes.

```
Select
Object_Name( i.id ) AS [Table Name],
i.name AS [Index Name],
i.keycnt as [Total Keys],
i.rows as [Total Rows],
Case Indexproperty( i.id , i.name , 'IsClustered') When 1
Then 'Yes' Elese 'No' End As [Clustered Index],
Case Indexproperty (i.id,i.name,'IsUnique') When 1 Then
'Yes' Else 'No' End As [Unique Index],
Sstats_Date( i.id , i.indid ) AS [Date Last Updated]
FROM sysindexes AS i
Where
Indexproperty ( i.id , i.name , 'IsClustered') = 1 And
Objectproperty ( i.id, 'IsMSShipped' ) = 0 And
Indexproperty ( i.id , i.name , 'IsStatistics') = 0 And
Indexproperty( i.id , i.name , 'IsAutoStatistics' ) = 0 And
Indexproperty( i.id , i.name , 'IsHypothetical') = 0 And
i.indid Between 1 And 250
```

In this excellent article Doug covers the basics of creating an Indexed View. He also goes into detail on sizing considerations and when and when not to use an Indexed

View. With SQL Server 2000, Microsoft has introduced the concept of Indexed Views, which can make your applications and queries run faster in the right circumstances.

INDEXED VIEWS

Views have been available throughout the history of Microsoft SQL Server. However, using views that return very large result sets can lead to poor performance, as the result set is not indexed and the entire result must be table scanned if the view is used in a join or a subquery of a T-SQL command. Additionally, products like Oracle have come out with the concept of a Materialized View that give an additional performance boost by being able to have indexes built on a view. So in the continuing evolution of the SQL Server product line and in response to Oracle's Materialized View, Microsoft SQL Server 2000 has a new feature called the View Index.

View Indexes give the product the capability to define an index on a view. Additionally, SQL Server View Indexes are dynamic in that changes to the data in the base tables are automatically reflected in the indexed view. Also the SQL Server query optimizer will try to use an indexed view even if the view is not referenced in the from clause of a T-SQL command. These features are not available in Oracle's Materialized Views.

BEFORE SQL SERVER 2000

Typically a view is thought of as a virtual table, or a stored query. The results of using a view are not permanently stored in the database. The data accessed through a view is actually constructed using standard T-SQL select command and can come from one to many different base tables or even other views.

This T-SQL select command is stored as a database object (a view). Developers can use the results from the view by referencing the view name in T-SQL statements the same way they would reference a real table. When referenced, the stored T-SQL that represents the view is merged with the referencing T-SQL code and executed to come up with the final results.

Views have additional benefits of:

- Views provide a security mechanism by subsetting the data by rows (All Active Customers, all customers in a certain state).
- Views provide a security mechanism by subsetting the data by columns (Payroll fields not shown in the Employee Phone List View).
- Views can simplify complex queries into a single reference. Complex Join operations that can make a normalized database design of several tables into a single row in the result set of the view. This is great for reporting tools like Crystal and Cognos.
- Views give us aggregation capabilities (Min, Max, Count, Sum) where the data is not stored but calculated.
- Views can create other calculated fields based on values in the real underlying tables.
- Views can reference another view as one its "Base Tables".
- Views can hide the complexity of partitioned data (Sales from 1998 are in the 1998 table, Sales from 1999 are in the 1999 table, Sales from 2000 are in the Current Table) .
- Views can be updateable in certain situations (only update to 1 of the base tables!).
- Views do not incur overhead of additional permanent storage.

SQL SERVER 2000 INDEXED VIEWS

Views in SQL Server 2000 are very similar to those in previous versions with a few major exceptions when using Indexed views. When a clustered index is created on the view, SQL Server immediately allocates storage space to store the results of the view. You can then treat the view like any other table by adding additional nonclustered indexes.

Requirements for Indexed views

There are several requirements that you must take into consideration when using Indexed views.

- View definition must always return the same results from the same underlying data.
- Views cannot use non-deterministic functions.
- The first index on a View must be a clustered, UNIQUE index.
- If you use Group By, you must include the new Count_Big(*) in the select list.
- View definition cannot contain the following
  - Top
  - Text, ntext or image columns
  - Distinct
  - Min, Max, Count, Stdev, Variance, Avg
  - SUM on a nullable expression
  - A derived table
  - Rowset function
  - Another view
  - UNION
  - Subqueries, outer joins, self joins
  - Full-text predicates like Contain or Freetext
  - Compute or Compute By
  - Cannot include order by in view definition

Notice that Indexed Views change the very essence of what a view was before this version of Sql Server. First, the data represented by the view is actually stored in the database. Secondly, the view definition must always return the same results for the same underlying data and all functions and expressions must be deterministic no matter what the current session settings.

To make sure that you can meet this requirement, the following session options must be set when you create an index view, when you modify any of the tables included in an indexed view or when the optimizer decides to use the indexed view as part of a query plan. Session Options that must be on

Ansi_Nulls
Ansi_Padding
Ansi_Warnings
Arithabort
Concat_Null_Yeilds_Null

Quoted_Identifiers
Session options that must be off
Numeric_Roundabort

Functions like GetDate(), rand() are non-deterministic because of different session settings can return different values and the settings for one user may not be the same as for another. The list of deterministic and non-deterministic functions will be included in the final version of Books Online for SQL Server 2000. (Look for topic Deterministic and Nondeterministic Functions in the Books Online)

Besides these restrictions, the underlying tables that make up the view must be protected from schema changes. Part of the syntax of the create view command is the "with SCHEMABINDING" phrase. This is required to create a View Index and this will prevent the dropping or altering of tables participating in an Indexed View. Note that dropping the clustered index of an Indexed View will return it to the standard SQL view as it was as described above in the section Before SQL Server 2000, what was a View?

Creating Indexed View

- Make sure that session properties are properly set.
- Create a deterministic view with new Schemabinding syntax.
- Create unique Clustered Index.
- Optionally, create additional nonclustered indexes.

Below you will find the code that you can paste into the Sql Server Query Analyzer to test this yourself. This example is based on the Northwind sample database.

```
Use the northwind database
USE NORTHWIND
GO
Make sure that all session settings are set
properly
IF sessionproperty('ARITHABORT')
= 0 SET ARITHABORT ON
IF sessionproperty('CONCAT_NULL_YIELDS_NULL')
= 0 SET CONCAT_NULL_YIELDS_NULL ON
```

```
IF sessionproperty('QUOTED_IDENTIFIER')
= 0 SET QUOTED_IDENTIFIER ON
IF sessionproperty('ANSI_NULLS')
= 0 SET ANSI_NULLS ON
IF sessionproperty('ANSI_PADDING')
= 0 SET ANSI_PADDING ON
IF sessionproperty('ANSI_WARNINGS')
= 0 SET ANSI_WARNINGS ON
IF sessionproperty('NUMERIC_ROUNDABORT')
= 1 SET NUMERIC_ROUNDABORT OFF
go
Create the view, it must comply with the rules
CREATE VIEW PRODUCTS_BY_CUSTOMER WITH
SCHEMABINDING AS
select customers.companyname,
products.productname,
sum(odetail.unitprice*odetail.quantity) as
TotalPurchase,
count_big(*) as cnt
from dbo."order details" as odetail
inner join dbo.orders as omain
on omain.orderid = odetail.orderid
INNER join dbo.customers as customers
on customers.customerid = omain.customerid
INNER join dbo.products as products
on products.productid = odetail.productid
group by
customers.companyname,
products.productname
go
the following statement will cause an error if
the view has not been
indexed
EXEC SP_SPACEUSED 'PRODUCTS_BY_CUSTOMER'
Server: Msg 15235, Level 16, State 1, Procedure
sp_spaceused, Line 91
Views do not have space allocated.
Check to see if the indexes can be created
```

```
if ObjectProperty(object_id ('products_by_
customer'),'IsIndexable') = 1
BEGIN
-- Create a clustered index, it MUST be unique
CREATE UNIQUE CLUSTERED INDEX
PRODUCTS_BY_CUSTOMER_UNIQUE ON
PRODUCTS_BY_CUSTOMER(COMPANYNAME, PRODUCTNAME)
EXEC SP_SPACEUSED 'PRODUCTS_BY_CUSTOMER'
Create NonClustered Indexes
CREATE INDEX PRODUCTS_BY_CUSTOMER_1 ON
PRODUCTS_BY_CUSTOMER(COMPANYNAME)
EXEC SP_SPACEUSED 'PRODUCTS_BY_CUSTOMER'
Create NonClustered Indexes
CREATE INDEX PRODUCTS_BY_CUSTOMER_2 ON
PRODUCTS_BY_CUSTOMER(PRODUCTNAME)
EXEC SP_SPACEUSED 'PRODUCTS_BY_CUSTOMER'
END
```

Object Property (object_id ('products_by_customer'), 'IsIndexable') = 1 in the above code listing. This command will tell you if all of the requirements for indexing a view have been met so that you can programmatically determine if a view can be indexed or not.

Also note that no space is allocated in the database for this view until the clustered index is created. If you try to use the SP_SPACEUSED stored procedure on a view that is not indexed, you get an error. The results of the SP_SPACEUSED commands that are sprinkled throughout the above code listing gives the following results on my test machine.

	# of Rows	Data	Index	Total Used
After Clustered Index Created	1685	168 kb	16 kb	184 kb
After NonClustered Index 1	1685	168 kb	168 kb	336 kb
After NonClustered Index 2	1685	168 kb	320 kb	488 kb

USING INDEXED VIEW

You can use the view like you would any other view. Also, the SQL Server query optimizer will attempt to use a View Index even if the view is not referenced in the from clause, although you can override this behaviour with the Expand Views hint. From the sample created in the above code example, you could use the view as follows

Example: select * from products_by_customer

Example above lets the query optimizer determine whether or not to use the view and its indexes or to use the base tables. Surprising on my test machine, this example uses the base tables, not the Indexed View. The query optimizer is a complex piece of technology but it isn't always perfect. Based on my testing with this sample data in the Northwind database, I had to use the (noexpand) hint seen in the next example to force the optimizer to use the View Index.

The speed of this on my test machine was about 3 times faster with 1685 records. By increasing the number of records in the base tables (orders 3000 records and order details 224,696 records), I found that the query optimizer did use the View Index without specifying the hint and the resulting query speeds where approximately 50 times faster. The # of records in the view, after adding all of these records in the base tables, was 1880 records. I conclude that the query optimizer with a small number of records in the base table (Orders had about 830 and order details had about 2155 records when I started) lean towards using the base tables instead of the View index. More testing would be needed to nail down the break even point but this just points out why the hints are still around and how much faster performance can be when the View Indexes are used.

USING VIEW INDEX

If you have an application that is a Data-Mart, Data-Mining or decision-support type application, you can improve performance with View Indexes.

Applications that do any of the following may benefit as well:

- Joins and aggregations of big tables
- Repeated patterns of queries
- Repeated aggregations on the same or overlapping sets of columns
- Repeated joins of the same tables on the same keys

Also, situations where you might consider de-normalizing a set of tables by storing aggregate information in the parent table may be good situations to consider creating an aggregate view on the child table and creating the appropriate View Index. In essence, the Indexed View replaces your de-normalized fields and all the work of keeping this de-normalized aggregate field up to date is taken care of by the database engine.

You obviously cannot use a View Index if you need to include syntax in the view definition that is not allowed. It seems to me that Top, Min, Max, Count, using another view, union, subqueiries and outer joins are serious restrictions that would disqualify a large number of views that I might want to optimize using the View Index.

Storage may also be a major consideration as the data in the view is physically and permanently stored not only in its base table, but in the clustered index of the View Index. Effectively, the data is stored twice, once in its base table and once in the clustered index of the Indexed View.

Also, On-Line Transaction Processing systems (OLTP) will actually suffer performance loss if you try to use View Indexes. Databases with frequent inserts, updates, deletes suffer as these commands must not only process the table, but any associated Indexed Views that the base table is participating in. Also, views that are simply subsets of rows or columns with no aggregation or computation provide no benefit over a standard SQL view or a T-SQL command directly against the base tables. This additional overhead to update the data in the clustered index of the view I believe is the reason that the clustered index must be unique for an Indexed view. It uses this unique value to quickly update the appropriate record in the Indexed View. Without a unique index, the processing for updating the Indexed View records could be unacceptably long.

PERFORMANCE BENEFITS

As I indicated earlier, I experienced query times 3 times quicker using the Indexed Views over the same query not using the Indexed Views on the sample data in the NorthWind database. With a much bigger data set and with the same database objects defined, I got query times as much as 50 times faster. Microsoft has reported performance improvements of 10 to 100 times with applications that access indexed views instead of base tables. I also experimented with using other queries that did not directly reference the Indexed View and got similar performance gains when the optimizer selected the Indexed View over other possible execution plans.

SQL SERVER VIEWS

Relational databases like SQL Server use indexes to find data quickly when a query is processed. Creating and removing indexes from a database schema will rarely result in changes to an application's code; indexes operate 'behind the scenes' in support of the database engine. However, creating the proper index can drastically increase the performance of an application.

The SQL Server engine uses an index in much the same way a reader uses a book index. For example, one way to find all references to INSERT statements in a SQL book would be to begin on page one and scan each page of the book. We could mark each time we find the word INSERT until we reach the end of the book. This approach is pretty time consuming and laborious. Alternately, we can also use the index in the back of the book to find a page number for each occurrence of the INSERT statements. This approach produces the same results as above, but with tremendous savings in time.

When a SQL Server has no index to use for searching, the result is similar to the reader who looks at every page in a book to find a word: the SQL engine needs to visit every row in a table. In database terminology we call this behaviour a table scan, or just scan. A table scan is not always a problem, and is sometimes unavoidable.

However, as a table grows to thousands of rows and then millions of rows and beyond, scans become correspondingly slower and more expensive. Consider the following query on the Products table of the Northwind database. This query retrieves products in a specific price range.

```
SELECT ProductID, ProductName, UnitPrice
FROM Products WHERE (UnitPrice > 12.5) AND
(UnitPrice < 14)
```

There is currently no index on the Product table to help this query, so the database engine performs a scan and examines each record to see if UnitPrice falls between 12.5 and 14. In the diagram below, the database search touches a total of 77 records to find just three matches.

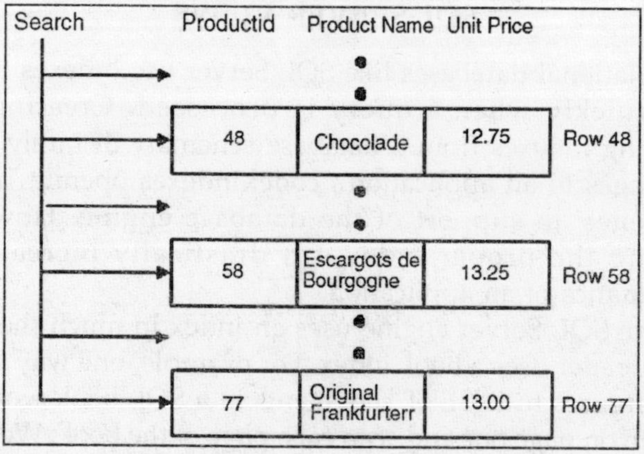

Now imagine if we created an index, just like a book index, on the data in the UnitPrice column. Each index entry would contain a copy of the UnitPrice value for a row, and a reference (just like a page number) to the row where the value originated. SQL will sort these index entries into ascending order. The index will allow the database to quickly narrow in on the three rows to satisfy the query, and avoid scanning every row in the table.

CREATE AN INDEX

Having a data connection in the Server Explorer view of Visual Studio.

Net allows us to easily create new indexes:

- Navigate to the Products table of the Northwind database.
- Right click the table and select Design Table from the context menu.

- With the design screen in focus, click the Indexes/ Keys item on the View menu of the IDE.

This should bring you to the following tabbed dialog box.

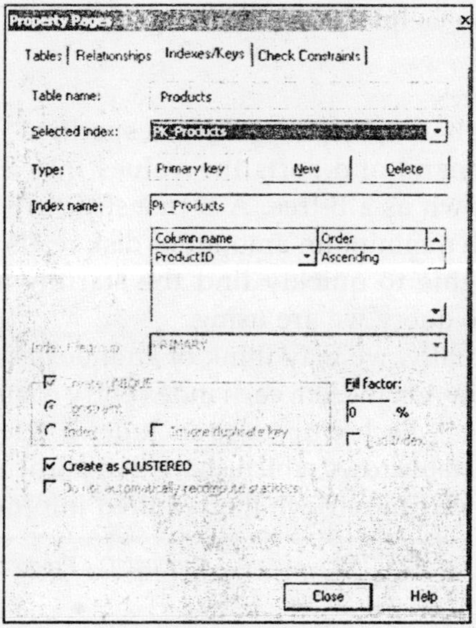

The dialog is currently displaying an existing index on the Products table: the PK_Products index. We will see later in this chapter how primary key fields are automatically indexed to enforce uniqueness in the key values.

- In the above dialog click on the New button, and in the Index name text box, replace the existing entry with IDX_UnitPrice.
- Beneath the text box is a control where we set the columns to index. Pull down the entry with ProductID and select the UnitPrice column instead.
- Leave all of the other options with default settings.
- Close the dialog and the table design view, making sure to save all of the changes when prompted to do so. The IDE will then issue the commands to create the new index.

We can create the same index using the following SQL. The command specifies the name of the index (IDX_UnitPrice), the table name (Products), and the column to index (UnitPrice).

Create Index [IDX_UnitPrice] ON Products (UnitPrice)

To verify that the index is created, use the following stored procedure to see a list of all indexes on the Products table:

EXEC sp_helpindex Customers

Working

The database takes the columns specified in a CREATE INDEX command and sorts the values into a special data structure known as a B-tree. A B-tree structure supports fast searches with a minimum amount of disk reads, allowing the database engine to quickly find the starting and stopping points for the query we are using.

Conceptually, we may think of an index as shown in the diagram below. On the left, each index entry contains the index key (UnitPrice). Each entry also includes a reference (which points) to the table rows which share that particular value and from which we can retrieve the required information.

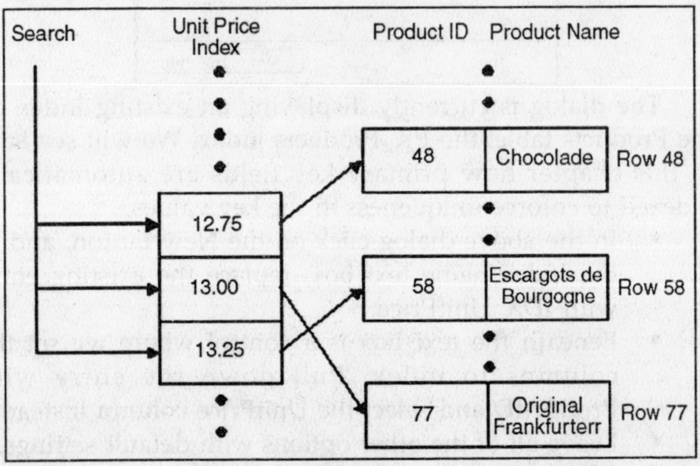

Much like the index in the back of a book helps us to find keywords quickly, so the database is able to quickly narrow the number of records it must examine to a minimum by using the sorted list of UnitPrice values stored in the index. We have avoided a table scan to fetch the query results. Given this sketch of how indexes work, lets examine some of the scenarios where indexes offer a benefit.

ADVANTAGE OF INDEXES

The database engine can use indexes to boost performance in a number of different queries. Sometimes these performance improvements are dramatic. An important feature of SQL Server 2000 is a component known as the query optimizer. The query optimizer's job is to find the fastest and least resource intensive means of executing incoming queries. An important part of this job is selecting the best index or indexes to perform the task. In the following sections we will examine the types of queries with the best chance of benefiting from an index.

Searching For Records

The most obvious use for an index is in finding a record or set of records matching a WHERE clause. Indexes can aid queries looking for values inside of a range (as we demonstrated earlier), as well as queries looking for a specific value. By way of example, the following queries can all benefit from an index on UnitPrice:

Delete From Products Where UnitPrice = 1
Update Products Set Discontinued = 1 Where Unit Price > 15
Select * From Products Where Unit Price Betweeb 14 AND 16

Indexes work just as well when searching for a record in Delete and Update commands as they do for Select statements.

Sorting Records

When we ask for a sorted dataset, the database will try to find an index and avoid sorting the results during execution of the query. We control sorting of a dataset by specifying a field, or fields, in an Oorder BY clause, with the sort order as ASC (ascending) or DESC (descending). For example, the following query returns all products sorted by price:

Select * From Products Order BY Unit Price ASC

With no index, the database will scan the Products table and sort the rows to process the query. However, the index we created on UnitPrice (IDX_UnitPrice) earlier provides the database with a presorted list of prices. The database can simply scan the index from the first entry to the last entry and retrieve the rows in sorted order.

The same index works equally well with the following query, simply by scanning the index in reverse.

Grouping Records

We can use a Group BY clause to group records and aggregate values, for example, counting the number of orders placed by a customer. To process a query with a Group By clause, the database will often sort the results on the columns included in the GROUP BY. The following query counts the number of products at each price by grouping together records with the same UnitPrice value.

SELECT Count(*), UnitPrice FROM Products GROUP BY UnitPrice

The database can use the IDX_UnitPrice index to retrieve the prices in order. Since matching prices appear in consecutive index entries, the database is able count the number of products at each price quickly. Indexing a field used in a GROUP BY clause can often speed up a query.

Maintaining a Unique Column

Columns requiring unique values (such as primary key columns) must have a unique index applied. There are several methods available to create a unique index. Marking a column as a primary key will automatically create a unique index on the column. We can also create a unique index by checking the Create UNIQUE checkbox in the dialog shown earlier. The screen shot of the dialog displayed the index used to enforce the primary key of the Products table. In this case, the Create UNIQUE checkbox is disabled, since an index to enforce a primary key must be a unique index. However, creating new indexes not used to enforce primary keys will allow us to select the Create UNIQUE checkbox. We can also create a unique index using SQL with the following command:

CREATE UNIQUE INDEX IDX_ProductName On Products (ProductName)

The above SQL command will not allow any duplicate values in the ProductName column, and an index is the best tool for the database to use to enforce this rule. Each time an application adds or modifies a row in the table, the database needs to search all existing records to ensure none of values in the new data duplicate existing values. Indexes, as we should know by now, will improve this search time.

Index Drawbacks

There are tradeoffs to almost any feature in computer programming, and indexes are no exception. While indexes provide a substantial performance benefit to searches, there is also a downside to indexing. Let's talk about some of those drawbacks now.

Indexes and Disk Space

Indexes are stored on the disk, and the amount of space required will depend on the size of the table, and the number and types of columns used in the index. Disk space is generally cheap enough to trade for application performance, particularly when a database serves a large number of users. To see the space required for a table, use the sp_spaceused system stored procedure in a query window.

```
EXEC sp_spaceused Orders
```

Given a table name (Orders), the procedure will return the amount of space used by the data and all indexes associated with the table, like so:

```
Name rows reserved data index_size unused
------- -------- ---------- ------ ---------- -------
Orders 830 504 KB 160 KB 320 KB 24 KB
```

According to the output above, the table data uses 160 kilobytes, while the table indexes use twice as much, or 320 kilobytes. The ratio of index size to table size can vary greatly, depending on the columns, data types, and number of indexes on a table.

Indexes and Data Modification

Another downside to using an index is the performance implication on data modification statements. Any time a query modifies the data in a table (INSERT, UPDATE, or DELETE), the database needs to update all of the indexes where data has changed. As we discussed earlier, indexing can help the database during data modification statements by allowing the database to quickly locate the records to modify, however, we now caveat the discussion with the understanding that providing too many indexes to update can actually hurt the performance of data modifications. This leads to a delicate balancing act when tuning the database for performance.

In decision support systems and data warehouses, where information is stored for reporting purposes, data remains relatively static and report generating queries outnumber data modification queries. In these types of environments, heavy indexing is commonplace in order to optimize the reports generated. In contrast, a database used for transaction processing will see many records added and updated. These types of databases will use fewer indexes to allow for higher throughput on inserts and updates.

Every application is unique, and finding the best indexes to use for a specific application usually requires some help from the optimization tools offered by many database vendors. SQL Server 2000 and Access include the Profiler and Index Tuning Wizard tools to help tweak performance.

Now we have enough information to understand why indexes are useful and where indexes are best applied. It is time now to look at the different options available when creating an index and then address some common rules of thumb to use when planning the indexes for your database.

CLUSTERED INDEXES

Earlier in the article we made an analogy between a database index and the index of a book. A book index stores words in order with a reference to the page numbers where the word is located. This type of index for a database is a nonclustered index; only the index key and a reference are stored. In contrast, a common analogy for a clustered index is a phone book. A phone book still sorts entries into alphabetical order. The difference is, once we find a name in a phone book, we have immediate access to the rest of the data for the name, such as the phone number and address.

For a clustered index, the database will sort the table's records according to the column (or columns) specified by the index. A clustered index contains all of the data for a table in the index, sorted by the index key, just like a phone book is sorted by name and contains all of the information for the person inline. The nonclustered indexes created earlier in the chapter contain only the index key and a reference to find the data, which is more like a book index. You can only create one clustered index on each table.

In the diagram below we have a search using a clustered index on the UnitPrice column of the Products table. Compare this diagram to the previous diagram with a regular index on UnitPrice. Although we are only showing three columns from the Products table, all of the columns are present and notice the rows are sorted into the order of the index, there is no reference to follow from the index back to the data.

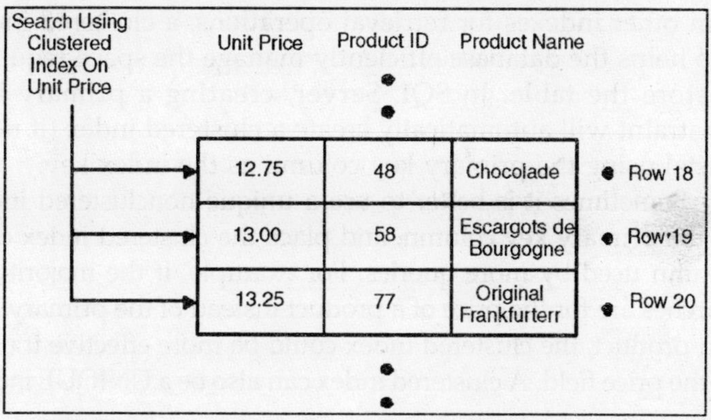

A clustered index is the most important index you can apply to a table. If the database engine can use a clustered index during a query, the database does not need to follow references back to the rest of\ the data, as happens with a nonclustered index. The result is less work for the database, and consequently, better performance for a query using a clustered index.

To create a clustered index, simply select the Create As CLUSTERED checkbox in the dialog box we used at the beginning of the chapter. The SQL syntax for a clustered index simply adds a new keyword to the CREATE INDEX command, as shown below:

CREATE CLUSTERED INDEX IDX_SupplierID ON Products(SupplierID)

Most of the tables in the Northwind database already have a clustered index defined on a table. Since we can only have one clustered index per table, and the Products table already has a clustered index (PK_Products) on the primary key (ProductId), the above command should generate the following error:

Cannot create more than one clustered index on table 'Products'. Drop the existing clustered index 'PK_Products' before creating another.

As a general rule of thumb, every table should have a clustered index. If you create only one index for a table, use a clustered index. Not only is a clustered index more efficient than other indexes for retrieval operations, a clustered index also helps the database efficiently manage the space required to store the table. In SQL Server, creating a primary key constraint will automatically create a clustered index (if none exists) using the primary key column as the index key.

Sometimes it is better to use a unique nonclustered index on the primary key column, and place the clustered index on a column used by more queries. For example, if the majority of searches are for the price of a product instead of the primary key of a product, the clustered index could be more effective if used on the price field. A clustered index can also be a UNIQUE index.

Disadvantage of Clustered Indexes

If we update a record and change the value of an indexed column in a clustered index, the database might need to move the entire row into a new position to keep the rows in sorted order. This behaviour essentially turns an update query into a DELETE followed by an INSERT, with an obvious decrease in performance. A table's clustered index can often be found on the primary key or a foreign key column, because key values generally do not change once a record is inserted into the database.

COMPOSITE INDEXES

A composite index is an index on two or more columns. Both clustered and nonclustered indexes can be composite indexes. Composite indexes are especially useful in two different circumstances. First, you can use a composite index to cover a query. Secondly, you can use a composite index to help match the search criteria of specific queries. We will go onto more detail and give examples of these two areas in the following sections.

Covering Queries with Index

Earlier in the article we discussed how an index, specifically a nonclustered index, contains only the key values and a reference to find the associated row of data. However, if the key value contains all of the information needed to process a query, the database never has to follow the reference and find the row; it can simply retrieve the information from the index and save processing time. This is always a benefit for clustered indexes.

As an example, consider the index we created on the Products table for UnitPrice. The database copied the values from the UnitPrice column and sorted them into an index. If we execute the following query, the database can retrieve all of the information for the query from the index itself.

SELECT UnitPrice FROM Products ORDER BY UnitPrice

We call these types of queries covered queries, because all of the columns requested in the output are contained in the index itself. A clustered index, if selected for use by the query optimizer, always covers a query, since it contains all of the data in a table.

For the following query, there are no covering indexes on the Products table.

SELECT ProductName, UnitPrice FROM Products ORDER BY UnitPrice

This is because although the database will use the index on UnitPrice to avoid sorting records, it will need to follow the reference in each index entry to find the associated row and retrieve the product name. By creating a composite index on two columns (ProductName and UnitPrice), we can cover this query with the new index.

Matching Complex Search Criteria

For another way to use composite indexes, let's take a look at the OrderDetails table of Northwind. There are two key values in the table (OrderID and ProductID); these are foreign keys, referencing the Orders and Products tables respectively. There is no column dedicated for use as a primary key; instead, the primary key is the combination of the columns OrderID and ProductID.

The primary key constraint on these columns will generate a composite index, which is unique of course. The command the database would use to create the index looks something like the following:

```
CREATE UNIQUE CLUSTERED INDEX PK_Order _
Details
    ON [Order Details] (OrderID, ProductID)
```

The order in which columns appear in a CREATE INDEX statement is significant. The primary sort order for this index is OrderID. When the OrderID is the same for two or more records, the database will sort this subset of records on ProductID.

The order of columns determines how useful the index is for a query. Consider the phone book sorted by last name then first name. The phone book makes it easy to find all of the listings with a last name of Smith, or all of the listings with a last name of Jones and a first name of Lisa, but it is difficult to find all listings with a first name of Gary without scanning the book page by page.

Likewise, the composite index on Order Details is useful in the following two queries:

```
SELECT * FROM [Order Details] WHERE OrderID = 11077
SELECT * FROM [Order Details] WHERE OrderID = 11077
AND ProductID = 13
```

However, the following query cannot take advantage of the index we created since ProductID is the second part of the index key, just like the first name field in a phone book.

```
SELECT * FROM [Order Details] WHERE ProductID = 13
```

In this case, ProductID is a primary key, however, so an index does exist on the ProductID column for the database to use for this query.

Suppose the following query is the most popular query executed by our application, and we decided we needed to tune the database to support it.

```
SELECT ProductName, UnitPrice FROM Products
ORDER BY UnitPrice
```

We could create the following index to cover the query. Notice we have specified two columns for the index: UnitPrice and ProductName (making the index a composite index):

```
CREATE INDEX IX_UnitPrice_ProductName ON
Products(UnitPrice, ProductName)
```

While covered queries can provide a performance benefit, remember there is a price to pay for each index we add to a table, and we can also never cover every query in a non-trivial application.

Additional Index Guidelines

Choosing the correct columns and types for an index is another important step in creating an effective index. In this section, we will talk about two main points, namely short index keys and selective indexes (we'll explain what selective indexes are in just a moment).

Keep Index Keys Short

The larger an index key is, the harder a database has to work to use the index. For instance, an integer key is smaller in size then a character field for holding 100 characters. In particular, keep clustered indexes as short as possible.

There are several approaches to keeping an index key short. First, try to limit the index to as few columns as possible. While composite indexes are useful and can sometimes optimize a query, they are also larger and cause more disk reads for the database. Secondly, try to choose a compact data type for an index column, based on the number of bytes required for each data type. Integer keys are small and easy for the database to compare. In contrast, strings require a character-by-character comparison. As a rule of thumb, try to avoid using character columns in an index, particularly primary key indexes. Integer columns will always have an advantage over character fields in ability to boost the performance of a query.

Distinct Index Keys

The most effective indexes are the indexes with a small percentage of duplicated values. Think of having a phone book for a city where 75% of the population has the last name of Smith. A phone book in this area might be easier to use if the entries were sorted by the resident's first names instead. A good index will allow the database to disregard as many records as possible during a search.

An index with a high percentage of unique values is a selective index. Obviously, a unique index is the most selective index of all, because there are no duplicate values. SQL Server will track statistics for indexes and will know how selective each index is. The query optimizer utilizes these statistics when selecting the best index to use for a query.

Maintaining Indexes

In addition to creating an index, we'll need to view existing indexes, and sometimes delete or rename them. This is part of the ongoing maintenance cycle of a database as the schema changes, or even naming conventions change.

View Existing Indexes

A list of all indexes on a table is available in the dialog box we used to create an index. Click on the Selected index drop down control and scroll through the available indexes. There is also a stored procedure named sp_helpindex.

This stored procedure gives all of the indexes for a table, along with all of the relevant attributes. The only input parameter to the procedure is the name of the table, as shown below.

```
EXEC sp_helpindex Customers
```

RENAME AN INDEX

We can also rename any user created object with the sp_rename stored procedure, including indexes. The sp_rename procedure takes, at a minimum, the current name of the object and the new name for the object. For indexes, the current name must include the name of the table, a dot separator, and the name of the index, as shown below:

```
EXEC sp_rename 'Products.IX_UnitPrice', 'IX_Price'
```

This will change the name of the IX_UnitPrice index to IX_Price.

Delete an Index

It is a good idea to remove an index from the database if the index is not providing any benefit. For instance, if we know the queries in an application are no longer searching for records on a particular column, we can remove the index. Unneeded indexes only take up storage space and diminish the performance of modifications. You can remove most indexes with the Delete button on the index dialog box, which we saw earlier. The equivalent SQL command is shown below.

```
DROP Index Products.IX_Price
```

Again, we need to use the name of the table and the name of the index, with a dot separator. Some indexes are not so easy to drop, namely any index supporting a unique or primary key constraint. For example, the following command tries to drop the PK_Products index of the Products table.

```
DROP INDEX Products.PK_Products
```

Since the database uses PK_Products to enforce a primary key constraint on the Products table, the above command should produce the following error.

An explicit DROP INDEX is not allowed on index 'Products.PK_Products'.

It is being used for PRIMARY KEY constraint enforcement.

Removing a primary key constraint from a table is a redesign of the table, and requires careful thought. It makes sense to know the only way to achieve this task is to either drop the table and use a CREATE TABLE command to recreate the table without the index, or to use the ALTER TABLE command.

VIEWING USEFUL TABLE

In DB2 9 there is a new administrative view called SYSIBMADM.ADMINTABINFO that can provide you with an easy way to find some useful information about your tables. For example you can easily see the size of the table object, the size of indexes on that table, the size of any LONG or LOB objects and the size of any storage for pureXML data types. As well you can see if there are any indexes on a table that still have a type 1 index on them, if tables are using large rids or large slots, or if any utility (like reorg, load, etc) are currently executing on the table.

Here are a few sample queries on this administrative view.

1. Show me the size of all tables in the EATON schema. Note that the values for object size are automatically displayed in KB.

```
SELECT SUBSTR (TABSCHEMA,1,10) AS SCHEMA,
  SUBSTR(TABNAME,1,15) AS TABNAME,
  INT(DATA_OBJECT_P_SIZE) AS OBJ_SZ_KB,
  INT(INDEX_OBJECT_P_SIZE) AS INX_SZ_KB,
  INT(XML_OBJECT_P_SIZE) AS XML_SZ_KB
  FROM SYSIBMADM.ADMINTABINFO
  WHERE TABSCHEMA='EATON'
  ORDER BY 3 DESC
```

A truncated result set is below:

SCHEMA	TABNAME	OBJ_SZ_KB	INX_SZ_KB	XML_SZ_KB
EATON	EMPMDC	1792	256	0
EATON	CL_SCHED	256	0	0
EATON	DEPARTMENT	256	256	0
EATON	EMPLOYEE	256	256	0
EATON	EMP_PHOTO	256	256	0
EATON	EMP_RESUME	256	256	0
EATON	CATALOG	256	256	256
EATON	ADEFUSR	256	0	0
EATON	PRODUCT	256	256	512
EATON	INVENTORY	256	256	0

```
EATON  CUSTOMER    256          256          512
```

2. Display the sum of all objects by schema

```
SELECT SUBSTR(TABSCHEMA,1,10) AS SCHEMA,
 SUM(DATA_OBJECT_P_SIZE) AS OBJ_SZ_KB,
 SUM(INDEX_OBJECT_P_SIZE) AS INX_SZ_KB,
 SUM(XML_OBJECT_P_SIZE) AS XML_SZ_KB
 FROM SYSIBMADM.ADMINTABINFO
 GROUP BY TABSCHEMA
 ORDER BY 2 DESC
SCHEMA    OBJ_SZ_KB   INX_SZ_KB        ML_SZ_KB
---------- ---------- ---------- ----------
EATON     10752        6400             1792
SYSIBM    7600         7728             400
SYSTOOLS 176           112              0
```

3. Display any tables that still have a type 1 index on them.

```
SELECT TABSCHEMA, TABNAME
 FROM SYSIBMADM.ADMINTABINFO
 WHERE INDEX_TYPE = 1
```

QUERIES AND SUB QUERIES

OVERVIEW

A query is an operation that retrieves data from one or more tables or views. In this reference, a top-level SELECT statement is called a query, and a query nested within another SQL statement is called a subquery. This chapter describes some types of queries and subqueries and how to use them. The top level of the syntax is shown in this chapter.

SELECT for the full syntax of all the clauses and the semantics of the keywords and parameters

select::=

Text description of select subquery.

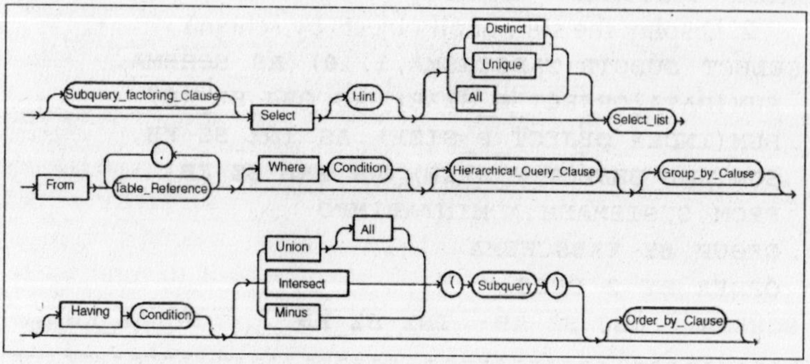

CREATING SIMPLE QUERIES

The list of expressions that appears after the SELECT keyword and before the FROM clause is called the select list. Within the select list, you specify one or more columns in the set of rows you want Oracle to return from one or more tables, views, or materialized views. The number of columns, as well as their datatype and length, are determined by the elements of the select list. If two or more tables have some column names in common, then you must qualify column names with names of tables. Otherwise, fully qualified column names are optional. However, it is always a good idea to qualify table and column references explicitly. Oracle often does less work with fully qualified table and column names.

You can use a column alias, c_alias, to label the preceding expression in the select list so that the column is displayed with a new heading. The alias effectively renames the select list item for the duration of the query. The alias can be used in the ORDER BY clause, but not other clauses in the query.

You can use comments in a SELECT statement to pass instructions, or hints, to the Oracle optimizer. The optimizer uses hints to choose an execution plan for the statement.

HIERARCHICAL QUERIES

If a table contains hierarchical data, then you can select rows in a hierarchical order using the hierarchical query clause:

hierarchical_query_clause::=

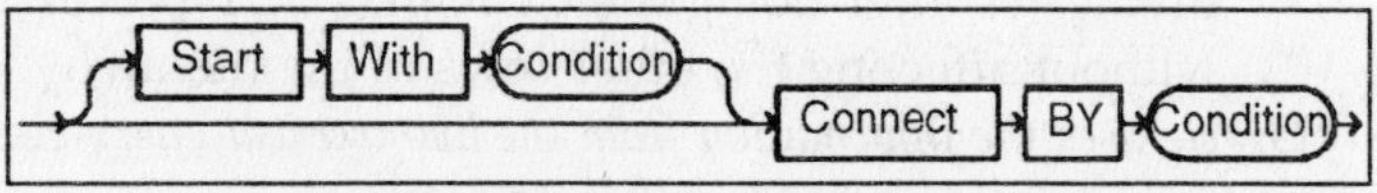

Text description of hierarchical_query_clause

- Start With specifies the root row(s) of the hierarchy.
- Connect By specifies the relationship between parent rows and child rows of the hierarchy. In a hierarchical query, one expression in condition must be qualified with the PRIOR operator to refer to the parent row. For example,
- ... Prior expr = expr
- or
- ... expr = PRIOR expr

If the Connect By condition is compound, then only one condition requires the PRIOR operator. For example: Connect By last_name != 'King' And Prior employee_id = manager_id

In addition, the Connect BY condition cannot contain a subquery. Prior is a unary operator and has the same precedence as the unary + and - arithmetic operators. It evaluates the immediately following expression for the parent row of the current row in a hierarchical query.

PRIOR is most commonly used when comparing column values with the equality operator. (The PRIOR keyword can be on either side of the operator.) PRIORcauses Oracle to use the value of the parent row in the column. Operators other than the equal sign (=) are theoretically possible in CONNECT BY clauses. However, the conditions created by these other operators can result in an infinite loop through the possible combinations. In this case Oracle detects the loop at run time and returns an error. The manner in which Oracle processes a WHERE clause (if any) in a hierarchical query depends on whether the WHERE clause contains a join:

- If the WHERE predicate contains a join, Oracle applies the join predicates before doing the CONNECT BY processing.
- If the WHERE clause does not contain a join, Oracle applies all predicates other than the CONNECT BY

predicates after doing the CONNECT BY processing without affecting the other rows of the hierarchy.

Oracle uses the information from the hierarchical query clause to form the hierarchy using the following steps:

- Oracle processes the WHERE clause either before or after the CONNECT BY clause depending on whether the WHERE clause contains any join predicates (as described in the preceding bullet list).
- Oracle selects the root row(s) of the hierarchy--those rows that satisfy the START WITH condition.
- Oracle selects the child rows of each root row. Each child row must satisfy the condition of the CONNECT BY condition with respect to one of the root rows.
- Oracle selects successive generations of child rows. Oracle first selects the children of the rows returned in step 3, and then the children of those children, and so on. Oracle always selects children by evaluating the CONNECT BY condition with respect to a current parent row.
- If the query contains a WHERE clause without a join, then Oracle eliminates all rows from the hierarchy that do not satisfy the condition of the WHERE clause. Oracle evaluates this condition for each row individually, rather than removing all the children of a row that does not satisfy the condition.
- Oracle returns the rows in the order shown in Figure. In the diagram, children appear below their parents. For an explanation of hierarchical trees, "Hierarchical Tree".

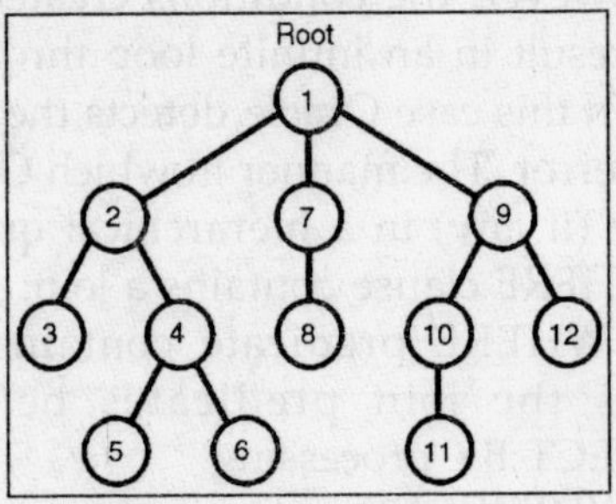

Fig. Hierarchical Queries

Text description of the illustration queries4.gif To find the children of a parent row, Oracle evaluates the PRIOR expression of the CONNECT BY condition for the parent row and the other expression for each row in the table. Rows for which the condition is true are the children of the parent. The CONNECT BY condition can contain other conditions to further filter the rows selected by the query. The CONNECT BY condition cannot contain a subquery.

If the CONNECT BY condition results in a loop in the hierarchy, then Oracle returns an error. A loop occurs if one row is both the parent (or grandparent or direct ancestor) and a child (or a grandchild or a direct descendent) of another row.

Note: In a hierarchical query, do not specify either ORDER BY or GROUP BY, as they will destroy the hierarchical order of the CONNECT BYresults. If you want to order rows of siblings of the same parent, then use the ORDER SIBLINGS BY clause

Examples

The following hierarchical query uses the CONNECT BY clause to define the relationship between employees and managers:

```
SELECT employee_id, last_name, manager_id
 FROM employees
 CONNECT BY PRIOR employee_id = manager_id;

EMPLOYEE_ID LAST_NAME            MANAGER_ID
----------- -------------------- ----------
 101  Kochhar                     100
 108  Greenberg                   101
 109  Faviet                      108
 110  Chen                        108
 111  Sciarra                     108
 112  Urman                       108
 113  Popp                        108
 200  Whalen                      101
.
.
.
```

The next example is similar to the preceding example, but uses the LEVEL pseudocolumn to show parent and child rows:

```
SELECT employee_id, last_name, manager_id, LEVEL
  FROM employees
  CONNECT BY PRIOR employee_id = manager_id;
EMPLOYEE_ID LAST_NAME   MANAGER_ID    LEVEL
----------- ---------------------- ----------
  101 Kochhar           100            1
  108 Greenberg         101            2
  109 Faviet            108            3
  110 Chen              108            3
  111 Sciarra           108            3
  112 Urman             108            3
  113 Popp              108            3
```

UNION, INTERSECT, MINUS OPERATORS

You can combine multiple queries using the set operators UNION, UNION ALL, INTERSECT, and MINUS. All set operators have equal precedence. If a SQL statement contains multiple set operators, then Oracle evaluates them from the left to right if no parentheses explicitly specify another order.

The corresponding expressions in the select lists of the component queries of a compound query must match in number and datatype. If component queries select character data, then the datatype of the return values are determined as follows:

- If both queries select values of datatype Char, then the returned values have datatype CHAR.
- If either or both of the queries select values of datatype Varchar2, then the returned values have datatype Varchar2.

Restrictions on Set Operators

- The set operators are not valid on columns of type BLOB, CLOB, BFILE, VARRAY, or nested table.
- The UNION, INTERSECT, and MINUS operators are not valid on LONG columns.
- If the select list preceding the set operator contains

an expression,then you must provide a column alias for the expression in order to refer to it in theorder_by_clause.

- You cannot also specify the for_update_clause with these set operators.
- You cannot specify the order_by_clause in the subquery of these operators.
- You cannot use these operators in SELECT statements containing TABLE collection expressions.

Note

To comply with emerging SQL standards, a future release of Oracle will give the INTERSECT operator greater precedence than the other set operators. Therefore, you should use parentheses to specify order of evaluation in queries that use theINTERSECT operator with other set operators.

The following examples combine the two query results with each of the set operators.

UNION Example

The following statement combines the results with the UNION operator, which eliminates duplicate selected rows. This statement shows that you must match datatype (using the TO_CHAR function) when columns do not exist in one or the other table:

```
SELECT location_id, department_name "Department",
  TO_CHAR(NULL) "Warehouse" FROM departments
  UNION
  SELECT location_id, TO_CHAR(NULL) "Department",
warehouse_name
  FROM warehouses;
LOCATION_ID Department   Warehouse
----------- ----------- -----------------
  1400 IT
  1400                  Southlake, Texas
  1500                  Shipping
  1500                  San Francisco
  1600                  New Jersey
```

```
1700                          Accounting
1700                          Administration
1700                          Benefits
1700                          Construction
```

More Example

The UNION operator returns only distinct rows that appear in either result, while the UNION ALL operator returns all rows.

The Union All operator does not eliminate duplicate selected rows:

```
SELECT product_id FROM order_items
UNION
SELECT product_id FROM inventories;
SELECT location_id FROM locations
UNION ALL
SELECT location_id FROM departments;
```

A location_id value that appears multiple times in either or both queries (such as '1700') is returned only once by the UNION operator, but multiple times by theUNION ALL operator.

INTERSECT Example

The following statement combines the results with the INTERSECT operator, which returns only those rows returned by both queries:

```
SELECT product_id FROM inventories
INTERSECT
SELECT product_id FROM order_items;
```

MINUS Example

The following statement combines results with the MINUS operator, which returns only rows returned by the first query but not by the second:

```
SELECT product_id FROM inventories
MINUS
SELECT product_id FROM order_items;
```

Sorting Query Results

Use the ORDER BY clause to order the rows selected by a query.

Sorting by position is useful in the following cases:

- To order by a lengthy select list expression, you can specify its position, rather than duplicate the entire expression, in the ORDER BY clause.
- For compound queries (containing set operators UNION, INTERSECT, MINUS, or UNION ALL), the ORDER BY clause must use positions, rather than explicit expressions. Also, the ORDER BY clause can appear only in the last component query. The ORDER BY clause orders all rows returned by the entire compound query.

The mechanism by which Oracle sorts values for the ORDER BY clause is specified either explicitly by the NLS_SORT initialization parameter or implicitly by theNLS_LANGUAGE initialization parameter. You can change the sort mechanism dynamically from one linguistic sort sequence to another using the ALTER SESSIONstatement. You can also specify a specific sort sequence for a single query by using the NLSSORT function with the NLS_SORT parameter in the ORDER BY clause.

Joins

A join is a query that combines rows from two or more tables, views, or materialized views. Oracle performs a join whenever multiple tables appear in the query'sFROM clause. The query's select list can select any columns from any of these tables. If any two of these tables have a column name in common, then you must qualify all references to these columns throughout the query with table names to avoid ambiguity.

Join Conditions

Most join queries contain WHERE clause conditions that compare two columns, each from a different table. Such a condition is called a join condition. To execute a join, Oracle combines pairs of rows, each containing one row from each table, for which the join condition evaluates to TRUE. The columns in the join conditions need not also appear in the select list. To execute a join of three or more tables, Oracle first joins two of the tables based on the join conditions comparing their columns and then joins the result to another table based on join conditions containing columns of the joined tables and the new table. Oracle continues this process until all tables are joined into the result. The optimizer determines the order in which Oracle joins tables based on the join conditions, indexes on the tables, and, in the case of the cost-based optimization approach, statistics for the tables.

In addition to join conditions, the WHERE clause of a join query can also contain other conditions that refer to columns of only one table. These conditions can further restrict the rows returned by the join query.

Equijoins

An equijoin is a join with a join condition containing an equality operator. An equijoin combines rows that have equivalent values for the specified columns. Depending on the internal algorithm the optimizer chooses to execute the join, the total size of the columns in the equijoin condition in a single table may be limited to the size of a data block minus some overhead. The size of a data block is specified by the initialization parameter DB_BLOCK_SIZE.

Self Joins

A self join is a join of a table to itself. This table appears twice in the FROM clause and is followed by table aliases that qualify column names in the join condition. To perform a self join, Oracle combines and returns rows of the table that satisfy the join condition.

Cartesian Products

If two tables in a join query have no join condition, then Oracle returns their Cartesian product. Oracle combines each row of one table with each row of the other. A Cartesian product always generates many rows and is rarely useful. For example, the Cartesian product of two tables, each with 100 rows, has 10,000 rows. Always include a join condition unless you specifically need a Cartesian product. If a query joins three or more tables and you do not specify a join condition for a specific pair, then the optimizer may choose a join order that avoids producing an intermediate Cartesian product.

Inner Joins

An inner join (sometimes called a "simple join") is a join of two or more tables that returns only those rows that satisfy the join condition.

Outer Joins

An outer join extends the result of a simple join. An outer join returns all rows that satisfy the join condition and also returns some or all of those rows from one table for which no rows from the other satisfy the join condition.

- To write a query that performs an outer join of tables A and B and returns all rows from A (a left outer join), use the LEFT [OUTER] JOIN syntax in the FROMclause, or apply the outer join operator (+) to all columns of B in the join condition in the WHERE clause. For all rows in A that have no matching rows in B, Oracle returns null for any select list expressions containing columns of B.
- To write a query that performs an outer join of tables A and B and returns all rows from B (a right outer join), use the RIGHT [OUTER] JOIN syntax in theFROM clause, or apply the outer join operator (+) to all columns of A in the join condition in the WHERE clause. For all rows in B that have no matching rows in A, Oracle returns null for any select list expressions containing columns of A.
- To write a query that performs an outer join and returns all rows from A and B, extended with nulls if they do not satisfy the join condition (a full outer join), use the FULL [OUTER] JOIN syntax in the FROM clause.

Oracle Corporation recommends that you use the FROM clause OUTER JOIN syntax rather than the Oracle join operator. Outer join queries that use the Oracle join operator (+) are subject to the following rules and restrictions, which do not apply to the FROM clause join syntax:

- You cannot specify the (+) operator in a query block that also contains FROM clause join syntax.
- The (+) operator can appear only in the WHERE clause or, in the context of left-correlation (that is, when specifying the TABLE clause) in the FROM clause, and can be applied only to a column of a table or view.
- If A and B are joined by multiple join conditions, then you must use the (+) operator in all of these conditions. If you do not, then Oracle will return only the rows resulting from a simple join, but without a warning or error to advise you that you do not have the results of an outer join.
- The (+) operator does not produce an outer join if you specify one table in the outer query and the other table in an inner query.
- You cannot use the (+) operator to outer-join a table to itself, although self joins are valid. For example, the following statement is not valid:
- The following statement is not valid:
- SELECT employee_id, manager_id
- FROM employees
- WHERE employees. manager_id(+) = employees. employee_id;

However, the following self join is valid:

```
SELECT e1.employee_id, e1.manager_id,
e2.employee_id
 FROM employees e1, employees e2
 WHERE e1.manager_id(+) = e2.employee_id;
```

- The (+) operator can be applied only to a column, not to an arbitrary expression. However, an arbitrary expression can contain one or more columns marked with the (+) operator.

- A condition containing the (+) operator cannot be combined with another condition using the OR logical operator.
- A condition cannot use the IN comparison condition to compare a column marked with the (+) operator with an expression.
- A condition cannot compare any column marked with the (+) operator with a subquery.

If the WHERE clause contains a condition that compares a column from table B with a constant, then the (+) operator must be applied to the column so that Oracle returns the rows from table A for which it has generated nulls for this column. Otherwise Oracle will return only the results of a simple join. In a query that performs outer joins of more than two pairs of tables, a single table can be the null-generated table for only one other table. For this reason, you cannot apply the (+) operator to columns of B in the join condition for A and B and the join condition for B and C.

Using Subqueries

A subquery answers multiple-part questions. For example, to determine who works in Taylor's department, you can first use a subquery to determine the department in which Taylor works. You can then answer the original question with the parent SELECT statement. A subquery in the FROM clause of a SELECTstatement is also called an inline view. A subquery in the WHERE clause of a SELECT statement is also called a nested subquery. A subquery can contain another subquery. Oracle imposes no limit on the number of subquery levels in the FROM clause of the top-level query. You can nest up to 255 levels of subqueries in the WHERE clause.

If columns in a subquery have the same name as columns in the containing statement, then you must prefix any reference to the column of the table from the containing statement with the table name or alias. To make your statements easier for you to read, always qualify the columns in a subquery with the name or alias of the table, view, or materialized view. Oracle performs a correlated subquery when the subquery references a column from a table referred to in the parent statement. A correlated subquery is evaluated once for each row processed by the parent statement. The parent statement can be a SELECT, UPDATE, or DELETE statement.

A correlated subquery answers a multiple-part question whose answer depends on the value in each row processed by the parent statement. For example, you can use a correlated subquery to determine which employees earn more than the average salaries for their departments. In this case, the correlated subquery specifically computes the average salary for each department.

Use subqueries for the following purposes:

- To define the set of rows to be inserted into the target table of an Insert or Create Table statement
- To define the set of rows to be included in a view or materialized view in a Create View or Create Materialized View statement
- To define one or more values to be assigned to existing rows in an Up Date statement
- To provide values for conditions in a Where Here clause, Having clause, or Start With clause of Select, Update, and Delete statements
- To define a table to be operated on by a containing query

You do this by placing the subquery in the FROM clause of the containing query as you would a table name. You may use subqueries in place of tables in this way as well in Insert, Up Date, and Delete statements. Subqueries so used can employ correlation variables, but only those defined within the subquery itself, not outer references. Outer references ("left-correlated subqueries") are allowed only in the FROM clause of a SELECT statement. Scalar subqueries, which return a single column value from a single row, are a valid form of expression. You can use scalar subquery expressions in most of the places where expr is called for in syntax.

Nested Subqueries

Subqueries are "nested" when they appear in the WHERE clause of the parent statement. When Oracle evaluates a statement with a nested subquery, it must evaluate the subquery portion multiple times and may overlook some efficient access paths or joins.

Subquery unnesting unnests and merges the body of the subquery into the body of the statement that contains it, allowing the optimizer to consider them together when evaluating access paths and joins. The optimizer can unnest most subqueries, with some exceptions. Those exceptions include hierarchical subqueries and subqueries that contain a ROWNUM pseudocolumn, one of the set operators, a nested aggregate function, or a correlated reference to a query block that is not the subquery's immediate outer query block.

Assuming no restrictions exist, the optimizer automatically unnests some (but not all) of the following nested subqueries:

- Uncorrelated IN subqueries
- IN and EXISTS correlated subqueries, as long as they do not contain aggregate functions or a GROUP BY clause

You can enable extended subquery unnesting by instructing the optimizer to unnest additional types of subqueries:

- You can unnest an uncorrelated Not In subquery by specifying the Hash_Aj or Merge_Aj hint in the subquery.
- You can unnest other subqueries by specifying the Unnest hint in the subquery.

Selecting from the DUAL Table

DUAL is a table automatically created by Oracle along with the data dictionary. DUAL is in the schema of the user SYS, but is accessible by the name DUAL to all users. It has one column, DUMMY, defined to be VARCHAR2(1), and contains one row with a value 'X'. Selecting from the DUAL table is useful for computing a constant expression with the SELECT statement. Because DUAL has only one row, the constant is returned only once. Alternatively, you can select a constant, pseudocolumn, or expression from any table, but the value will be returned as many times as there are rows in the table.

Distributed Queries

Oracle's distributed database management system architecture lets you access data in remote databases using Oracle Net and an Oracle server. You can identify a remote table, view, or materialized view by appending @dblink to the end of its name. The dblink must be a complete or partial name for a database link to the database containing the remote table, view, or materialized view.

Restrictions on Distributed Queries

Distributed queries are currently subject to the restriction that all tables locked by a FOR UPDATE clause and all tables with LONG columns selected by the query must be located on the same database. For example, the following statement will raise an error:

```
SELECT employees_ny.*
 FROM employees_ny@ny, departments
  WHERE employees_ny.department_id =
departments.department_id
 AND departments.department_name = 'ACCOUNTING'
 FOR UPDATE OF employees_ny.salary;
```

The following statement fails because it selects long_column, a LONG value, from the employees_review table on the ny database and locks the employees table on the local database:

```
SELECT employees.employee_id, review.long_column,
employees.salary
 FROM employees, employees_review@ny review
   WHERE employees.employee_id =
employees_review.employee_id
 FOR UPDATE OF employees.salary;
```

Chapter 5

Data Representation

DATA SUIT

INTERACTIVE DATA TEST SUITE

The purpose of the public test suite is to assist developers of software that must validate Interactive Data prior to its submission to EDGAR. The test suite consists of many small Interactive Data instances, schemas and linkbases that are categorized as to whether they violate a validation check, and if so, what validation check they violate and whether that would resulting a warning, or in an error that would cause the Interactive Data to be rejected.

Filers that attach Interactive Data files to EDGAR submissions as EX-101 attachments are responsible for compliance with all validations in Chapter 6 of Volume II of the EDGAR Filer Manual ("the Manual"). Automated validation by preparation software can make it more efficient for filers to verify compliance before sending their filings to EDGAR itself. Nothing in this test suite is intended to create new requirements or change existing requirements for EDGAR submissions; filers should consult the Commission rules and the Manual for submission requirements.

ALPHA AND BETA REPRESENTATION

CUSTOMER INVOLVEMENT

We want you to be involved! Customer Involvement is one of our core goals - read About Us and Our Philosophy for a summary of our goals. By being involved in the testing and development of our products, you will ultimately benefit from a product that more closely matches your needs, and you will receive a product that is of higher quality.

ALPHA PRODUCT

An Alpha product is very new! It is so new, that it has not yet reached the stage where it can be sold. It is still being developed. However, it HAS reached the stage where those who enjoy cutting-edge technology can download the product as-is, and try it out for themselves!

BETA PRODUCT

A Beta product is one where new feature development has stopped, and the focus is on polishing the product and ironing out any kinks, ready for sale.

We still encourage you to suggest ideas for improvement during this stage, but they will most likely be logged for development in a future version. Of course, if you find any bugs, please tell us!

ALPHA OR BETA TESTING PHASE

During the "Alpha" or "Beta" phase of a product: You can download and install the product to see whether it suits your needs. You automatically get a 7-day evaluation license at installation time, during which period the product is fully functional.

SIGN-UP

If you wish to continue using the product after the 7-day evaluation period has expired, you must sign-up to become an "Alpha Tester" or "Beta Tester", depending on which phase the product is currently in.

Signing up is free. You will be prompted to sign up when you launch the product. All you need to provide is your name and email address. In addition, as a reward for participating in the Alpha Testing phase, you will be entitled to a discount on the retail price of the product when it goes on sale.

DISCUSSION FORUMS

You can suggest ways to improve the product! You should do this by participating in our Discussion Forums. During the Alpha phase, suggestions for improvement will be actively taken on board. When a product moves to the Beta phase, then new feature development stops. However, suggestions for improvement are still considered and discussed, and may be logged for development in a future version. We welcome any ideas for improving our products.

Report Bugs

If you find any bugs with the software, please report them! There is sophisticated bug-reporting capability built-in to the software, in the event that application errors should occur. For other issues that you consider to be bugs or problems with the software you should submit a bug report via email.

Product Tracking

Keep up to date with each product via the Product Tracking page. From this page you can get a list of all issues logged, and find out whether that bug for which you logged a bug report has been fixed yet.

STATIC TESTING STRATEGIES

INTRODUCTION

Static testing is a form of software testing where the software isn't actually used. This is in contrast to Dynamic testing. It is generally not detailed testing, but checks mainly for the sanity of the code, algorithm, or document. It is primarily syntax checking of the code or and manually reading of the code or document to find errors.

This type of testing can be used by the developer who wrote the code, in isolation. Code reviews, inspections and walkthroughs are also used. From the black box testing point of view, static testing involves review of requirements or specifications. This is done with an eye toward completeness or appropriateness for the task at hand. This is the verification portion of Verification and Validation. Bugs discovered at this stage of development are less expensive to fix than later in the development cycle.

ALPHA/BETA USABILITY AND ACCEPTABILITY

Quality Logic can implement and manage your customer alpha, beta and gamma product testing programs, providing quality and timely feedback from real customers in real-world environments. We can manage the entire programme from customer selection and product delivery, through customer support and data gathering, to final data analysis.

Customer Management and Support

QualityLogic will work with your customers to ensure continuous programme involvement and feedback. We can provide pre-release product support, product upgrades and issue troubleshooting.

Data Analysis

Quality Logic can gather customer environment and usage information, satisfaction trends and product strengths and weaknesses. We make comparisons to competitive offerings and conduct root cause analysis on issues, providing actionable data.

Support Analysis

With our extensive product support experience, Quality Logic's staff provides feedback on product support effectiveness on released products.

Competitive Analysis Testing

Quality Logic's experienced staff can implement and manage part of or all your competitive intelligence testing. We can manage the entire programme from competitor selection and acquisition, through test design andimplementation, to final data analysis and reporting. Reporting can be used for either internal or external communications.

STRATEGIES

TESTING OF DATA

Static testing is a form of software testing where

the software isn't actually used. This is in contrast to Dynamic testing. It is generally not detailed testing, but checks mainly for the sanity of the code, algorithm, or document. It is primarily syntax checking of the code or and manually reading of the code or document to find errors.

This type of testing can be used by the developer who wrote the code, in isolation. Code reviews, inspections and walkthroughs are also used. From the black box testing point of view, static testing involves review of requirements or specifications.

This is done with an eye toward completeness or appropriateness for the task at hand. This is the verification portion of Verification and Validation. Bugs discovered at this stage of development are less expensive to fix than later in the development cycle.

CODE ANALYSIS

Static code analysis is the analysis of computer software that is performed without actually executing programs built from that software (analysis performed on executing programs is known as dynamic analysis).

In most cases the analysis is performed on some version of the source code and in the other cases some form of the object code. The term is usually applied to the analysis performed by an automated tool, with human analysis being called programme understanding or programme comprehension.

The sophistication of the analysis performed by tools varies from those that only consider the behaviour of individual statements and declarations, to those that include the complete source code of a programme in their analysis.

Uses of the information obtained from the analysis vary from highlighting possible coding errors (e.g., the lint tool) to formal methods that mathematically prove properties about a given programme (e.g., its behaviour matches that of its specification).

Some people consider software metrics and reverse engineering to be forms of static analysis. A growing commercial use of static analysis is in the verification of properties of software used in safety-critical computer systems and locating potentially vulnerable code.

FORMAL METHODS

Formal methods is the term applied to the analysis of software (and hardware) whose results are obtained purely through the use of rigorous mathematical methods. The mathematical techniques used include denotational semantics, axiomatic semantics, operational semantics, and abstract interpretation.

It has been proven that, barring some hypothesis that the state space of programs is finite and small, finding possible run-time errors, or more generally any kind of violation of a specification on the final result of a programme, is undecidable: there is no mechanical method that can always answer truthfully whether a given programme may or may not exhibit runtime errors.

This result dates from the works of Church, Gödel and Turing in the 1930s (see the halting problem and Rice's theorem). As with most undecidable questions, one can still attempt to give useful approximate solutions.

Some of the implementation techniques of formal static analysis include:

- Model checking considers systems that have finite state or may be reduced to finite state by abstraction;
- Abstract interpretation models the effect that every statement has on the state of an abstract machine (ie, it 'executes' the software based on the mathematical properties of each statement and declaration). This abstract machine overapproximates the behaviours of the system: the abstract system is thus made simpler to analyse, at the expense of *incompleteness* (not every property true of the original system is true of the abstract system). If properly done, though, abstract interpretation is *sound* (every property true of the abstract system can be mapped to a true property of the original system).
- Use of assertions in programme code as first

suggested by Hoare logic. There is tool support for some programming languages (e.g., the SPARK programming language (a subset of Ada) and the Java Modeling Language — JML — using ESC/Java and ESC/Java2).

DESCRIPTION

Static Testing is a well-known and beneficial concept within the testing space, but tightened budgets and looming deadlines can hinder the benefits. Here are few suggestions on how taking a risk-based approach to static testing can help realize the benefits.

Implementing Static Testing

Implementing static testing, it is advisable to create a small dedicated implementation team with specific roles. It should include the Process Champions who would be backing the process, the Trainers, and most importantly the Implementers, who will need to develop and document the process; examples of the process materials and collateral required are, Static Testing Policy, Strategy; Review Process, Review Techniques and Guidelines; Templates – Review Logs, Review Metrics, Document Review Matrix; Training courses.

The other factors to consider for the implementation are, verifying the internal materials by using the process and templates and involving people from different projects/teams in the development of the materials.

When actually implement-ng Static Reviews, experience has shown that a phased approach is often best, both in terms of minimizing the impact and also being able to demonstrate early benefits as a result.

For this reason AppLabs recommends an approach making use of a pilot and then a full implementation: The strategy behind the pilot approach is to provide a least risk environment which will allow early demonstration of some or all of the benefits of Static Testing.

Having experienced at first hand how this approach can provide a successful basis for further implementation(s),

AppLabs has recognized some essential factors that will contribute to success.

FORMAL TECHNICAL REVIEWS

Formal Technical Reviews (FTR) are processes used to improve work products through team effort. Any deliverable that is produced during the development life-cycle is eligible to be reviewed and should be at an early stage, beginning in the specification stage and recurring at each identifiable milestone.

A description of the review process as implemented at Fermilab is available as well as a list of reviews that have been held. Many additional references are available. Unless otherwise stated all Fermi FTR documentation will include the symbol shown at the top of this page to distinguish it from outside information.

The following guidelines should help in setting up an FTR:

- Choose the work product to be reviewed.
- Determine the type of FTR to use.
- Follow the description of the specific FTR in question.

It is important to remember when determining the type of FTR to use that no process will work for every organization. Feedback to the review process is an important part of having a *process*. The process evolves as experience and participant comments are folded back into it.

In some sense it is not only the work product which is being reviewed but the review process as well. What is important is to develop an FTR process that works for your organization and to stick with that process when performing a review.

TECHNICAL METHODS

- A planned and systematic pattern of all actions necessary to provide adequate confidence that an item or product conforms to established technical requirements.
- A set of activities designed to evaluate the process by which products are developed or manufactured"

When discussing software quality very little changes from the above statement, the goal is still to produce a usable product, which is capable of performing the task it was designed to do.

Formal technical reviews involve the analysis of an artifact by a group of technically skilled people following a specified and documented process. Michael Fagan first wrote about the idea of formal technical reviews in software quality in the 1970's whilst working for IBM, and the majority of all technical review methods have evolved in some way from Fagan's Code Inspection.

Background

A formal technical review is a method used to identify defects in an artifact before progressing to the next stage of development. Unlike system testing, formal technical reviews can take place at any stage in the development life-cycle, and as such allow for the identification, documentation and correction of defects earlier rather than later, therefore saving the company both time and money.

An example of such a cost saving is provided by Robert Grady and Tom Van Slack (1994) where they claim that software inspections saved Hewlett-Packard 21 million dollars, clearly showing there are long term cost gains to be made by implementing formal technical reviews.

It is commonly accepted that not all organisations implement formal technical reviews for various reasons ranging from ignorance of the benefits they provide through to the effects they may have on time management aspects of the project. However, standards organisations such as ISO and CMM are pushing companies in the direction of formal technical reviews by insisting on some form of inspection to be in place before offering certification.

An informal survey, which was carried out by Philip M Johnson (1996) regarding the use of formal technical reviews in the workplace, showed that despite the benefits offered by formal technical reviews, 80% of replies claimed that formal technical review methods in their place of business were infrequently carried out and in some cases not at all. Popular alternatives to formal technical reviews can be found in the form of structured walkthroughs and code reading. A structured walkthrough consists of a short meeting with one or more developers and the author to discuss the quality and suitability of the artifact.

No documentation is required and no data collection to assist in process improvement takes place during or after the meeting. Whist this process is not generally considered as "good" as a formal technical review, however, just because it is not a measured process does not mean it is not effective, simply more confidence is placed on the experience of the reviewers.

Laitenberger and Jean-Marc DeBaud (1999) supported this view when they identified that audits and walkthroughs, while informal may be equally as effective as a formal technical review, but due to the lack of structure and many variations, a direct comparison of the two is not possible. Code reviews involve two or more developers reading code independently then meeting with the author to discuss any findings. Again, this relies heavily on the experience of the reviewer knowing what to look for in a review.

Methods

Formal technical review methods began in 1976 with the publication of Fagan's code inspection techniques. Fagan inspections consist of 4 pre-defined roles, moderator, scribe, inspector and author.

Given the opportunity to follow the basic steps - overview, preparation, inspection, rework and follow up - this method allows for a controlled and documented review, with findings easily referred to and checked upon. This method was considered a major step forward in the field of software quality, and provided IBM with substantial cost savings during the development process.

As a result of this formal technical reviews became popular, and a wide variety of alternatives have since been developed although often a link to Fagan's code inspection can be seen. The first step of Fagan code inspections is the overview, this is where the inspection team are handed any design documents or code listings that are relevant, and given an outline of the project as a whole.

Following on from this is the preparation stage, where each member of the inspection team works independently to read and understand the documentation they have been given, during this phase a checklist is sometimes used to increase the chances of a defect being discovered.

The inspection phase generally involves a meeting including the inspection team and the author Where the documentation is systematically gone over as a group documenting any defects. These are then fixed by the author during the next phase, rework.

The final step is to check the defects have been corrected this is the Follow-up stage. Tom Gilb took this idea one step further, with an extension to Fagan code inspection. Gilb added process improvement and defect prevention to the list of goals, this helped companies identify reasons as to why defects were occurring, and if possible remove the cause, not just the defect. A study by Martin Höst and Conny Johansson (1999) showed that when a checklist based review was introduced into an organisation most defects were detected by a single inspector. They conclude this could be due to the experience of the inspector or time commitments of other inspectors.

Due to the costs associated with arranging a meeting when every member of the inspection team is available, Watts Humphrey created Humphrey's software review method, this consists of the producer talking the inspection team through the background material, following this each inspector performs the inspection alone in order to complete an error checklist. The producer then compiles this list before the group review meeting is held.

Due to the fact that members of the inspection team have all understood the artifact under inspection there is no longer a need for the producer to explain each line of code, this results in shorter group meetings. Group meetings are completely removed in active design review, produced by David L Parnas and David M Weiss. This inspection method involves the producer giving a brief overview or the project, and providing all the inspectors with a questionnaire, which they complete in order to ensure their understanding.

Next the inspectors individually analyse the artifact each focusing on a specialised area. The producer then meets with each inspector individually to collect the results of the inspection.

The producer then collates all the findings and produces a report regarding the inspection. Knight and Myers proposed a phased inspection technique taking some of the ideas of Humphrey and some of the ideas from active design review by splitting the inspection into 2 phases.

The first phase, single inspection phase, involves a simple yes or no checklist and can be carried out by anyone, not just a developer. The second phase, multi inspection phase, is carried out by each inspector following a checklist covering his or her own area of expertise. Upon completion of this a meeting is held to compare and analyse the findings.

With the problem of time available for reviews still remaining Shinji Kusumoto et al. carried out an experiment to accurately estimate the time needed in order to carry out a formal technical review.

They proposed taking samples of the producers code and inspecting them, the results of this sample inspection enabled them to estimate the time needed for a complete inspection of the entire product based on the knowledge that the lower the quality of a product the higher the effort needed to complete the inspection.

The results from this experiment showed that the defect detection rate increased from 28% to 40% when this procedure was applied. A study carried out by Oliver Laitenberger and Jean-Marc DeBaud concluded that the reading method used during an inspection could significantly contribute to the defect detection rates.

This study also uncovered evidence to suggest that when applying perspective based reading, the experience of the inspector plays a far smaller part in the overall defect detection rate as opposed to using a checklist based system Perspective based reading involves setting each inspector a different area or perspective to inspect the artifact from, for example an end user or code maintenance.

This allows for better coverage of artifacts under inspection as each inspector is focused on one specific area of expertise. A different study by Laitenberger et al. focusing on the application of perspective based reading to UML documentation found that an inspector's perceived understanding of an artifact was increased when perspective based reading was applied.

The increased understanding provided by the use of perspective based reading could explain the increased defect detection rate as a study by A Dunsmore, M Roper and M Wood (1999) identified a link between inspector comprehension of an artifact and the defect detection rate when using checklist based methods.

Another finding of Laitenberger et al. was that on a cost per defect ratio, it worked out cheaper for the company to use a perspective based reading technique. Victor R Basili et al. conducted an experiment, the comparison of various reading techniques within the perspective based reading family, as they consider this fundamental to defect detection.

During this controlled experiment with professional software developers, two teams. were formed one using perspective based reading, the other using their usual technique. The results from these experiments show that overall the team using perspective based reading techniques performed better than the control team.

REVIEWS

In an attempt to provide easier implementation and automatic capture of metric data relating to the inspection process, data needed in order to improve the inspection process, a range of computer tools to assist in formal technical reviews quickly became available. With the computer assistance the time needed to record this data is removed from the inspection process, it is also more accurate and can record the amount of time spent by each inspector and on which area of the artifact.

One of the first such tools was a system by ITT in 1982; this prototype was both a hardware and software solution, creating a workstation to assist in reviews. However, no documents concerning the use of this system have ever been released. ITT have since sold off their research labs to Alcatel who closed them down.

The first inspection tool to have published results regarding its use was developed by Bellcore and called ICICLE (Intelligent Code Inspection in a C Language Environment). ICICLE allows for a 2 phases of inspection, individual inspections and inspection meetings, unfortunately no support for distributed meetings was included in ICICLE and all meetings needed to be held with the inspectors all in the same room.

During the inspection process ICICLE attempts to remove errors it is aware of in the code in an attempt to assist with the inspection process. ICICLE was designed to support inspections of the C/C++ language following Fagan's inspection method, which restricts the possible applications of the programme significantly.

Scrutiny adds support for geographi-cally distributed inspections, potentially allowing for large cost savings if used on a national/ international project, allowing members of the team to hold inspections without the need for travel. An attempt to remove the language barrier was also implemented in Scrutiny as any plain text file is accepted by the system for inspection.

The University created an inspection support tool named CIS (Collaborative Software Inspection) in order to support Humphrey's software reviews. Like Scrutiny CIS is an on-line based tool allowing for geographically distributed development and inspection teams.

The on-line bases of CIS allows it to support meetings not only over. Different geographic locations, but also across different time zones in that all members of the inspection team can do their inspection when it suits them. CIS uses hyperlinks to link the inspection documents to defect logs and notepads etc. With the use of computer support becoming more and more common Knight and Myers developed InspeQ - an inspection support tool designed to support their phased inspection technique.

InspeQ was designed for use by an individual inspector, and as such contains no meeting support tools, and generates a checklist for each inspector without any link being made between them.

In order to utilise the full potential of using computer support during an inspection process CSRS (Computer Supported Review System) was developed along with its own inspection technique FTArm (Formal Technical Asynchronous review method). CSRS allows the user to model existing or future inspection methods with the goal of allowing CSRS to support and assist any inspection method.

The default method FTArm allows for the inspection of any document type. The exclusion of on-line meetings from CSRS renders this tool unusable to any development or inspection teams that are unable to meet face to face for inspection meetings.

The idea of supporting any review method was also upheld by F. Macdonald and J Miller, the creators of ASSIST (Asynchronous/Synchronous Software Inspection Tool). ASSIST was designed with the goal of providing support for any inspection technique, to achieve this a process definition language was created so new inspection techniques could be added as and when they became available.

ASSIST contains 3 major stages, organisation, detection and completion these 3 stages can be applied to almost any current formal technical review method. With the growing demand for software inspection support tools it was inevitable that off-the-shelf software would soon appear an example of this is ReviewPro developed by Software Development Technologies Corporation.

A web based inspection tool ReviewPro includes the web server needed to host an inspection with ReviewPro will run on both Windows NT and Unix providing a solution for cross-platform development environments.

TECHNICAL VIEWS

In observing peer technical review processes over the past two decades, it has become obvious that no one review process is best for all. There are many variations on the general theme, which may be appropriate in some organizations and not in others [CRA].

This observation is in direct contrast to the SEI's (Software Engineering Institute) CMM (Capability Maturity Model), which basically prescribes a style of review process to be implemented at a particular point in an organization's overall process maturity. Characteristics of the process outlined follow the lines of the IEEE's standard for reviews [IEE].

In our deliberations over that standard in the early 1980's, only the most generic parts of a review process were retained, from the many successful variations with which the standards committee was familiar. The process defined basically elaborates on: *"You plan, prepare, review, and follow-up"*. Little guidance is provided on exactly *how* to do those activities. The real action of a review process, however, is in those details. Regardless of an organization's maturity level, however, there is a review process appropriate for it.

In an organization with absolutely no formally defined development process, people can sit down together, look over one another's work, and productively find flaws in their acts of software design and construction. In such an organization, that is probably the single most important thing to do to improve the quality of a delivered system.

As an organization matures (by whatever scale chosen), however, so should its technical review process. As an organization documents its processes, defining roles & responsibilities for people and entry & exit criteria for activities, so too should this be done for the review process. As measurement and baselines are established, the review process should be updated to track data. As root cause analysis becomes understood, it should be integrated with reviews.

And as the overall development process becomes better understood and more finely tuned, the standard review process has been seen to evolve into several processes, each appropriate to the very different types of workproducts within the development cycle. Another dimension of variation among review processes is influenced by an organization's management style. Just as the varying cognitive styles of people influence how best they learn and mature, the management style of organizations influence the maturing of their review process. In an autocratic organization, a process, once somehow defined or selected, is imposed and changed by executive fiat. Management with a participative or consensual focus will have processes designed (at least in part) by the technical staff, thus opening the door to nearly unlimited process variations. In the body of this paper, review processes for differing maturity levels are delineated.

The basic outline of the CMM's process plateaus is used here, providing a common framework with the SEI's work. The influence of management style is then highlighted. My particular expertise in technical review processes comes from a long consulting relationship across a diversity of development organizations. My intuition tells me that a multi-level model of a review process, as discussed herein, has analogues in other software development practices. I hope others with a breadth of experience across these other practices can profit from this model and apply it within their realms.

PROCESS

What follows is a typical, generic story of a review process, as it matures along with the overall set of an organization's development practices. The basic outline of the CMM is preserved, as a common framework. For any one development organization, the details may vary, but the general outline of the levels remains.

INITIAL PLATEAU

In an ad hoc development, peer reviews can prove particularly important. Any professional realizes that mistakes are likely in developing complex systems, and the independent perspective of another person is key in discovering oversights and blind spots. Babbage and von Neuman, long before "software development" was a phrase, reviewed with their peers the logic they attempted to implement on the earliest of computers.

An early model of software peer reviews was that familiar from referred journals: circulate a draft and consolidate returned commentary. To be effective for software, this model relies on the software artefact to be reasonably stand-alone and self explanatory. Another model, the buddy-check or desk-check, has roots in the multi-person office, where one could turn to a peer and ask them to, *"look this over, could you?"* In this case, as questions arose, the author was close at hand to fill in missing context and detail. Too close, some would argue. Often these practices were "recommended" to be followed during software systems development, but the general lack of fine-grained project scheduling and tracking typical of organizations at this level precluded strict following of what actually occurred.

Some of the problems noted in the ad hoc practices of this stage were that of inconsistent practice both within and across teams, and a feeling among some that the time spent reviewing was wasted since it took away from time which could be otherwise be spent coding (which is the only real productive activity at this level, of course). Generally, the code's author runs the review, since the product *is* their responsibility.

Index

I

L

M

N

O

P

R

S

T

U

V

W